Stevie Wonder

RHYTHMS OF WONDER

Stevie Wonder

RHYTHMS OF WONDER

SHARON DAVIS

**ROBSON
BOOKS**

This paperback edition first printed in 2006

First published in hardback in Great Brtain in 2003 by
Robson Books
141 Freston Road
London
W10 6TH

An imprint of Anova Books Company Ltd

ISBN 1 86105 965 5

10 9 8 7 6 5 4 3 2

Designed by Richard Mason and Claudia Schenk

Typeset by SX Composing DTP, Rayleigh, Essex
Printed by Creative Print & Design (Wales), Ebbw Vale

This book can be ordered direct from the publisher
Contact the marketing department, but try your bookshop first

www.anovabooks.com

This book is dedicated to the memory of Marvin Gaye, Dusty Springfield and Gloria Marcantonio

I wish you luck on your telling of Stevie's trials and celebrations. He is worthy. Thanks for caring. All of your books are so elegantly done. I know you will make him proud.

Martha Reeves
(Martha Reeves and the Vandellas)

If there's a place that's beyond genius, that's where I'd put Stevie's music. His music is creative, innovative and absolutely timeless. Artistry such as Stevie's comes few and far between. You can't be still and listen to his music, something has to move. I'm so very proud to say I know, love, and respect the man and his music.

Sundray Tucker
(ex-member of Wonderlove and the Flos)

I was raised on Little Stevie's music and went on to include some of his songs in my act. Lyrically, he's a megastar; his melodies and range are awesome. *Songs In The Key Of Life* actually inspired my future work. I was honoured to join in his birthday celebrations at the NEC Birmingham – something I'll never forget [. . .] Sharon, girlfriend, you are so good. A story well told and to be proud of.

Jaki Graham
(Singer)

I was a new entertainer/musician and EMI Records decided that Sharon was to be my mentor (or is that tormentor). She introduced me to many cool musicians, but the biggest surprise was when she told me she'd secured the final invite for Stevie's birthday party. I became fourteen years old instantly! Then reality hit me when I realised I was being photographed with the man himself. He was holding my hand in quite a grip until I reluctantly plied myself away. On returning home there was a call for me from Stevie's suite at the Holiday Inn inviting me to a crew party. I thought about it but as I'd already had a wonderful experience that would last for a good few years I declined and said maybe next time. So Stevie, if you need my number Sharon has my permission to pass it on.

Dottaye Green
(Singer/Composer)

One of my fondest memories of Stevie happened about a year after I started working for him exclusively as his publicist. There was something I found troubling but I just could not identify it [. . .] Then, one night after a show in Idaho we were discussing the next day's activities in Stevie's luxury suite, when he excused himself to go to the bathroom. He left the table, walked to the bathroom, turned on the light, walked in and closed the door. It was at that time a light clicked on in my head. Why does he need a light? Now I knew what it was that had been bothering me for almost a year. I was so used to hearing the familiar click of the bathroom light that it didn't register with me. So when he returned I had to ask him 'Why do you turn on the light when you go to the bathroom?' His answer was, 'I thought you'd never ask. Now you can see with your ears, welcome to my world.' And I've been seeing with them ever since. What a great experience, what a man.

Ira Tucker Jr

(ex-Stevie Wonder Publicist and Road Manager)

Stevie Wonder had such an impact on me that Motown Records had me 'on the shelf' for several years. That is to say, they wouldn't record me because 'they' thought I sounded too much like him! Stevie promised to produce me many years ago and I'm still waiting for it to happen. One day I was at the company and Stevie was approaching. We were introduced and, perceiving he was not particularly impressed, I knew I had to do something quick because he was leaving. I ducked into one of the rooms that had a piano and started singing my little heart out, playing the only three chords that I knew. Would you believe it, that wonderful man came all the way back, peeked into the room and exclaimed, 'You sound just like me!' Wow – what a rush, what a compliment! I will always treasure meeting the beautiful person and incredibly talented human being. Sharon helped me get around fabulous England many years ago. We became friends and, for many years, lost touch with each other. I remember how sensitive, thoughtful, attentive and smart she was, and still is. We are friends for life.

Tata Vega

(Singer/Composer)

CONTENTS

INTRODUCTION

Martha Reeves first introduced me to Stevie Wonder at London's Hammersmith Odeon during the seventies when he burst into her dressing room where she and the two Vandellas were changing into their stage clothes. This fact didn't deter the young singer from staying around to chat, laugh and flirt with his friends. I didn't move a muscle or speak but Stevie knew I was there. Before long I too was fooling around, enjoying the banter.

It was almost a decade later when Stevie and I met again: the first of several occasions. He was an international success and I was Motown's publicist who, with the dedicated team at Motown's London office (Noreen Allen, Gordon Frewin, Les Spaine and Chris Marshall), was organising a *Hotter Than July* playback at the Abbey Road Studios. Stevie was less accessible in 1980. He was a heavily shielded man. With his chin thrust forward and one arm straight ahead touching the shoulders of the person before him, Stevie was ushered around. He shook my hand upon introduction, clasping his hands around mine, talking as he did so. 'The voice and feel of the hands are extremely important,' he explained.

By the late eighties Stevie had enjoyed 28 top ten American singles, placing him third behind Elvis Presley with 38 and The Beatles with 33. And according to *Billboard* magazine, nine of his 23 albums had been top ten hits and three had won Grammy awards for Album of the Year. He'd come a long way from the Hammersmith Odeon when he supported Martha and the Vandellas!

This book is a celebration of Stevie Wonder's music and his

astounding career, which very nearly didn't happen. But his music isn't just about selling records, it's about bringing people together, by demolishing ethnic barriers. Through his tireless work much has been achieved, including his triumph over the American Congress to honour the late Dr Martin Luther King with a national holiday. Encouraged by the continued support of the American people, his ongoing plan is to ensure equality and respect for all people.

Remarkably, Motown's founder Berry Gordy identified the youngster's raw talent and rode the success and despair, the triumphs and tragedies, until Stevie found his foothold in the world. As Gordy struggled to find the right musical niche for Stevie, the singer was having fun, with his vitally energetic style and screechy voice mesmerising audiences. But the boy grew up, his voice broke and his outlook mellowed. In his early teens he was recognised as the most creative musician of his generation, and by his thirties he had forty million record sales to his credit. He's now the most consistently successful artist alive.

There are very few artists who, from adolescence, have mastered most musical instruments known to man and of these, very few have been blind from birth. Stevie refused to let his blindness be a handicap as he strode forward to fulfil his personal and professional ambitions. Reaching maturity he embraced the public with his love and, of course, his music. 'One only needs to listen to hear the depth of his thoughts and perceptions of life,' ex-Supreme Lynda Laurence tells me. 'The way he sees life is meaningful and it shows through the lyrics of his music. I'm reminded of a song he wrote, "Do Yourself A Favour". The lyric goes, "Do yourself a favour, educate your mind. Get yourself together. Hey there ain't much time." And this from a teenager!' She has a point.

He's not an easy subject to write about because – other than his rare interviews – little is forthcoming from the Wonder camp and his private life is, as he says, private. So this is why I'm extremely grateful to the following artists for their input via interviews, phone calls and emails to help me tell the story – Martha Reeves, Dave Godin, the late Marvin Gaye, Edwin Starr, Mary Wells and Dusty Springfield, Tata Vega, Gary Byrd, Jermaine Jackson, Diana Ross, Lynda Laurence, Kim Weston, Syreeta, Dottaye Green, Boy

George, The Temptations, Smokey Robinson, Mary Wilson, Stephen Moore and Rockwell. And, of course, the man himself.

To the following highly recommended publications, my sincere thanks – *Dancing in the Street: Confessions Of A Motown Diva* by Martha Reeves; *Temptations* by Otis Williams; *To Be Loved: The Music, the Magic, the Memories of Motown: an Autobiography* by Berry Gordy; *Dreamgirl: My Life As A Supreme* by Mary Wilson; *Nowhere To Run: The Story of Soul Music* by Gerri Hirshey; *Where Did Our Love Go?: The Rise and Fall of the Motown Sound* by Nelson George; *Divided Soul: The Life of Marvin Gaye* by David Ritz; *Aretha: From These Roots* by Aretha Franklin, David Ritz; *Call Her Miss Ross: The Unauthorized Biography of Diana Ross* by J Randy Taraborrelli; *Eddie Murphy: The Life And Times Of A Comic On The Edge* by Frank Sanello; *Take It Like A Man: The Autobiography of Boy George* by Boy George; *The Billboard Book Of Number One R&B Hits* by Adam White & Fred Bronson; *Lead Us Not Into Temptation* by Tony Turner; *Rock 'N' Roll Babylon* by Gary Herman; *Be My Baby* by Ronnie Spector; *Smokey: Inside My Life* by Smokey Robinson; *Women of Motown: An Oral History* by Susan Whitall and David Marsh and *Stevie Wonder* by John Swenson.

My further thanks to Phil Symes for his 1970s interviews; to the staff, notably editor Bob Killbourn, of *Blues & Soul* magazine, whose pages are a constant source of inspiration – especially my own articles! To Graham Betts for compiling the discography, such an important feature in a book of this nature. To Universal/ Motown's Silvia Montello for the music; to my business colleague Gerry Constable for the book's title and Julie Rough for her researching skills; John Pawsey for inspiring me to rise to the challenge and to the staff of Robson Books for believing in the project.

And as a final word, Stevie Wonder is working on a new album as I write this. There, I've said it!

Sharon Davis
April 2003

LONELY BOY

'Many underestimated the power of Stevie Wonder and music'
Kenny Gamble

'The sensation of seeing is not one I have, so I don't worry about it'
Stevie Wonder

'I didn't know that God would take his eyesight for the gift of music'
Lulu Mae Hardaway

On 15 January 1981 Stevie Wonder led a rally in Washington to celebrate the birthday of the late Dr Martin Luther King, the American civil rights leader who was assassinated on the balcony of the Lorraine Hotel in Memphis in April 1968.

Between 150,000 and 200,000 people shrugged off the thirty-degree weather to participate. Crowds arrived in 250 buses from thirty cities nationwide, including twenty vehicles hired by Johnson Publications' radio station, Chicago's WIPV which carried almost its entire staff, and sixteen coaches hired by the Philadelphian chapter of People United to Save Humanity. Several record company executives such as Kenny Gamble (also president of the Black Music Association), George Clinton and Curtis Mayfield, and artists including Teddy Pendergrass, Dizzie Gillespie, Johnnie Taylor and Bootsy Collins lent their heavyweight support. Most black-owned radio stations also devoted their airwaves to the cause. For example, New York's inner city broadcasting FM outlet, WBLS, cancelled all advertising for the day to play Dr King's speeches. Stevie Wonder's own station in

Los Angeles chartered a plane to transport two hundred passengers to Washington.

The march started at 10 a.m. from the Capitol steps, down Constitution Avenue to the Washington Monument grounds, where the two-hour programme started at noon. Wonder told the crowd 'Martin Luther King Junior is a man America can be proud of and the words he spoke spring from the vast and eternal ocean of true principles – a message of peace, love, human dignity and freedom.' The singer then performed 'Happy Birthday', a song he had conceived in King's memory, followed by a rousing version of the civil rights anthem 'We Shall Overcome'.

At the close of his performance Wonder said, 'It was a very moving day for us all, and the people who came to join in the celebration gave me a lot of satisfaction in confirming what I believe to be a just and rightful cause in honouring such a man. The very least the American people can do is to officially acknowledge and celebrate the birthdate of such a humane and caring person.'

His wish came true in 1986. It was Stevie Wonder's finest hour.

Twenty-seven years earlier, in Detroit, Michigan, a young enterprising black man – Berry Gordy Jr – opened his own record label, Tamla, to release his first single, titled 'Come To Me', by Marv Johnson.

Berry Gordy Jnr was one of eight children, and his family – like thousands before them – moved in search of a better life from the cotton plantations of Georgia to Detroit, Michigan, where he was born on 28 November 1929. Once settled in the city's black-dominated west side, the Gordy family opened a print store and a grocery shop where the children worked, while their father started a plastering business and their mother found employment in real estate. Berry Gordy Jnr refused to work in his parents' shops, preferring to develop his growing passion for music. He listened to the radio all day, humming songs and making notes about the music he heard. This encouraged him to compose and his debut attempt titled 'Berry's Boogie', won him first prize at a local talent show. However, the young Gordy was prevented by his father from developing his musical leanings, so he dropped out of school and followed in the footsteps of his brothers Robert and Fuller, joining one of Detroit's amateur boxing teams. With rigorous training, Berry Gordy eventually qualified as a featherweight, left school and turned professional. Boxing attracted many black youths because it was one of the rare professions in which they could earn good money, and was an alternative to the car factory assembly lines that kept Detroit's heart pumping. During his many fights, Gordy met the Golden Gloves champion Jackie Wilson, who was, ironically, instrumental in Gordy's later music career.

Boxing was abandoned when Gordy joined the Army during 1951 for the Korean War. In 1953 he was discharged with a high-school equivalency degree and married nineteen-year-old Thelma Louise Coleman in Toledo. During the day Gordy worked for his parents, while his nights were spent in local clubs mingling with Detroit's jazz musicians. With his small Army savings and a $700 family loan, Gordy forged his interest in music into reality by purchasing the 3-D Record Mart specialising in jazz records, his prime love. However, after two years of selling jazz to a limited market the Record Mart went bankrupt, leaving a disappointed Gordy no option but to take a job as a trimmer in Ford's Wayne Assembly Plant. The boredom of daily life only made him more determined to succeed with his musical ambitions. He experimented further with songwriting, his most notable composition being 'You Are You', which he paid $25 to have transferred into sheet music. Gordy explained, 'I'd been inspired by seeing a film with Danny Thomas on the life of Gus Todd. Doris Day was in it and I wrote this song for her after seeing the movie. So I was inspired by her and Danny Thomas of all people!'

Berry Gordy's marriage ended in divorce in 1956 and, prior to him opening his own recording operation, his ex-wife launched two labels, Thelma and Ge-Ge, with limited success. Gordy went to live with his sister Loucye, while two of his other sisters, Anna and Gwen, worked for The Flame Show Bar (a prestigious theatre for black entertainers) having secured the cigarette and photography franchises. As Gordy frequented this and other clubs regularly he became aware of the wealth of raw, untapped Detroit talent and this further inspired him to pursue a life in music. Gwen and Anna also pushed his compositions through their contacts at The Flame Bar.

When ex-boxer-now-R&B-singer Jackie Wilson embarked upon a recording career he was desperate for original material. Gordy approached him with songs he had composed with Billy Davis (who also used the pseudonym Tyron Carlo). Wilson recorded several of these, including 'To Be Loved', 'Lonely Teardrops' and 'Reet Petite'. Wilson remembered Gordy as a little man with a big dream, who was more into publishing than recording. Gwen Gordy remembers, 'We were all musically inclined, and Berry and I would often work as a team writing songs in the late fifties . . . I always wanted to be in the record business and I knew Berry was interested, so I was constantly asking him if he was ready to venture into the business full-time, but at that time he wasn't ready.' Part of Gordy's reluctance was that Detroit already had numerous artists – John Lee Hooker and Dinah Washington in the forties, Lavern Baker and Della Reese in the fifties, and the Franklin family, the Reverend C L Franklin's daughters Erma, Carolyn and Aretha, who were preparing to take over the sixties – and independent R&B labels such as Jack and Devorah Brown's Fortune, with subsidiaries including Hi-Q which had limited local success. Gordy wanted to move beyond those boundaries.

Following the release of 'Reet Petite' for which Gordy earned $1,000, he met a young poet, Janie Bradford, a meeting that fuelled a future writing commitment together. Bradford, with others in Gordy's musical family, unwittingly conceived the raw basis of the future 'Motown Sound'. Encouraged by Jackie Wilson's success, Gordy swapped his trimmer's job for full-time music, and in 1958 met fellow music enthusiast and future second wife Raynoma Liles after she won an amateur singing contest in a Detroit club. Liles went on to join her husband's musical team now comprising Bradford, Robert Bateman and Brian Holland, and, formed and fronted The Rayber Voices who added vocals behind the singers they worked with. Herman Griffin's 'I Need You', issued in 1958 on the House of Beauty label, was the first single to carry a Rayber Voices label credit. It was also the first song to be published by Jobete, Gordy's future publishing company, named after his children from his first marriage – Hazel Joy, Berry and Terry.

In time Gordy recruited other talents to work with him and

gradually built up a prolific working team to license his finished master recordings to large white-owned record companies, such as United Artists. He rented a studio and hired a second-hand disc-making machine, charging singers $100 to use his facilities. He also frequently worked with Detroit-born Marv Johnson, a former clerk at the 3-D Record Mart, and during 1958 the Detroit-based Kudo Records released Johnson's Gordy-penned track 'My Baby-O' and Brian Holland's 'Shock'. Holland's brother, Eddie, also recorded a Gordy composition for Mercury Records. Unbeknown to the Holland brothers, they were destined to become key influences in shaping Gordy's music. However, before that happened, Gordy met William 'Smokey' Robinson.

From the age of six, Smokey (so nicknamed by an uncle) experimented with songwriting and became a dedicated reader of popular song books. While at school he formed his first group, The Five Chimes, later The Matadors. During 1957 Robinson, Claudette Rogers, her brother Bobby and friends Ronnie White and Pete More auditioned for Jackie Wilson's manager Nat Tarnopol and his songwriter Berry Gordy. The group failed the audition, featuring original Robinson compositions, because Tarnopol felt Claudette and Smokey should perform together, as duettists were popular at the time. Berry Gordy disagreed and offered to manage the group. Following a handful of local gigs, Gordy and Robinson began collaborating as songwriters, whereupon their first song, 'Insane', was recorded by Wade Jones. They then worked with The Matadors to release their debut single 'Got A Job' under the name The Miracles. The single was distributed by the New York-based End Records in November 1957, as was its follow-up 'Money', not to be confused with the Barrett Strong single of the same name.

Berry Gordy was an ambitious man; he pined to have his own record label like his sister Gwen who, encouraged by her working relationship with Billy Davis, had started the Anna label in 1958. The label was named after her sister, who was also a partner, and was enjoying limited success despite radio airplay restrictions (the number of black acts achieving high sales figures was spasmodic at this time because whites re-recorded black originals and radio airplay was given to the white cover-versions). The Anna label's biggest-selling single was the Gordy/Bradford-penned 'Money (That's What I Want)', recorded by Barrett Strong and leased by Gordy to his sister in 1959.

Having his records scattered about different companies for distribution and promotion was not an ideal working environment for Gordy. His only answer was to found his own company. With encouragement from Smokey Robinson, Gordy once again persuaded his family to loan him money, this time $800 in 1959 from the family Ber-Berry Co-op fund, to open the Tamla label, a subsidiary of his future Tamla Motown company. 'Tamla' was a spin-off from the Debbie Reynolds' hit of the time, 'Tammy's In Love'; Gordy intended to use 'Tammy' but it was already registered as a label. And 'Motown' was the abbreviation of Detroit's nickname 'motor town'.

The Motown label was launched in 1961 when Tamla had released over twenty singles, the first being Marv Johnson's 'Come To Me' in January 1959, although Johnson wasn't strictly speaking a Tamla act. When Gordy secured his licensing arrangement with United Artists he had to withdraw his rights to Johnson, although he continued working with him. In a short time, however, Gordy would cut his ties with the powerful white-owned companies and press, promote and distribute his own product from his small, but slowly expanding business on 2648 West Grand Boulevard, in a once-affluent Detroit neighbourhood. Gordy's second wife, Raynoma, transformed the near-derelict two-storey building, slotted between a funeral parlour and a beauty shop in a row of houses, into a pulsating music concern. Berry, his wife and their young son Kerry lived in the upstairs of the house, while the Tamla Motown offices were downstairs. The dining room was gutted to become the sales and distribution office, the kitchen became the control room, and the book-keeping staff took over the one-time living room. The house already had a studio built on the back, which had been used for photography; a sign reading 'Hitsville USA' was hung over the front porch and a large poster in the front window proudly declared 'The Sound Of Young America'.

With Tamla Motown underway, the Gordy family businesses were closed down so that everyone could be involved in the new enterprise. Gordy's father 'Pops' became the leading figure in the daily running of the operation, while Berry's sister Esther handled administration and later, with Thomas 'Beans' Bowles headed ITM (International Talent Management), the in-house management company. Esther had, in fact, worked as her brother's secretary prior to joining Tamla Motown. Another Gordy sister, Loucye, was the company's first head of sales, and her musician husband, Ron Wakefield, became a copyist in the arranging department, before transferring to artist co-ordination. Sadly, Loucye died in 1965 without seeing her brother's company enjoy international acclaim. Berry's brother Robert became apprentice studio engineer and enjoyed a short recording career under the pseudonym Robert Kayli in 1958 and 1959. While Tamla Motown's reputation was being established, weekly salaries averaged $3 with a daily hot meal. Raynoma Gordy recalls, 'Nobody complained. This is how interested everyone was in just being a part of it and watching it grow. It was fun, something that was in our blood . . . it was a bunch of people who really believed, working together for a specific goal.'

Berry Gordy carefully chose his early musicians, writers and producers. The musicians were mostly native Detroiters with jazz backgrounds, while the composers wanted a permanent base to work from. However, like Gordy, most of his creative staff couldn't read or write music, so William 'Mickey' Stevenson was hired to oversee the Artist & Repertoire (A&R) department run by writer/producer Clarence Paul. Brian Holland, who recorded 'Shock' in 1958, began his Tamla Motown career as a recording engineer before switching to songwriting, although his talent for creating a commercial sound was not fully realised until he was joined by his brother Eddie and colleague Lamont Dozier. Eddie actually joined Tamla Motown as a singer (his debut single 'Jamie' was issued in January 1962), while Dozier, a member of The Romeos, later The Voicemasters, was a solo artist recording under the pseudonym Lamont Anthony. In 1962 he recorded one single, 'Fortune Teller Tell Me', before teaming up with Freddie Gorman (who later fronted The Originals) and Brian Holland. Mickey Stevenson recognised the potential of a writing/producing trio and encouraged Eddie Holland to replace Gorman, whereupon the famous team of Holland/Dozier/Holland was born, creating million-selling titles for

The Supremes, The Four Tops and Martha and the Vandellas, among others.

The company's back-room staff, especially the musicians, were more important to Gordy than the artists themselves, although they were afforded no public recognition until later years. This tight group ran the studio in their own style, guiding inexperienced staff when required. There were several priceless musicians who played an integral role in building Gordy's company into an empire, including keyboardist/bandleader Earl Van Dyke, who also headed his own touring band and recorded several records in his own right such as *That Motown Sound* album in 1965. Along with Van Dyke were bassists Bob Babbit and James Jamerson, keyboardists Joe Hunter and Johnny Griffin, percussionist Jack Ashford, guitarists Joe Messina, Eddie Willis and Robert White, and saxophonists Eli Fountain and Choker Campbell, who, like Van Dyke, was a recording act in his own right. Joining these and others in Studio A were Eddie 'Bongo' Brown on congas and drummer extraordinaire William 'Benny' Benjamin, also known as Papa Zita (because he looked like a Cuban and swore in Spanish), whose ability to play numerous rhythms simultaneously earned him the respect of colleagues and artists alike. When he was unable to work two drummers trained by him (Uriel Jones and Richard 'Pistol' Allen) replaced him. Interestingly, it was Stevie Wonder who introduced Benjamin and Uriel in 1966, as the latter remembered: 'Stevie could play drums and one day he came in [to the studio] with a drum part he wanted to play. He tried Benny and he couldn't play it. He tried me and I couldn't play it. So then he split it up between us. He sat us both down and said, "Well, you do the foot in this part, and you do the cymbal in this part."'

Other musicians, such as Hank Cosby, David Van De Pitte and Paul Riser, were later promoted to writers and arrangers. These musicians played on almost every Tamla Motown recording during the sixties and were the very foundation of the distinctive Motown Sound, although Jamerson once commented, 'We were doing more of a job than we thought we were doing and we didn't get any songwriting credit. Motown didn't start giving musicians credits on the records until the seventies.' Often known as the Funk Brothers, they recorded live with the singers.

The Temptations' Otis Williams wrote in his autobiography, *Temptations* – '[They] must go down in history as one of the best groups of musicians anywhere. Each of them was a master in his own right and sometimes I'd get so wrapped up listening to them, I'd miss my cue and forget to sing.' It was usually Jamerson who reprimanded him.

As the salaries Gordy paid to musicians were below union rates, many of them moonlighted for Ed Wingate's labels Golden World and Ric Tic. Gordy found out, increased the wages to a reputed $25,000–$50,000 a year, and later purchased both of Wingate's labels, whose artists he signed to Tamla Motown. (Tamla Motown will be referred to as Motown hereafter despite the official name change not taking place until 1976.)

Meanwhile, Motown's music continued to be heard from the basement studio at 2648 West Grand Boulevard, known as 'the snake pit'. It was well named, being a poky, claustrophobic room with soundproofed walls, which did little to contain the music within. A nearby toilet acted as an echo chamber, while a cubicle large enough for a solo singer stood near the console board, where producers would control recording sessions. Backing singers would fight for space and spare microphones. An assortment of instruments, speakers, chairs and other items were crammed in, together with tin cans, bells and other improvised musical instruments. 'Generally, we could cut a track in three to four hours and wrap up a whole album inside a week,' recalled Otis Williams. 'Even though today technology affords artists the chance to make perfect records, they still haven't come up with the machine that puts in that special electricity and energy of those live records.'

Berry Gordy kept a tight rein on all his employees. He introduced a general fines system for absenteeisim, below-standard work and so on, and pinched the idea of a punch clock and card system from his Ford assembly-line days. A stickler for perfection, a strict boss, yet generous to a fault, Gordy was fighting for his life in a white-dominated musical world. Every song recorded had to be a potential number one single, so in-house competition between writers and producers was intense. The acts weren't involved in this rivalry, they were simply the mouthpiece for the music. 'The people at Motown had a choice of sitting in a studio creating something that would make them feel good and proud, or they could be out robbing somebody's house or taking dope,' Berry Gordy once said. 'Or doing some of the things that people do when they're bored.' Once a song was recorded it would be subjected to the Friday meeting of high-ranking marketing staff, headed by Gordy, where its fate was decided. If the vote was unanimous the single was issued. If not, the song was returned to its originators or canned for an album track. Once a song was considered suitable for release, it would be played at a local dance hall where punters would be asked for their opinions.

When artists signed a recording contract, Gordy also secured their publishing rights via Jobete and handled their careers with ITM. These contracts were invariably incomplete and did not guarantee that the signatories' records would actually be released. In essence, Motown's contracts differed little from those offered by other companies at this time, although Clarence Paul thought otherwise, as he told author David Ritz: 'Just about everyone got ripped off at Motown. The royalty rates were sub-standard. Motown had their own songwriting contracts, which were way below the rest of the industry. Tunes were stolen all the time and often credit wasn't properly assigned.' While Smokey Robinson, in his autobiography *Inside My Life* stressed: 'I saw the contracts, I knew that the deals offered were straightforward and, for those days, standard as the twelve-bar blues.'

And it was one of these contracts that Stevie Wonder's mother, Lulu Mae Hardaway, signed on his behalf in 1961, legally binding her eleven-year-old son to Motown for five years. Esther Edwards worked closely with the Michigan Department of Labor in the structuring of the contract to ensure it fell within the tight specifications of the child labour laws. With stipulations that he would receive special schooling in between recording and touring commitments, that Motown would handle all his business affairs and that his royalties, administered by Jobete, would be held in trust for him until he was 21 years old, the contract allowed Wonder to be given a weekly allowance while his mother received regular money for his upkeep and clothing, a godsend to her because she had to escort her son back and forth to the offices. The trust was regularly monitored by government representatives dealing with minors and Motown's own accountants until Wonder was twenty-one years old.

Stevie Wonder was born four weeks premature on 13 May 1950 in a Saginaw hospital. He was Lula Mae Hardaway's third son, and was perfect but tiny. She named him Stevland. His natural father's surname was Judkins, although his birth certificate shows Morris. Hardaway was the surname of his two elder brothers, Milton and Calvin. Baby Stevland was kept alive in an incubator in the hospital's special care unit for a month; it was during this time that he lost his sight. Excessive amounts of oxygen were pumped into the incubator, causing the baby to develop retrolental fibroplasia, a condition in which a fibrous membrane develops behind each eyeball, causing blindness.

Neither of the brothers' fathers lived with Lula Mae, leaving her to struggle to raise her three sons in a grim environment. She supplemented her state benefit with a variety of domestic jobs, and with the support of family and friends was able to clothe and feed her family. Wonder has little, or no, memory of his young life in Saginaw except that he was raised in the Baptist faith and had the love of a wonderful mother who was, he often said, 'fortunate enough to be married to more than one man'.

However, in time the fight for survival became so desperate that Lula Mae moved her young family to Detroit, one hundred miles northwest of Saginaw, for a better life. They moved into a small house on Breckinridge Street, on the city's west side. 'You'd call it lower middle class or upper lower class. We had enough to get by,' Wonder remembered. 'Sometimes we'd go without eating, some-times for days. I can prove it by the pain I felt in my stomach . . . In the winter my mother, brothers and I went to this dry dock where there was coal and steal some to keep warm. To a poor person that's not stealing, that's not a crime. That's a necessity.' As the family settled into their new lifestyle, Lula Mae was reunited with Paul Hardaway, the father of her first two sons. He found work in a nearby bakery, while she continued her domestic chores and raised two further sons, Timothy and Larry, and their one daughter, Renee.

During his young life, Wonder and his mother consulted doctors and specialists to see whether his sight could be restored. Time and again they were given hope, hanging on to the fact that medicine was changing, cures were being found, but more often than not, the answer was the same – there was nothing to be done. 'They talked crazy stuff. They couldn't wake up the dead,' Wonder later said. 'There are things that they said they could do, but I went to more doctors that said if there was any way that they could return my sight they would try. It's one thing when you're blind from birth, you don't know what it's like to see, so it's just like seeing anyway . . . The sensation of seeing is not one I have, so I don't worry about it.' Lula Mae was more upset than her son and often sought guidance from her Baptist ministers, who eventually convinced her that Stevland's sight was not lost in vain. He would have other, more treasured, qualities in life, they said. Lula Mae expressed it thus: 'I didn't know that God would take his eyesight for the gift of music. It really did hurt.' Especially, she recalled, when she watched her son stumble around, courageously trying to be independent. When Wonder sensed her total despair he would smile, convincing her he was happy to be blind because it was, after all, a gift from God Almighty.

As he grew, the youngster became increasingly aware of his special needs and the protective arm of his family, which, on occasion, suffocated him. He also realised his other senses were becoming more acute, and this gave him the confidence to become more adventurous: 'I used my hearing to find out where people are, whether they're young, old, even if they're really happy. All from their voices and what they say.' As an adult, he believes he has more insight into a person's real nature than those with sight, because he cannot judge from appearance: 'Maybe I can find the truth about them . . . because people who see often tend to choose the book by the cover. I have to do it my way. Maybe a person is also beautiful inwardly and that's the side I'll know first.' Wonder's growing curiosity about reality, his surroundings and the people who touched his life, fuelled his positive attitude in tackling everyday life without fear. The essence of that development was simple: his blindness wasn't abnormal to him, only to other people. He learnt to swim, ride a bike and skate. And he held his own in a fight. In fact, he said, as a child he was no different from others of his age:

> I spent all my time like other kids, playing, fighting and going out on the railway tracks. Everything they did I did, even down to playing Cowboys and Indians. I went through a few stages of 'here comes the blind man' but then the kids didn't understand and I used to whomp them anyway. I had a sling shot and I used to like to hear it hit the rocks. It sounded just like a gun. I used to take tyres off abandoned cars and roll them down the alley. Yeh, it was a good childhood.

He also joined in the popular pastime of hopping barns. This entailed jumping on and across the roofs of small sheds in his neighbours' gardens: 'In the ghetto where I lived we'd hop atop them, one to the other . . . I remember one time my aunt came and said "OK, Steve, Mama said don't be doin' that," and I said, "Aw, fuck you."' Neighbours heard and reprimanded his aunt for allowing the youngster to be foul-mouthed. This incensed Lula Mae who whipped him with her ironing cord, a punishment often administered. But it was playing 'doctors and nurses' with the neighbourhood girls that got him into most trouble, as he recollected to *Rolling Stone* magazine in 1973:

> We used to sneak and do it to little girls. I used to get into a lot of shit. I got caught trying to mess with a girl, she was eight years old. I really was . . . taking the girl's clothes off . . . I don't understand how I did that stuff. I mean, I was in it. I had her in my room with my clothes off. And she gave it away cause she started laughin' and gigglin' 'cause I was touching her.

Calvin and Milton would contribute to their younger brother's behaviour by playing on his blindness, enticing him into situations they knew would incur their mother's wrath. One such escapade related to his brothers deciding he needed more light in a room at home. The situation got dangerously out of hand when the boxes of matches they ignited to provide the extra light almost burned down their house. Although Wonder is quick to point out that his early memories of Detroit are of happier, fun-packed times, he also admitted to experiencing dark episodes of panic and gnawing loneliness, particularly when finding himself outside his familiar environment. Up to the age of ten, he was never allowed to wander unescorted, and when given the freedom to do so would invariably have difficulty in finding his way home.

However, there was one consuming passion in Wonder's young life – music. Due to the family's breadline existence, they couldn't afford to buy him a musical instrument, so Lula Mae encouraged him to listen to the radio. Wonder remembers, 'I started school when I was four and as soon as I came home I'd turn the radio on. By the time I was six, I was spending my evenings listening to R&B.' His favourite station was the local Detroit WCHB, and he religiously listened to the evening programme, *Sundown*. 'Detroit had the best cross section of music and different cultures,' he once said, and cited The Five Royales, The Staple Singers and Del Shannon as prime examples of that diversity. He took his listening to the streets, where he sang his version of songs by Johnny Ace, and others he had memorised. Or he disappeared into a neighbour's house to spend hours playing the piano until the occupant could stand it no more. 'I started on things like "Three Blind Mice" and then started playing tunes I heard on the radio,' he recalls. 'It seems that everything I heard I was able to play. Folks used to say to my parents, "He's gonna be a great musician", but I never really thought about it.' (When that neighbour later moved from the locality, she gave Wonder the piano, much to his mother's annoyance.)

His musical ear also brought him promotion from choir lead singer to junior deacon at the local Whitestone Baptist Church, where his family prayed. Despite the minister's hope that his young prodigy would follow in his ministerial footsteps, Wonder's ambitions lay elsewhere. 'I decided to be a sinner instead,' he quipped, 'to follow my love of R&B!'

Learning music stood Wonder in good stead at school, because he demonstrated the same enthusiasm in his studies. Registered as Stevland Judkins, he was a bright pupil. When he became bored with the daily routine of basic teaching, he turned his interest to science and world history; he remembers, 'The most interesting to me was about civilisations before ours, how advanced people really were, how high they had brought themselves only to bring themselves down because of missing links. The weak foundations. So the whole thing crumbled, and that's sad.'

When Wonder was four years old, an uncle gave him his first musical instrument. It was a four-holed harmonica taken from a key chain on which he used to emulate the harmonica sequences from songs heard on the radio. His incredible ear for sound enabled him to learn quickly, and with constant practice he began mimicking the Blues, in the style of Bobby Bland and Jimmy Reed: 'I took a little of everybody's style and made up my own . . . I kept finding new things, new chords and new tunes. It was like searching in a new place you've never been before.' However, his first passion was the drums. 'I've always loved them. When I was seven or eight I used to beat holes in the walls trying to get the hang of it.' He also improvised on tin cans, bottles, any object that would make a noise. Then his prayer was answered at a family reunion, when one of the guests arrived with a drum kit. Wonder says, 'He took me by the hand and showed me where everything was and I thought then I had to master them. The next year I got a set for Christmas and wore the skins out in one day. I beat the hell out of them in the back yard. I had a girlfriend at the time who couldn't stand the noise. She threatened to cut them up with a knife. She went in a hurry!'

Playing and singing his improvised songs on street corners and being appreciated by passing neighbours, gave the young Wonder confidence. Gradually, other musically minded youngsters joined him, to take their music to local functions, parties, and so on. Wonder was being noticed for something other than his blindness. He felt his music made him belong and, maybe, this was what the Baptist ministers meant – his lost sight was replaced by another talent, that of producing music.

One local youngster in particular, John Glover, joined Wonder in his musical adventures. Glover's harmonies complemented his friend's lead and before long they were dubbed 'Stevie And John', the neighbours' favourite duettists. Wonder also played drums and harmonica, and John, the guitar, as they performed Marvin Gaye and Smokey Robinson material. 'This was a special part of my life,' remembers Wonder, 'because I owe a lot to the neighbours, and John's mother, Ruth Glover, who was actually responsible for us getting to Motown.'

Gerald White was one of the boys' regular followers. 'He told his brother Ronnie [a member of The Miracles] about me and when Ronnie got back from touring I sang and played for him my composition *Lonely Boy*. He said he'd introduce me to Berry Gordy.' Not an easy thing to do because Gordy was protected by a personally chosen team who first had to be convinced of the youngster's talent. A further audition, therefore, was arranged with Brian Holland, Motown's then talent scout, which left him sharing Ronnie White's enthusiasm. Holland then told the company's A&R director Mickey Stevenson, 'Stevie is the most gifted singer I've seen and he has a real feel for his music.' Mickey Stevenson, in turn, consulted Berry Gordy. Meanwhile, a bewildered youngster had no idea he was auditioning for a future career in music; as he said, 'Singing for me was fun, that's all!'

Berry Gordy was eating breakfast when Mickey Stevenson burst into his office, insisting he hurry to the nearby studio. Leaving his meal, Gordy found Ronnie White with a young blind boy. Gordy later wrote in his autobiography *To Be Loved* – 'He was singing, playing the bongos and blowing on a harmonica. His voice didn't knock me out, but his harmonica playing did. Something about him was infectious.' Wonder too remembered his first meeting with Gordy: 'I didn't know he was the same guy I'd heard a lot about. But I did know he was a black man and someone who was making a good, positive direction in the black community. Anybody who would let me come into their studio and let me play so many instruments had to be a good person.'

Signed to Motown in 1961, The Supremes' Mary Wilson remembered seeing the young Stevie arrive at the offices with his mother and brother. As Gordy ushered the party into the studio, Wilson heard him ask the youngster to play with the instruments. 'Stevie would jump up, find his way to something else, and start playing that – keyboards, horns, percussion. Nothing seemed beyond him,' she wrote in her autobiography *Dreamgirl: My Life As A Supreme*, 'I especially remember him playing a harmonica he'd brought with him. Of course we were all dumbstruck with amazement. At the time, the Supremes were still the youngest artists on the roster. To see someone as young as Stevie was something else.'

When contracts were signed and exchanged, Stevland Morris was eleven years old. Berry Gordy's Motown was two.

LITTLE WATER BOY

'At first we were told . . . to stay away from [Stevie] because we might be a bad influence'

Martha Reeves

'Everyone loved [Stevie] and that was a good thing, because he was always full of mischief'

Mary Wilson

'They were a comical version of everything in me'

Berry Gordy, speaking of Stevie Wonder and Marvin Gaye

Berry Gordy gradually built up his roster of acts to include The Temptations, Mary Wells, Marvin Gaye, The Miracles, Martha and the Vandellas and The Contours who, with The Marvelettes and The Supremes, would work with his supportive and enthusiastic in-house team of musicians, producers and writers. 'The Motown Sound' or 'The Sound Of Young America' that was to become known internationally was in its early stages. And Stevland Morris was to become a part of this growing family company.

Part of the youngster's grooming process was a name change. Stevland Morris held no commercial ring; it was cumbersome and dull. As often happens, a new name came by accident, when, after attending one of his rehearsals, an excited Esther Edwards dubbed him 'a little Stevie Wonder'. In contrast, Clarence Paul recalls that the name change happened when he chanced to call the youngster 'little Stevie', while the musicians chose 'the boy wonder'. However it came about, the name Little Stevie Wonder stayed until 1964.

With encouragement from Berry Gordy, Lula Mae escorted her son to Motown after school and during the weekends. He would be welcomed by the musicians, particularly Benny Benjamin, from whom Wonder learnt a great deal. Indeed, decades later, his influence can distinctly be heard in Wonder's drumming style. 'I remember the first time I recorded in the studio I cried,' Stevie recalled in later life. It was a song called "Thank You Mother" which I wrote to show my mother I appreciated all she'd done for me.'

The A&R (Artists & Repertoire) department was another of Wonder's favourite haunts, where he spent time after school with Martha Reeves who was then the department's secretary but who, in a short time, fronted her own successful trio, the Vandellas. She told author Gerri Hirshey in *Nowhere To Run*, 'At first we were told by some of the administration to stay away from [Stevie] because we might be a bad influence. But it was OK to be his friend around the office.' If Reeves was busy, the youngster made a nuisance of himself, by disassembling her office, until she had little choice but to spend time with him, exchanging jokes, discussing music, teaching him to dance and duetting. Regrettably, these impromptu sessions were never taped. Reeves recalls, 'I remember sitting with him, day after day, with this little old tape recorder he liked to play with. It was fun. Stevie at this Hammond organ, he'd play those silly chords.' More seriously, she told DJ Alan Taylor, 'He would play rhythms and melodies which no child of his age should even know, he was that creative.' On other occasions, he would sneak up on Reeves while she was on the phone, or play tricks at her expense. They enjoyed a brother–sister relationship that exists to this day. Reeves remembers:

He used to come over to my house after sessions at Motown when [his mum] didn't pick him up. He knew and loved my family just like he's a member, because we took him in. It's not like he was a little blind kid. Stevie was active . . . he would beat everybody up. He was taller than most of them. They'd tear my mama's house up. They made Stevie ride a bike. That's something he'll never forget.

Years later, when Reeves' mother died, the adult tearaway sang the Lord's Prayer at her funeral.

During Wonder's grooming process, he was given a free run of the Motown building, but spent most of his time in and around the studio. This meant that some recording sessions were a nightmare because the participating artists never knew when a wandering blind kid would sneak in. Many a take was ruined when Wonder traipsed in, unable to see the red light shining above the outside studio door. Many songs, therefore, actually feature an uncredited Wonder as a vocalist, drummer, hand-clapper, box banger or chain rattler. In fact, any item that would make an unusual sound.

Berry Gordy's first white artist, fifteen-year-old Connie Van Dyke, who recorded for the Motown label told John O'Dowd:

> I was recording 'Oh Freddy' with Mickey Stevenson producing, Stevie came bursting through the back door of the studio, right in the middle of my session – the door led out to an alleyway and he used to come in that way because at the time I think he lived just down the street. He started making funny faces at me and turned the place upside down with his cutting up.

He actually disrupted the recording session so much that Van Dyke threatened to sabotage one of his sessions in retaliation. The youngster simply laughed at her, saying, 'Yeh, but I won't be able to see you [do it]'. Unfortunately, Van Dyke's single 'Oh Freddy' sold poorly. The singer's Motown career only spanned eighteen months, so she probably never carried out her threat.

The Supremes' Mary Wilson also remembered the young boy's antics:

> Learning every inch of the place, [Stevie] eventually got to the point where he didn't need help getting from room to room, and before long he was pulling his practical jokes. Everyone loved him and that was a good thing, because he was full of mischief. Stevie seemed to always know who was standing near him, and one of his favourite pastimes was to run up and pinch ladies on their bottoms.

His other pastime was to feel women's breasts. Upon introduction he'd first feel their faces, arms, hands enabling him to recognise them again. Then, invariably, he would drop his hands to their breasts, as Berry Gordy confirmed – 'Stevie would [then] quickly apologise to the girl for his "mistake". Then he'd smile in our direction as if to say "eat your heart out fellas!"'

Even Berry Gordy himself wasn't spared these antics, Wonder's gift of mimicry was mercilessly practised, enabling him to perfect different accents and voices:

> I knew the com-line numbers of everyone at Motown and would change my voice and say 'this is Berry Gordy and I want you to get Stevie that tape recorder.' [He had already broken four recorders trying to establish how they worked.] After they fell for this about three times and never got the recorder back, they gave me one of my own.

Gordy, who believed Wonder inherited his humour from Lula Mae, was horrified to learn that his staff believed he actually sounded like Wonder's vocal impersonation and went to great lengths to change his accent. But it wasn't just Wonder who earmarked the Motown boss for the butt of his jokes. Fellow Motowner Marvin Gaye was also a believable mimic, and the two regularly had competitions at Gordy's expense. 'They were a comical version of everything in me!' he once admitted, while other artists complained they were 'a pain in the arse!'

As Stevie Wonder played and annoyed, unaware that his career was being planned, Gordy mulled over the problem of presenting him on record, and of how to train his voice to cope with a full musical accompaniment. In the end he assigned writer/producer Clarence Paul to Wonder: the perfect combination. Paul became the youngster's surrogate father and was the most important figure in his early career. It was this unique relationship that balanced personal ambitions and professional expectations. As Motown guitarist Dave Hamilton told author Nelson George in *Where Did Our Love Go?* – 'Clarence shaped Stevie. I remember when Stevie would be at Clarence's house and Clarence would teach him to sing those standard tunes like "Masquerade", those tunes that he was singing that the people would be amazed to see a kid his age singing. Clarence was teaching him because he was a helluva singer himself'. Even at his tender age, Wonder recognised the importance of Paul in his life: 'Everyone over eleven was a parent. Clarence Paul loved me like his own son. Esther Edwards, all the musicians and artists watched over me.' Being part of the Gordy family also had its downside, because he would regularly be scolded for eating too much candy. Wanda, of The Marvelettes, would often reprimand Wonder but not the supplier, in-house composer Hank Cosby, who recalled, 'Stevie always asked me if I'd brought him candy, and that went on for years until he was about eighteen or nineteen and he didn't want nobody to see me bring him the candy.'

It took a year to groom the boy Wonder sufficiently to record his first single. By this time, he'd not only stockpiled his own compositions, but had mastered the drums, harmonica and piano. 'I'd written a lot of songs by the age of ten but I forgot most of them because I didn't have any way of keeping them,' the singer later recalled. 'I'd write tunes every time I met a girl I thought I'd like. They used to love me playing them songs I'd written especially for them.' To ride on the tailcoat of Ray Charles seemed the obvious route to take, whereupon Clarence Paul, Brian Holland and Mickey Stevenson provided the Charles-inspired 'You Made A Vow', which was re-named 'Mother Thank You', a love song suited to Wonder's young age. Nelson George wrote: '[The song's] cutesy melody and hokey lyrics set an unenviably shlocky standard that too many of his subsequent records would match.' However, before the single could be pressed, it was pulled as unsuitable. Yet, the title would later find its way as the B-side of Wonder's sixth single, 'Castles In The Sand'. And, for the record, it was re-titled for the second time to 'Thank You (For Loving Me All The Way)'!

Clarence Paul teamed with Hank Cosby to write Wonder's official debut single on the Tamla label (where he would stay until 1981), which hit the record stores in August 1962. Titled 'I Call It Pretty Music (But The Old People Call It The Blues) (Part I)', it featured Marvin Gaye on drums, was packaged in a picture sleeve but had no selling power. Two months later, 'Little Water Boy' followed, a duet between Wonder and Paul, who also composed the title. The mediocre song likewise disappeared without trace.

While the singles bombed, Motown already had two finished albums ready for release, but Berry Gordy was undecided which to issue first. So, for public-familiarity reasons *Tribute To Uncle Ray* became Little Stevie Wonder's debut album. An obvious ploy perhaps, in view of how successful the blind Blues artist was in America and later the world, where he was revered as the master of his art. *Tribute To Uncle Ray* was actually scheduled for an October 1962 release, a month following what should have been Wonder's original debut *The Jazz Soul Of Little Stevie*.

With a seated youngster, dressed in white jumper and black trousers (which failed to reach the top of his blue socks), and holding his harmonica, the album's front cover was as incongruous as most produced by Motown at the time. In the sleeve notes for *Tribute To Uncle Ray*, Billie Jean Brown wrote, 'In this album, Stevie forgoes his playing of the harmonica, piano, organ, drums and bongos in favour of his vocal abilities. He displays soulfulness that few adults, and fewer still 11-year-olds, will ever attain. Though it has been said, and is admittedly true, that no one can sing these tunes like Ray Charles, it must be concluded that here Stevie does one whale of a job . . .' Kicking off with the Charles classic 'Hallelujah I Love Her So', (in which Charles' name in the song was replaced by Little Stevie's), Wonder's strained voice then battled through 'Ain't That Love', yet settled with ease into the Blues-tinged 'Don't You Know'. The often-rehearsed ballad 'The Masquerade Is Over' portrayed young emotion, and the gospel-styling of the folk song 'Frankie & Johnny' proved the youngster was quickly learning vocal versatility. With hard-hitting Blues dictating the rhythm of 'Drown In My Own Tears', Wonder turned his emotions upside down to capture the feelings behind another Charles' R&B hit 'Come Back Baby', while Berry Gordy's composition 'My Baby's Gone' was Motown-styled Blues. 'Sunset', written by Paul and Wonder, who was credited as Judkins, was a ballad of some note, showing a maturity beyond his young years. However, the general consensus was simple: little Stevie's voice was no match for Charles' superior material, and, tribute or not, without a hit single to catapult sales, the album stagnated until August 1963.

By contrast *The Jazz Soul Of Little Stevie* (carrying another picture of the young artist from the white jumper photo shoot, but this time from the waist up) was more significant. Included on the album was the original version of 'Fingertips', the re-worked title that would launch Wonder as a successful recording artist. His expertise on harmonica, drums, piano, organ and bongos can be heard throughout this adventurous but mediocre release, particularly via 'Square' and 'Soul Bongo', co-written by Marvin Gaye. The Latin-influenced 'Manhattan At Six' was bearable, leading into 'Paulsby', a showcase for his inspired musicianship. The remaining tracks crossed from Blues to soul, with Wonder's co-writing credits with Paul on 'Wondering' and 'Session Number 112', while Berry Gordy's solitary composition 'Bam' closed the album. The true spirit of the project to display Wonder's instrumental maturity on a big-band jazz project, was not realised until years later when it became a Motown collector's item. Once again Billie Jean Brown gushed sleeve notes, which included: 'Adored and acclaimed by all who witness his amazing performance, Stevie is touted as a musical genius. Not only are outside observers amazed by his versatility, but Tamla-Motown artists and employess are kept limp as he energetically sings and plays for hours . . .' Brown noted that Wonder was thirteen years old on this album, while on *Tribute To Uncle Ray* he was eleven!

Meanwhile, on the singles front, and sandwiched between The Miracles' 'You've Really Got A Hold On Me' and Marvin Gaye's 'Hitch Hike', Brian Holland, Janie Bradford and Lamont Dozier were recruited for Wonder's third single in December 1962. The changeover worked – 'Contract On Love', with The Temptations' melodious support vocals, sold better than its predecessors, although it bombed miserably against The Miracles' number eight position in the mainstream chart (number one in the R&B listing), and Gaye's hit at numbers ten and twelve respectively.

Nevertheless, 'Contract On Love' marked a more confident vocalist, with positive expectations for the future, even though the single's mini-success may, many believe, be attributable to its exposure on Motown's first American touring revue.

Chapter 3

THE TWELVE-YEAR-OLD
GENIUS

'There were lots of drugs around Motown in the early sixties'
Clarence Paul

'Realistically, there was nothing for me . . . but to make rugs for a living'
Little Stevie Wonder

'You really had to start paying attention to Stevie after "Fingertips"'
Marvin Gaye

Berry Gordy knew that the best way to sell records was to present his artists before the public. As many of Motown's albums did not carry pictures of the acts on the packaging, only if they played live would they cease to be faceless names. Audiences could enjoy not only their live performances but also the choreographed stage routines. Very few booking agencies were interested in handling black artists so Gordy had to find an alternative means of exposure. With the help of his creative staff, he put together his own touring package of major acts, and late in 1962 was able to convince certain promoters to book his package, which he dubbed 'The Motown Revue'. Most dates were booked on the 'chitlin' circuit, which comprised venues catering for black audiences, while a handful were frequented by mixed races.

Before leaving Detroit, Gordy assembled his artists together and instructed them that they should act with dignity as they were representing his company, that male performers should sit at the back of the bus, with the girls and their chaperones in front. Of course, once the battered bus, resembling a relic from a nearby scrapyard, with 'Motor City Tour' blazoned along its sides, crossed the Michigan state line, the occupants mingled.

The Marvelettes, The Contours, Mary Wells, Martha and the Vandellas, The Miracles, Marvin Gaye, The Temptations, Singin' Sammy Ward, The Supremes and Little Stevie Wonder were the participating acts, backed on stage by Choker Campbell and His Show of Stars Band. Bill Murray was MC, and Thomas 'Beans' Bowles (who assisted Gordy in the tour's itinerary) travelled with them as tour manager and stand-in saxophonist. 'Berry packed far too many people on the bus,' 'Beans' Bowles told author David Ritz in *Divided Soul*. 'We were always overcrowded. And he booked way too many dates. The strain was bad. We had a bad accident in November '62, my driver was killed and we were lucky not to have others [killed]. There might have been a little weed around but no coke. Who had the money?'

Berry Gordy prided himself that Motown was a drug-free company, a picture painted for the media, but, in reality, many staffers were regular users, as Clarence Paul recalls: 'There were lots of drugs around Motown in the early sixties, just like there were lots of drugs around any black neighbourhood. Marvin and I did our fair share of cocaine beginning in the early sixties. We were into it early on. Other artists, like Little Stevie, hated the stuff.'

The tour kicked off at the Howard Theater, Washington DC, and took in 94 performances through the Midwest, down south and back to Harlem's Apollo Theater. Segregation still operated in southern states, which meant blacks were often confined to theatre balconies. Or, as Otis Williams remembered, 'From the stage you could look out across the auditorium and see a rope running smack down the middle of the aisle – blacks one side, whites the other. We couldn't believe it. Angry, we asked "what the fuck is this rope for?" but we knew the answer.' Weapons were openly carried into the theatres by both races, and rivalry between the two could have ignited at any time, yet when the music started, both races united as one. It was when the music stopped that the artists experienced life-threatening situations. Bullets were frequently dug out from the sides of the travelling bus and the musicians encountered racial hatred at its most degrading. They were refused admission to restaurants and hotels, and were banned from using outside toilets at petrol stations. As Martha Reeves puts it, 'It's an insult when you've got money in your pocket and you can't eat. Have you ever had a meal of sardines and popcorn?'

Not being allowed to stay in certain hotels meant sleeping sitting up on the bus because there wasn't sufficient room to stretch out. In an eighties interview, The Temptations' Melvin Franklin remembered, 'I used to sleep in the luggage rack. Wasn't any of us under 6ft 1in. I can't climb like I did then, got rheumatoid arthritis. Maybe it's from being a 6ft 1in sardine all them years.' Mary Wilson also recollected those heady days when people paired off, while others gambled, smoked pot, slept or rehearsed. They usually dressed for the stage en route or in a public toilet. 'Every few days we would stop at a cheap motel to bathe and wash some clothes. We seldom got to sleep one in a bed, but compared to sleeping sitting up on a hard bus seat, being able to lie on any mattress was heaven.'

Little Stevie adapted well to his first major tour. His fellow artists went to great lengths to protect and care for him off-stage, but their patience was stretched at times. For instance, sitting at the rear of the bus with the musicians, he often played his harmonica for hours non-stop, usually when everyone else wanted to sleep. Otis Williams recollects:

Then it got to be about two or three in the morning. Someone would yell 'Stevie man, put that damn harmonica down and go to sleep.' If that didn't work, we tried 'Steven, we're gonna beat your ass if you don't take that damn harmonica . . .' and he'd laugh because he knew we'd never do that. Not that the thought didn't cross our minds now and then!

Play-acting also got Little Stevie into trouble. An example of this is recalled by Martha Reeves, when she says that, having been primed by his cohorts, he would yell from the bus window at a young girl, then describe her clothes and hair colouring:

The startled girl would look around and see Stevie with his dark glasses on. 'Are you talking to me?' she would inquire. We'd be killing ourselves trying to suppress our laughter. We all knew Stevie had no way of knowing what she was wearing or how she looked, yet he was a master at pulling off these gags with a straight face.

On a more serious note, touring disrupted the youngster's education. His teachers complained to the Detroit Board of Education that his studies had lapsed and that if this continued he would need to reconsider his working situation. It was true that quality learning time was in short supply while touring because Stevie's days were crammed with travelling, performing, playing and sleeping, plus, his adolescent excitement meant he wanted to be involved in all aspects of this adult musical family. This was a situation that was later resolved following a showdown with the authorities.

The 'Motown Revues' were non-stop entertainment Motown-style: slick stage acts, pulsating dance rhythms and strong melodies, from young and enthusiastic artists whose sole aim was to press home 'The Sound Of Motown'. New single releases were performed alongside established tunes, each accompanied by corresponding choreography and backed by the company's finest musicians. Little Stevie usually opened the show, because of the labour laws relating to performing minors. The opening hour changed from state to state, which resulted in erratic showtimes. Audiences adored the little blind guy, who displayed such expertise playing the harmonica as he jumped around the stage, swaying his head in time with the musicians' pounding, hard beat. He sang, squealed, laughed; his infectious enjoyment in performing bouncing from stage to auditorium. Mary Wilson recalls, '[He] never failed to get a crowd going. So much so, he was a difficult act to follow.'

When the Revue hit New York, it stayed at the Apollo for a week, where the shows were taped and later released on the album *Recorded Live At The Apollo*, and re-titled *The Motortown Revue* for British release in May 1965. Wonder's contribution was an electrifying 'I Call It Pretty Music (But The Old People Call It The Blues)' and the mellow 'Moon River'.

Having touched success with 'Contract On Love' and armed with positive feedback from Little Stevie's live performances, Berry Gordy was desperate to sustain that interest. With the youngster's energetic act in mind, he decided to record his show at Chicago's Regal Theater, a move that angered other artists, because, in their opinion, Little Stevie was attracting too much personal preference for a no-hit artist. He was unaware of these feelings at this time, although sensed an unspoken animosity from certain quarters. In all honesty, he was too young to understand, believing everyone at Motown to be friends. He would learn otherwise.

While Little Stevie toured Hank Cosby worked on a big-band style tune, developed from a jamming session with Wonder, 'Beans' Bowles and Benny Benjamin. Cosby had dubbed the tune 'Fingertips' because it featured Wonder playing bongos. As neither Cosby nor Wonder could adapt the tune for lyrics, it had remained unfinished. However, Little Stevie was so smitten with the instrumental that he used it as his finale in his Chicago show and ad libbed his way through the high-octane performance before allowing Clarence Paul to escort him off stage, against a backdrop of a roaring audience begging for more of the same. The next act, Mary Wells and her conductor Joe Swift (each act had its own conductor) waited in the wings for their entrance. 'When the crowd demanded an encore, Clarence pushed Stevie back on stage,' Mary Wilson recalled. 'It was a choreographed ploy to make the audience think that Stevie didn't know where he was. Joe Swift had already taken over the conductor's spot, and when Stevie started the reprise of "Fingertips" Joe was shouting "What key, Little Stevie, what key?"'

Berry Gordy's ploy to record his protégé live worked; the whole album, but particularly 'Fingertips', fully captured the thrill and electric energy of his spontaneous performance. Titled *Recorded Live – The 12 Year Old Genius*, the album featured a seven-minute version of 'Fingertips' but when issued as a single Gordy split it into two parts. Radio DJs preferred the B-side, which included the 'what key' sequence, so the topside became 'Fingertips Part 2'. Berry Gordy crossed his fingers.

'Fingertips Part 2', boasting a picture sleeve, marked Little Stevie's debut British release on the Oriole label in August 1963.

It passed by unnoticed to all except Motown's devoted cult followers. In America, the story was very different: Gordy's gamble had worked. 'Fingertips Part 2' was the first live recording to top the singles chart, a position it held for three weeks, and was Motown's second number one single (The Marvelettes' 'Please Mr Postman' was first in December 1961). Interestingly, while Wonder sat at the pole position, a song that he was later to record held the number four slot – 'Blowin' In The Wind' by Peter, Paul and Mary. 'When "Fingertips" was number one,' Little Stevie later commented, 'I didn't realise and understand how many people had bought it, how much it all meant, how many other artists had broken their hearts and died trying to achieve exactly that . . . and there were so many other good records around at the time. The Chiffons were big with "He's So Fine" and Major Lance was up there with "Monkey Time".'

'You really had to start paying attention to Stevie after "Fingertips"', Marvin Gaye told David Ritz. 'No matter what else you might be doing, you'd always know that Stevie had a superior musical intelligence and was learning just as fast as you.'

For the time being at least, Little Stevie had found his niche in music but instead of basking in the accolade, he once more felt the weight of The Board of Education, which demanded his schooling take precedence over his career. The Board, encouraged by his father, considered he'd neglected his education to such an extent they had no choice but to legally bind him to stay in Detroit's public school until he was nineteen years old. It was a dumbfounded Little Stevie who said, 'One teacher told me that I had three big disadvantages in life – I was poor, blind and black. Realistically, there was nothing for me, indeed for any uneducated blind guy, but to make rugs for a living.' The teacher later apologised, but the damage had been done. Wonder rebelled against the system and fought with his fellow students who taunted him. The odds were against him:

> The main thing was that [The Board] wanted me to be with kids of my own age. But the travelling didn't harm my education; in fact, it helped me a lot, especially with things like history. When I went to Europe I'd make tapes about places I visited like the

Eiffel Tower or the Tower of London. I recorded the sounds of the places to get the atmosphere and interviewed people who worked there. I was [later] awarded credits for the tapes when I got to school and they were played to the other kids.

In a last-ditch attempt to save her son's career, Lula Mae took matters into her own hands by contacting the Michigan School for the Blind, based at Lansing, 150 miles from Detroit. 'We saw Dr Thompson and he said he didn't see why I couldn't get the two things together,' Wonder remembers. 'It would save my career and I'd still be able to go to school. In the music field you can't say "let's wait". It's a rat race and won't wait for anyone.' A study programme was compiled that included the private tutor Ted Hull, himself partially sighted. This confined Little Stevie to two weeks' study out of four at the Michigan School and, when touring, two hours tutorial nightly. Motown and Lula Mae agreed to the stipulations. Ted Hull also acted as liaison officer between Motown and the school until 1969, during which time he taught his pupil the value of money with a small weekly allowance, and familiarisation of personal space, like hotel rooms which invariably were identical, comprising a bed, bathroom, minimal furniture and a phone. Starting at six in the morning, Hull prepared his pupil's schedule, usually allocating ten to one o'clock for studies to ensure he didn't lag too far behind other students, before juggling other duties into the day and often the night. Always he was at Little Stevie's side acting as valet, driver or personal assistant. Later on in his career, the singer acknowledged Ted Hull as his mentor:

Having experienced travelling around the world, he helped me a great deal to communicate with people . . . If Ted had been a different person he might have felt that as long as we got the studies done and toured a little that would be enough. But he explained foreign currencies to me, taught me about the electric currents and their differences. He connected the blind world with the sighted world.'

Meanwhile, to capitalise on his debut American chart-topper, Little Stevie's third album *Recorded Live – The 12 Year Old Genius* was issued in June in America and Britain during August 1963. Produced by Berry Gordy, Wonder played harmonica, bongos, drums and piano throughout the project, which included many magical live moments like 'Soul Bongo', 'Don't You Know', 'Hallelujah I Love Her So', 'Drown In My Own Tears', together with his immature interpretations of standards like 'The Masquerade Is Over'. Typical of Motown's incongruous album sleeves at this time, *The 12 Year Old Genius* showed three oblong-shaped pictures of Little Stevie on the front cover: one swiped from the *Tribute To Uncle Ray* cover, with a second to be recycled in negative form for the future *With A Song In My Heart* album. It was the music that counted and no one was more pleased than Berry Gordy when the album repeated the success of 'Fingertips Part 2' by dominating the American R&B chart. To all intents and purposes, Little Stevie Wonder was on his way!

Three months on from the album's American release, reality set in once more with an attempt to recapture the vital rawness of 'Fingertips Part 2'. As a follow-up Gordy chose the Cosby/Paul composition 'Workout Stevie, Workout' which stalled at number 33 in the R&B listing. Not a promising result by any means, but when set against the larger picture of his artist's expanding popularity outside America, he felt it was only a matter of time before his investment paid dividends.

Britain was rapidly becoming Motown's second major market and Stateside Records, which replaced the Oriole label as Motown's European licensee, asked that Little Stevie promote 'Workout Stevie, Workout' in person. With expenses paid, he appeared on ITV's groundbreaking live music show *Ready Steady Go!* and the more mainstream *Thank Your Lucky Stars*. Although audiences warmly greeted this young black kid, record sales remained sluggish. Since 1959 selected Motown records had been released in Britain. The first was Marv Johnson's 'Come To Me' on the London American label. In November 1961, the releases were switched to the Fontana label with The Marvelettes' 'Please Mr Postman' and from 1962 to 1963 the acts moved to Oriole with 'You Beat Me To The Punch' from Mary Wells. The EMI Records subsidiary Stateside took over with Martha and the Vandellas' 'Heatwave' in October 1963, and in 1965 EMI Records itself secured a licensing deal to open the Tamla Motown label in Britain, combining the names of two of Berry Gordy's American labels, and catering for British releases on all his labels. The debut single, 'Stop! In The Name Of Love' by The Supremes, released during March 1965, reached the top ten. This was the start of Motown's revolutionary step into the world market and with the music now more slanted to commercial black/soul sounds, EMI Records could promote much of it as mainstream music. Not every record was successful but on average Tamla Motown held its own. Through EMI Records' international network the product was available in most territories of the world on the Tamla Motown label. America was the only country not to use it.

With A Song In My Heart, Little Stevie's second album of 1963 (a year when Motown would gross $4.5 million in record sales), upset many fans because the progress he'd made into the R&B field was squashed with an album of show tunes. Whatever the reasoning behind this project, produced by Clarence Paul and Mickey Stevenson, it was poorly received despite the efforts of sleeve-note writer Susan Lynn Mathison, who enthused, '[Stevie] has succeeded with this album, in bringing new identities to old standards, but singing them with strictly his interpretation. The result is a very appealing collection of "soulful" sounds, rendered by one of the most outstanding musicians in the field of popular sounds today . . .' The album's title started the debatable journey through theatreland, stopping off for tracks like 'When You Wish Upon A Star', 'Smile', 'Put On A Happy Face', 'On The Sunny Side Of The Street' and 'Without A Song', among others. The stark brown cover boasted the recycled photo negative of the singer from the neck upwards singing into a microphone hanging from the top right-hand corner.

ABC-TV's high-profile entertainment programme *The Ed Sullivan Show*, gave Little Stevie his first major television appearance of 1964. His first single of the year was an unsophisticated 'Castles In The Sand', written by the quartet of Wilson, Davis, Gordon and O'Brien, recorded in Los Angeles. Even its picture sleeve couldn't push it higher than the R&B top sixty during April. Nonetheless, the single marked a landmark in the young boy's career. It was the last time he'd be marketed as

Little Stevie Wonder – a relief, as he loathed the name. Lee Garrett, who went on to compose with Wonder, recalls, 'We were doing a show together and the MC called out "Little Stevie Wonder". Stevie exploded "Little! Little! Little Stevie Wonder! I'm not going on that fucking stage. I'm not Little Stevie Wonder!" I put my hand on [his] shoulder and said "That's OK, you've got to let them grow out of it." '

The year 1964 introduced the not-so-'little' singer to the film world, albeit confining him to the current popularity of flimsy beach party films with banal storylines. Linking up with American International Pictures, Wonder sang in two movies directed by William Asher and starring Frankie Avalon and Annette Funicello. He performed 'Happy Feelin'' in *Bikini Beach* and 'Happy Street' in *Muscle Beach Party*; both soundtracks issued by Buena Vista. Needless to say, the songs had a longer shelf life than the movies – thankfully!

Two further singles were released during 1964, namely, 'Hey Harmonica Man' as a taster from his pending album, and 'Happy Street'. The former was an R&B top thirty hit; the latter bombed. Once again, both titles were too insignificant for words and certainly not representative of Wonder's previous work. It was becoming clear that, like other Motown artists before him, he was suffering from inferior material and lazy ideas, a situation that could kill an artist's career within months. Many believed this was Stevie Wonder's destiny.

To cash in on his film involvement, his first album as Stevie Wonder was the predictably titled *Stevie At The Beach* and as the title suggested the tracks enjoyed the seashore spirit: 'Castles In The Sand' (vocal and instrumental), 'Ebb Tide', 'Red Sails In The Sunset', 'The Party At The Beach House', 'Beachstomp', 'The Beachcomber' and 'Beyond The Sea'. Plus 'Happy Street' with its B-side 'Sad Boy'. A small picture of the cross-legged artist sitting on a sandy shore, surrounded by sea-blue, attempted to grab record buyers' imagination, but the plan failed. Produced by Hal Davis and Marc Gordon, the album was released on the Stateside label in Britain under the title *Hey Harmonica Man*. The name change didn't work either; but all due respect to Berry Gordy for trying yet another musical avenue for his protégé to stroll down.

Wonder recalls, 'I felt bad because I wasn't successful in writing or singing but that didn't discourage me. It never made me feel like giving up. Rather it made me try even harder. You must have bad times to know what good times are.'

Thankfully, other artists were breaking ground because by 1964 Motown music was hitting headlines, with three-quarters of its sixty or so releases entering the American charts. The company enjoyed four number one singles – 'My Guy' (Mary Wells) and three from The Supremes: 'Where Did Our Love Go', 'Baby Love' and 'Come See About Me'. When Berry Gordy first savoured healthy record sales, he realised he needed to streamline his team of artists, composers, producers and musicians, and introduced a methodical working practice for recording and releasing product. Keeping control of The Temptations and The Supremes for the time being, he assigned certain writers to particular acts. 'They would go through the list of artists and give assignments to the various producers' producer/composer Sylvia Moy told Adam White and Fred Bronson. 'When they reached Stevie Wonder's name, volunteers were sought. None came forward.' This new practice didn't really help Stevie Wonder but did lead to the introduction of the Quality Control team – all intended singles were submitted by their producers for final approval at Friday morning meetings. It was a ruthless measure by any standards, but upheld Gordy's ruling that every single released by Motown had to be a potential number one title. And competition bred winners. However, that thinking was to backfire on Gordy – and in public.

Berry Gordy had recently purchased the Graystone Ballroom, a five-storey structure on 4237 Woodward Avenue for $125,000 and spent a further $25,000 on immediate improvements. He intended to use the ballroom for Motown's Christmas parties and other company functions, such as previewing records on dance nights and staging the Battle Of The Stars, in which two acts competed against each other by each performing three songs. Audience response decided the winner. One particular competition put Marvin Gaye, who had enjoyed a handful of hits to date, against Stevie Wonder, and his one hit. Stevie began with 'Workout Stevie, Workout', accompanying himself on harmonica; Gaye followed with 'Hitch Hike' and, because he was determined to win, surprised the audience by whipping out and playing a melodica. Wonder's next, 'I Call It Pretty Music (But The Old People Call It The Blues)' into which he spliced 'Fingertips Part 2', competed against 'Stubborn Kind Of Fellow'. However, instead of receiving the wild audience response Wonder had before him, Gaye suffered a tirade reproaching him for taking advantage of a little blind kid! He hadn't expected this. Attempting to win the audience round, the embarrassed Gaye plunged into 'Pride And Joy', but it was pointless. He had no choice but to leave the stage. 'Though I still felt competition bred champions,' Berry Gordy explained at the time, 'I could see that it also had a downside. And in this particular case of putting a grown man against a little blind kid, I had blundered badly. That was the last Battle of the Stars at Graystone.'

Chapter 4

MY CHERIE AMOUR

'I'm a poor blind black kid with a stick on his arm and a cup in his hand!'

Stevie Wonder

'King wasn't doing anything but trying to bring people together'

*Otis Williams on the death of
Dr Martin Luther King*

'[Stevie] had to feel the presence of people. If there were none around, his vocal was just dead'

Sylvia Moy

The next two years saw three significant milestones in Motown's history. The first happened in New York, where one of America's top DJs, Murray The K, staged one of his spectacular shows at the Brooklyn Fox Theater in 1964. This particular event broke all previous box-office records by earning $204,000. Dusty Springfield and The Searchers performed in the show alongside The Shangri-Las, The Ronettes, The Dovells and Little Anthony and the Imperials. The Temptations, The Supremes, The Contours, Martha and the Vandellas, The Miracles, Marvin Gaye and Stevie Wonder were part of the Motown contingent. Springfield said, 'I couldn't believe the fantastic performances. Each act had routines for every number and even between performances – and we'd be doing up to six shows a day – they'd be working out new ones.'

The Ronettes' lead singer Ronnie Spector wrote in *Be My Baby* that there was a great feeling behind the scenes at the Brooklyn Fox, where all the acts spent twelve hours a day at the venue:

> So everyone tried to make the best of it. The dressing rooms were all next to each other on this long hall, so the acts couldn't help but mingle. Diana Ross would come in to borrow our lipstick and I remember little Stevie Wonder loved to play tricks on us. 'You girls sure look great tonight in those red dresses,' he'd say, making light of the fact that he was blind and couldn't have seen our dresses if they were on fire.

Like Spector, participating artists laughed at or tolerated Wonder's many antics because of his obvious growing talent, displayed in his high-octane performances on stage. But unlike his peers, including Dusty Springfield who suffered greatly from pre-stage nerves, he itched to be before an audience, although at one point he harboured worries about being pulled off stage by over-enthusiastic fans – some of whom forgot about his blindness. However, as his confidence increased he established a two-way mutual respect and affection to the point of poking fun at himself – 'I'm a poor blind black boy with a stick on his arm and a cup in his hand!' More often than not, the youngster would be carried off stage because he would not stop performing. A regular, contrived part of the act, as Hank Cosby remembered: 'He'd pretend he didn't want to leave and someone would have to pull him off. He just loved that. He loved the attention of the audience.'

His love of audience attention attracted criticism when Wonder started touring in Britain. The public actually refused to accept his blindness, saying it was impossible for him to jump around on stage without sight. In typical Wonder style, he rose to the occasion – 'This blindness business is just a gimmick I use!' – which didn't quell the rumours at all! Later, in a more serious mood, he said, 'Maybe audiences are a bit worried when I jump up and down and off my chair, but it doesn't worry me. I'm well taken care of, nothing goes wrong.' Despite his assurances, this subject was raised time and again in Britain.

Motown's second milestone was probably the riskiest in financial terms. Berry Gordy sent a specially compiled Revue to

Britain during March 1965. The 21-date tour started at Finsbury Park Astoria, London, and closed at the Guildhall in Portsmouth on 12 April 1965. Taking part were Stevie Wonder (who arrived three days earlier than the others), The Supremes, Martha and the Vandellas, The Miracles, Earl Van Dyke and his Soul Brothers, The Temptations, with British artist Georgie Fame adding (so-called) credibility. Dave Godin said, 'The Motortown Revue has broken box office records all over the USA, and the phenomenal sales of these artists' recordings placed the Motown organisation second in singles sales in the USA in 1964. It's fortunate they should begin their overseas conquest at this time.'

British Motown enthusiast Dave Godin was the first British visitor to Detroit's 2648 West Grand Boulevard during 1964. During his short stay he enjoyed a guided tour around the offices and spent time with the artists. Through his meticulously operated Tamla Motown Appreciation Society, where, with support from Detroit, he regularly promoted the music and artists via newsletters and magazines, a British Revue was the vehicle he was promised to help in his tireless efforts to publicise the new American sound.

Martha Reeves remembers well when she stepped on to the tarmac at London's Heathrow Airport in 1965: '[There] were huge crowds waiting there to meet us with banners waving, all thanks to Dave. There were hundreds of well-wishers and we were almost buried alive with bouquets of fresh flowers. In this chilly climate, we were met with warm hugs and kisses.' Bundled up in winter clothes, the artists rode in open-roof cars through London to their hotel, and she added, 'Several streets were blocked off to allow our motorcade to pass. I was stunned by the enthusiasm of all our fans . . . It felt like a homecoming, only we were the kings and queens!'

The tour was a financial disaster, as The Supremes' Mary Wilson explained at the time: 'It was a flop. There's no use in denying it. The audiences were good but they were kinda thin . . . in my opinion the show was too specialised for British audiences.' She was also concerned at the complacent attitude of audiences, despite being warned by Godin beforehand. As he explained, 'I've seen the Revue in America and the acts rely so much on audience participation. They are more exuberant, they dance and sing and make a lot more noise. If this happened here, I think the theatre manager would pull down the curtain. So I've warned them that our audiences are much tamer.'

Scanty publicity and scattered dates were the major cause of poor ticket sales, but the Revue did give the audiences a chance to see the artists behind the music. However, as one promoter explained, 'By the time people got to know how good the show was, the Revue had moved to another venue. I didn't make any money at all but I have to admit those Motown people know how to put on a very good show.' The British had a lot to learn.

The final milestone in Motown's history was also reached in Britain with the revolutionary television show *The Sound Of Motown*, organised and presented by Dusty Springfield. After working with the artists in America, she persuaded Rediffusion to build a show around the acts she loved so much. The TV executives eventually agreed whereupon a show starring The Supremes, Martha and the Vandellas, The Temptations, The Miracles, Stevie Wonder and the Earl Van Dyke Sextet was screened on 28 April 1965 at 9.40 p.m. It was not only the first show of its kind to be screened on British television, but was the only one devoted to a particular style of music or record company.

Meanwhile, back in Detroit, Motown continued to work as a 24-hour operation. Daytime was reserved for business; nighttime for recording, because most of Gordy's staff and artists worked at either the Ford or Chrysler factories. There was more activity from eleven o'clock to four in the morning than at any time during the day – much to the neighbours' disgust!

Robert Dennis, who joined Motown as a studio technician in 1963, told *Chatbusters* magazine: 'The stars were very ordinary people and many had jobs in the day-to-day running of the company. When The Contours went out for a series of shows, we lost our shipping department!' Dennis also recalled weekly visits from a little blind kid, whose purpose was to keep himself up to date on the workings of the Engineering Department: '[Stevie] would always be greeted by the boss or the shop foreman saying "Are you getting any yet Stevie?" '. . . We managed to "jive around" and have no significant dialogue during the visits. Stevie was a comical and steady victim of Motown's expansion.' In an attempt to add extra work areas in the same square footage, 'Pops' Gordy regularly changed the floor plans to the (now) three houses on West Grand Boulevard. 'Stevie's favourite trick was to give the slip to his assigned guide and go off on his own to discover the changes. You would regularly see him walk into walls where doors had been a month ago. After finally finding his way into an area, he would ask, "So what's in this area now?"'

With touring now a major part of Stevie Wonder's professional life, it was inevitable that he'd be drawn into all aspects of the lifestyle of the travelling artist. He shied away from drugs (following an unhappy experience with marijuana) but did enjoy his first sexual encounters. As a thirteen-year-old, he was goaded by the musicians to participate in hotel groupie parties. It was reported that once Ted Hull had retired for the night, Wonder was paired off with a suitable guest and would often pay for her services afterwards. Dave Godin, however, recalled Wonder actually losing his virginity to The Soul Sisters when they initiated him into carnal pleasures at a very early age.

Unbeknown to the young Wonder at this time, his life also changed in another way when he met Dr Martin Luther King, leader of the Civil Rights Movement in America. During the mid-fifties King became leader of the movement. He advocated non-violence and his visionary speeches, dominated by his desire for peaceful harmony between black and white, endeared him towards Congress and the president of the day, John F Kennedy, who, for all his personal failures, was a humanitarian and a believer in equal rights for all.

Much of the violence between the races was instigated by the police or a hardcore element of white thugs, but King persevered most memorably with his message with his 1963 deliverance of 'I Have A Dream', one of the most significant and most quoted speeches in the world of politics. A year after President Kennedy's assassination in 1963, King's dream became reality when the bill forbidding any form of racial discrimination became law. For his tireless work in reaching this historical goal, King was awarded the Nobel Peace Prize. Of course, he would later pay the ultimate price.

Now in Detroit, Stevie Wonder needed new material. His last single, 'Kiss Me Baby', which he co-wrote with Clarence Paul (Wonder's first A-side composition), released in March 1965, struggled for recognition. This replaced the previously scheduled single 'Pretty Little Angel', which was used for radio promotion purposes. As the resulting feedback was negative, the planned commercial release was aborted. For his next single Berry Gordy reverted to a live recording, edited by his brother Robert and titled 'High Heel Sneakers'. A spoken word introduction was used on the American release (though deleted from the British version); but the 'magic of live' didn't work this time. The single crawled into the American top sixty in October 1965. Nothing seemed to succeed for Gordy's protégé. It was decision time.

The support given to Wonder up to this juncture turned against him when his fellow artists once again objected to his preferential treatment. Any other artist with his poor track record would have been dropped by the company, and they felt their own careers were suffering as a result. This time, though, Wonder was aware of the animosity:

> Many people felt I was getting too much too soon . . . but I didn't realise that it was all happening. I just enjoyed singing. Sometimes when it was time for an interview or rehearsal. I just wanted to go play or have a few cookies . . . I didn't care about interviews. I wanted to do other things. That might have made some feel I was a brat, but not true. I was just a normal kid.

Even as a fifteen-year-old he felt he should be allowed greater control over the material he was instructed to record. He'd already accumulated a stockpile of songs that he had written under the name Judkins because that was his father's name and because, he said, 'I signed the song contract in his name but I don't know why. On later recordings I decided I wanted people to know that I'd written the songs and used Wonder.' Therefore, he felt he knew better than most what his capabilities were: 'The people who produced me used to say, "Now come on Stevie, I want you to scream on this part of the song, 'cos that's you man." And I used to scream my head off. Then I thought, well, shit, maybe, maybe not. If I feel it, I'll do it, but don't make me scream before the break on every song.' His protestations fell on deaf ears. Artists who toed the Motown line were rewarded with hits, notably The Supremes who in 1965 enjoyed three number one singles – 'Stop! In The Name Of Love', 'Back In My Arms Again' and 'I Hear A Symphony'. The Temptations' 'My Girl' and The Four Tops' 'I Can't Help Myself' likewise topped the American listing. A further six titles were top ten entrants.

To be fair, Berry Gordy was extremely reluctant to free Stevie Wonder from his recording contract because he had an absolute faith, a gut feeling that, with the right break, Stevie would become a major influence in international music. After all, hadn't he already enjoyed a number one single? 'We had opened doors,' he says, 'and we hadn't taken advantage of it. That was a no-no for our company.' Clarence Paul said 'I had exclusive production on Stevie, but we were cold. I didn't have no hits. I couldn't think of nothing, and he couldn't think of nothing.' Stevie Wonder's voice was breaking which was another worry for the already troubled Berry Gordy. But in time he believed it to be a godsend: 'That young, undeveloped, high-pitched sound that I hadn't loved when I first met him turned into a controlled, powerful, versatile instrument.' Wonder recalls, 'My voice was high then low. Fortunately I had a lot of records in the can which they put out on me while my voice was changing keys and some of the things I did on stage I couldn't do any more.' All Motown needed was a hit single.

As it transpired, it was Stevie Wonder himself who solved the problem. In December 1965, he produced 'Uptight (Everything's Alright)', which he wrote with Hank Cosby and Sylvia Moy. Within a month, the title had returned Wonder to the upper regions of the American singles chart. 'Uptight (Everything's Alright)' also marked his British chart debut in the top twenty, thanks to the exposure it received during his third tour of the country in January 1966. Sylvia Moy remembered the actual recording of the track: 'I would stand in the control room. Stevie would be at the mike in the studio and I would sing the song to him with the lyric. He'd be listening on his headset to one line ahead, and singing the previous line, without missing a beat or a note.'

Conceived from a jamming session, the song was formulated

around Wonder's upbeat chorus, inspired, he said, by The Rolling Stones. With Hank Cosby and Mickey Stevenson replacing Clarence Paul as producers, the beloved harmonica was replaced by a sharp rhythm sympathetic to Wonder's optimistic vibrato vocals marking his escape from the poor black boy syndrome. Also 'Uptight (Everything's Alright)' was to date the nearest he had come to recording his personal music – and the experiment worked. With this unexpected, but welcome, success, the composing team rushed to record the follow-up single. Another energetic slice of early Wonder at his best, although, perhaps, too similar to its precedessor, 'Nothing's Too Good For My Baby' peaked in the American top twenty in May 1966, the same month that the *Uptight* album was released. Its British outing came four months later. Produced by Cosby, Stevenson and Paul, *Uptight*, a compilation of tried-and-tested material, included his next single 'Blowin' In The Wind' and flipside 'Ain't That Asking For Trouble'. 'Nothing's Too Good For My Baby', its B-side 'With A Child's Heart'; the three-year-old bomber 'Contract On Love', and 'Music Talk' (B-side of 'High Heel Sneakers') were also on the album. A 'Dancing In The Street' clone titled 'Love A Go Go', and 'Hold Me' and 'Teach Me Tonight', medium pacers in the Sam Cooke mode, offered soulful reflections. Of particular interest, however, were 'I Want My Baby Back', hinting at The Four Tops' most recent hit sound, and the nondescript 'Pretty Little Angel'. How could one artist sound so different . . . and so bad? The answer was easy – the album was hastily compiled to cash in on the single's success, with little thought of how it would affect Wonder's fragile career.

The front packaging was split between blue and orange, showing three pictures of the youngster performing at the piano, drums and with the harmonica (the instruments he played on the album), while Ed Aaronoff waffled in his sleeve notes along these lines: 'While still in his teens, Stevie Wonder joined the ranks of other sightless great artists who have left their mark in the popular music world – Alec Templeton, George Shearing and Ray Charles.'

No one was prepared for the drastic change in style in Wonder's next single – a re-working of Bob Dylan's civil rights anthem 'Blowin' In the Wind', with Clarence Paul as duettist. The Four

Tops' lead singer, Levi Stubbs, assisted with support vocals. Within seven months, Wonder had changed tact, confusing his fans with a popular non-Motown song, which had been rehearsed with Paul away from the Motown studios. As Wonder was now skilled at re-working mainstream material, it was, they felt, an obvious choice to test his versatility. Berry Gordy, on the other hand, believed that releasing a song worshipped by the hippy element of Dylan's public would be a grave error, but was beaten down by Wonder's associates who insisted it was a highlight of his live shows. The popular song peaked in the American top ten and British top forty. But, more importantly for Stevie Wonder and Motown, it soared to pole position in the American R&B singles chart, confirming the singer's convictions that black singers need not be confined to the limited soul market and could successfully record white-originated material. Clarence Paul was admonished by Berry Gordy for promoting his own singing career on the record. The angry composer retaliated: 'The reason I was on [the single] was because of the lyrics. On stage I led Stevie in because he didn't know the second verse. That's how it got started, and he said, "Man, keep doing that", so we put it in the song.' As the single peaked, Stevie Wonder was planning a three-week European tour, before joining his fellow artists at Detroit's Fox Theater for a series of Christmas shows.

An optimistic 'A Place In The Sun', penned by Ron Miller and Bryan Wells, quickly followed the Bob Dylan tribute, and returned him to the number nine position in the American chart during December 1966. It became a top twenty British hit in January 1967, heralding his third hit in that country, cementing his growing popularity, and proving that regular touring stints sold records. His final American single of 1966 was 'Someday At Christmas', contributing to the festive season, which he included in his Fox Theater act. Miller and Wells wrote this song for Wonder following the surprise success of 'A Place In The Sun', and like those of its predecessor, the lyrics weren't what they appeared to be! A year later, 'Someday At Christmas' became a compilation, produced by Hank Cosby, where Motown originals complemented festive favourites. Ron Miller co-wrote most of the company's contributions – such as 'Bedtime For Toys', 'A Warm Little Home

On The Hill' and 'One Little Christmas Tree' – while the singalong contemporaries included 'Ave Maria', 'The Little Drummer Boy' and 'Silver Bells'. The album was nothing more than a cosy Christmas present. Unconvinced of its sales potential, Motown in Britain put the compilation on hold until December 1968.

Fellow artist and lead singer with The Miracles, Smokey Robinson, noted that at this point in time Stevie Wonder 'was having absolutely no trouble whatsoever in making the adjustment from child star to mature young man'. Even those artists who felt cheated at the unjustified attention showered upon him now had to acknowledge that he was a rising artist who could, at any time, overtake them in the popularity stakes. Interestingly, those same artists would later beg Wonder for his compositions to boost their flagging careers.

The final album of 1966 was *Down To Earth*, produced by Cosby and Paul, with its front cover showing a more mature artist sitting in a doorway, playing the harmonica. His casual dress befitted an older boy, down to his oversized gold ring which matched the colour of his short-sleeved shirt. Thankfully, banal sleeve notes were omitted this time; perhaps the music spoke for itself. Was anyone listening though? Once more, confusion arose as the project spanned pop tracks like Sonny & Cher's 'Bang Bang (My Baby Shot Me Down)', Bob Dylan's 'Mr Tambourine Man' (a duet with Clarence Paul) and a clone of The Supremes' hit 'My World Is Empty Without You'. Needless to say, this strange collection of material was basically held together by the recent 'A Place In The Sun' and the album's title track. Stevie Wonder co-wrote four tracks – 'Thank You Love', 'Be Cool, Be Calm (And Keep Yourself Together)', 'Sylvia' and 'Hey Love' with Cosby, Paul, Sylvia Moy and Morris Broadnax. The combination of sweet soul R&B attempted to complement the blues element of 'Sixteen Tons', but, to be honest, it was a collection of changing moods and singles. A 'leftover' track, 'Travelin' Man', was the next single in February 1967. Its poor-selling top forty position sent warning signals to Motown that the public had overdosed on mellowness.

Happily, Stevie Wonder was one step ahead. His instincts told him to rebel against Motown's complacency in releasing similar-sounding singles, and when he presented his next to the public, their support returned, with faith rekindled. Wonder explained, 'It kinda speaks of my first love to a girl called Angie. A very beautiful woman. She got married and later had three children, I think.' With Hank Cosby and Sylvia Moy, he took ten minutes to pen his song for Angie titled 'I Was Made To Love Her', a vigorously exciting track, with a compelling dance rhythm, a firey James Jamerson bass, and racing vocals. The single shot to number two in the American chart during July 1967 and number five in Britain, while its mother album, bearing the single's title, forged a top 45 place in America. As an aside, it was reported that Hank Cosby took Stevie Wonder to a local Detroit Baptist church to hear the minister's rousing and inspiring voice because it was this that he wanted Wonder to emulate on the song. '[It] had so many catchy little phrases in it,' Martha Reeves told DJ Alan Taylor, 'but it was what everybody could relate to and I thought he was ingenious, he and Clarence Paul, to write that wonderful song.'

A full-colour front sleeve, showing the singer in live action, housed the music of the *I Was Made To Love Her* album released in August 1967, four months later in Britain. The Hank Cosby-produced project appeared to pay tribute to Wonder's peers like Little Richard ('Send Me Some Lovin''), Marvin Gaye ('Can I Get A Witness', 'Baby Don't You Do It'), Aretha Franklin ('Respect'), Ray Charles ('A Fool For You'), James Brown ('Please Please Please'), suggesting he still needed familiar tracks to sell his albums. These were interspliced with Jobete titles where, on one, Wonder borrowed riffs from The Supremes for 'Every Time I See You I Go Wild', while 'I'd Cry', was one of four co-written by him. The others were innocuous, namely, 'Everybody Needs Somebody (I Need You)' and 'Every Time I See You I Go Wild'. It was a pot-pourri of interesting sounds, appealing to a wider audience than previous releases, a move he'd craved since duetting with John Glover on street corners those few short years ago.

The follow-up to 'I Was Made To Love Her' was the more frenetic, almost tuneless, single 'I'm Wondering', a play on his name. Released during September 1967, it failed to match its precedessor's success, by stalling at number twelve in the American listing; 22 in Britain. But no one was overly bothered, Stevie Wonder was still a charting artist.

The re-established singer then joined The Marvelettes, Gladys Knight and the Pips, Edwin Starr, Chris Clark, The Miracles, Willie Tyler & Lester, with a full support band, on an end-of-year special upbeat 'Motown Revue' for Detroit's handicapped people. The performance sold out , and all proceeds went to local charities. But Christmas celebrations this year were muted in the black and soul fraternities, after Otis Redding died on 10 December. A small plane in which he and the Bar Kays were travelling crashed into Lake Monona, a short distance from the airport at Madison, Wisconsin. At his highly charged funeral, Stevie Wonder mourned with Aretha Franklin, Percy Sledge, Little Richard, James Brown and hundreds of others.

The year of 1968 was one of more change and tragedy. On the personal front, Stevie Wonder graduated with honours from the Michigan State School for the Blind, freeing him from tutors and enabling him to concentrate fully on his music. One of his first major appearances of the year was to participate (with Esther Edwards as escort) in the biggest ever Motown Festival in Japan, where he co-starred with Martha and the Vandellas, among others. It was reported that Wonder mesmerised the packed houses, where audiences danced in the aisles and between seats. He rehearsed during his free time, while Martha Reeves shopped in Tokyo. One of her purchases was a kimono, which she wore on stage, a move greatly appreciated by the Japanese fans.

On the singles front, in March 1968 Wonder released the typesetter's nightmare 'Shoo-Be-Doo-Be-Doo-Da-Day'. The single, an R&B number one, marked a further change of mood: an easy sound with an instant hookline, which returned the singer to number nine in the American chart, number 46 in Britain. Wonder was annoyed when the single was released, because the record credit was wrong. In the song he sings 'shoo-be-doo-don-day'. The credit read '. . . *da*-day'. Sylvia Moy said at the time that he had exhausted his supply of song titles but believed 'this song's message was like a little scat. It says something and then it doesn't, and yet it says a lot.'

As the single climbed the American chart, the unthinkable happened – Dr Martin Luther King was assassinated in Memphis, Tennessee, as he prepared to lead a march of workers protesting against unfair treatment by their employers. King's murder ignited riots in several American cities, including Detroit, when his dictates for peace were overshadowed by destructive and bloody revenge. Motown acts heard of the tragedy at their various touring venues. The Temptations were told hours before they were due to perform in Charlston, South Carolina, as Otis Williams noted:

> I remember saying, 'I don't know if I want to go out.' There was concern that King's assassination would spark violence and it went without saying that nobody was going to be in the mood to have a good time. We ended up going ahead with the show anyway . . . I was more angry than anything else, because King wasn't doing anything but trying to bring people together, preaching equality not only for blacks and whites, but for everyone.

A heartbroken Stevie Wonder shared The Temptation's senti-ments, and in time, King's ideals and later assassination would filter into his future compositions, as his passion grew for love and peace in the world. In fact, Wonder would eventually (inadvertently?) become a major figure on the civil rights movement, a fighter for causes and minorities, and, ultimately, a figurehead to respect. It wasn't a responsibility he took lightly.

A short time after Dr King's death, his widow, Coretta, asked Berry Gordy to arrange a benefit concert in honour of The Poor People's Campaign. With two days' notice to organise a show in Atlanta, Gordy included Stevie Wonder, Gladys Knight and the Pips, and The Temptations, with The Supremes as headliners. To coincide with this benefit before an estimated 13,000 people in the Atlanta Civic Center, King's album *Free At Last* was released on the Gordy label; the first was '*The Great March To Freedom*' in 1963, which was an adventurous move for Motown at the time. The company took a further stand for its race in 1970 by opening the Black Forum label, which was a public platform for black activists. A further Martin Luther King album, *Why I Oppose The War In Vietnam* was issued, alongside others by Stokley Carmichael, Langston Hughes and Elaine Brown. Otis Williams said of the Atlanta benefit: 'Even though we did nothing special, just our regular show, it felt good to be supporting Mrs King and the cause, and giving back something to her husband's memory.' Following the concert, the artists joined in The Poor People's march, which ended in Washington.

As a nation mourned and Detroit's streets burned, Motown's music played on. By March 1968 Stevie Wonder was finally qualified to release his *Greatest Hits* compilation; the British release followed in August. As the title suggested, the charters were included: 'Uptight (Everything's Alright)', 'I'm Wondering', 'I Was Made To Love Her' through to 'A Place In The Sun', 'Contract On Love', 'Fingertips Part 2' and 'Castles In The Sand'. The British release had a change of tracks and cover design, but Scott Regen's sleeve notes were identical – more's the pity! For a 'greatest hits' package the American sales were disappointing; Motown floundered with a top forty placing, yet in Britain, sales were much healthier, with a top thirty entry – his first ever charting album. Wonder's next single, 'You Met Your Match', which was his debut as a producer, stalled in the American top forty. Despite attractive vocal interplay between the singer and back-up vocalists, this funk rocker, also penned by Wonder, his mother and Don Hunter, was, perhaps, too busy to be melodic.

Also in March, Motown moved offices from West Grand Boulevard to 2547 Woodward Avenue, into what was formerly the Donovan Building. The company transferred premises because it was outgrowing the original property, and, more importantly, the now high-profile Motown deserved an uptown address and not one in a renovated ghetto area. The original buildings continued to be used and maintained, until years later when they were transformed into The Motown Museum, one of Detroit's most popular tourist attractions.

On the music front, bizarre suggestions were being thrown Stevie Wonder's way. Berry Gordy wanted him to record an instrumental version of the Burt Bacharach and Hal David composition 'Alfie'. Remarkably, Hank Cosby agreed to the idea, but quipped, 'How many Motown tracks carry a harmonica solo on a Bacharach track!' And when Wonder also rose to the challenge, the single grew into an album of instrumentals. As it was necessary to avoid confusion with the singer's current work, another name was used – Eivets Rednow – Stevie Wonder spelt backwards. Cosby recalled, 'The idea came from the marketing department. We create the product but they have to sell it. And it's difficult for me to say if it would have been done in the same way if there was no other current product.'

'*Eivets Rednow*' exemplified Wonder's determination to escape categorisation. He loathed the prevalent attitude of the time that black artists played for black people, and white artists for whites. If music was to grow, he argued, barriers had to be broken down and new music routed to an all-race audience. In defence of Motown's musical strategy, huge inroads had been slowly carved thanks to commercially slanted R&B releases by The Supremes, The Four Tops, The Temptations, and so on, while the purer, spiritual sound was left to artists like Gladys Knight and the Pips, The Originals, Brenda Holloway, Marvin Gaye and Kim Weston. Wonder acknowledged that his fans would realise 'Eivets Rednow', was him, so it came as a surprise when he listened to a young man moaning, 'This Eivets dude needs to be sorted, Stevie! He's trying to copy you.' The artist smiled and walked on.

'A House Is Not A Home' was the second Bacharach and David track on the album. Stevie Wonder composed four, namely, 'More Than A Dream', 'How Can You Believe', 'Which Way The Wind' and 'Bye Bye World' (Wonder says, 'I wrote that track for Wes Montgomery. I told him about the song and then, not long after, there was his tragic death') with filler tracks of 'Never My Love', 'Ask The Lonely', 'Ruby' and 'Grazing In The Grass'. Both the album (with a drum kit on its front cover) and the single were issued on the Gordy label, and not his usual Tamla outlet in America, in late 1968. There was no British release. Cosby told journalist Alex Kanakaris: 'That album demonstrated Stevie's talent at playing the various instruments. Basically he played the harmonica, piano, different keyboards, drums and all the percussive instruments. Primarily, it was to demonstrate his skill.' Skilled or otherwise, the project bombed and many bemoaned Motown's lack of conviction.

With that debatable project behind him, Stevie Wonder's recordings returned to normal with another Ron Miller song. Titled 'For Once In My Life', which Miller wrote to celebrate the birth of his daughter and which was previously recorded by Tony Bennett, it was earmarked for Wonder's next album. Motown, however, had other ideas, and a month prior to the album's release date, issued 'For Once In My Life' as a single. Without doubt, it was another slice of Ron Miller magic; the depth of the melody gave the feeling of a familiar song, a ballad of class, as borne out by its soaring to number two in the American chart, held off the pole position by Marvin Gaye's 'I Heard It Through The Grapevine'. In Britain it was Wonder's biggest-selling single to date, peaking at number three. By recording middle-of-the-road material of this ilk, Berry Gordy was able to steer his older acts, like The Supremes, Marvin Gaye and The Temptations into the lucrative nightclub arena. The problem with Wonder, however, was his age, but that didn't prevent Gordy from priming his protégé for that market when his time arrived.

Carrying another front-cover shot from the session used on the British *Greatest Hits* compilation, the *For Once In My Life* album included the following sleeve notes from Allan Rinde: 'Stevie Wonder is still growing and his music is growing with him, and this album captures that growth.' For once, listeners agreed with him. *For Once In My Life*, produced by Hank Cosby (with the exception of two tracks from Don Hunter and Wonder, namely, 'You Met Your Match' and the future single 'I Don't Know Why (I Love You)', and included the familiar 'Shoo-Be-Doo-Be-Doo-Da-Day' and 'You Met Your Match'. The next two titles, 'I Wanna Make Her Love Me' and 'I'm More Than Happy (I'm Satisfied)' combined up-tempo and ballad, while a smooth version of Bobby Hebb's classic 'Sunny' led into the slow rhythm of 'I'd Be A Fool Right Now' and 'Ain't No Lovin''. A heartfelt cover of Billie Holiday's passionate 'God Bless The Child' contrasted badly with a throwaway love ditty 'Do I Love Her' which was followed by Wonder's second version of 'The House On The Hill'. Playing harmonica, keyboards and percussion, Stevie Wonder had again gelled easily with Motown's finest musicians.

This was an extremely productive period in Wonder's career. As with his fellow acts, time not spent touring was used for recording. Material was stockpiled to ensure an ample supply of releases to cover those long periods spent on the road. Indeed, Wonder always had songs to record, although of late, he had chosen to work with other artists, or actually given away material intended for his own use. To date, several happy Motown artists had benefited from his work: The Contours' 'Just A Little Misunderstanding', Marvin Gaye's 'You're The One For Me', The Four Tops' 'Loving You Is Sweeter Than Ever' and Smokey Robinson and the Miracles' 'The Tears Of A Clown', which was, in fact, the fourth song he'd co-written for the group. The others were 'Can You Love A Poor Boy?' on the *Away We A Go-Go* album, and 'My Love Is Your Love (Forever)' and 'After You Put Back The Pieces (I'll Still Have A Broken Heart)' on the group's *Make It Happen* album. Stevie Wonder loved working in the studio with others because he fed off their presence. Subsequently, when he recorded his own work, he regularly demanded that someone be in the studio with him all the time. Sylvia Moy believes this was due to his blindness: 'He had to feel the presence of people. If there were none around, his vocal was just dead. At times, I had to go outside and stop people who were passing to bring them in, so Stevie could feel their presence. Once we got that, he could fire into that feeling.'

Arguably, one of the finest tracks lifted from the *For Once In My Life* project was the next single, 'I Don't Know Why (I Love You)' with 'My Cherie Amour' on the flipside. The top title, clearly influenced by the late Otis Redding, was a compelling declaration of love, prompting the late British journalist Penny Valentine to enthuse, 'It's the sexiest record I have ever heard.' It was typical of the artist's hard-edged music, but wasn't the single's most popular side. Peaking at number 39 in the American chart (number fourteen, and then upon re-entry, number 43, in Britain), it was 'My Cherie Amour' that proved to be the selling item, thanks to constant radio exposure. Motown, sensing a huge cash-in, flipped the single to 'My Cherie Amour' and promoted it as a new release. As such, Stevie Wonder enjoyed a top four American and British hit, probably due to record buyers not being quick enough to spot the switch, and ending up with two singles containing the same tracks! An excited singer admitted the song had grown from sadness: 'I wrote it when I was sixteen after me and my sweetheart broke up. It took me thirty minutes to write, but I never did give it to anyone because it was too personal.' The single also changed Stevie Wonder, the person: 'I was young and carefree. I didn't think about anything, not even the money I was making. I didn't take anything seriously. I changed with "My Cherie Amour". I suddenly realised it was time I calmed down and started behaving responsibly.'

Naturally, an album, hastily retitled *My Cherie Amour* quickly followed in August 1969; five months later in Britain. Another dark cover of a singing artist, in the same coloured printing as the British *Greatest Hits* package. And, once again, producer Hank Cosby agreed to the inclusion of tried-and-tested material like 'Light My Fire', 'The Shadow Of Your Smile' and 'Hello Young Lovers', which Wonder, now an adept performer, capably handled in his acceptable mature mode. He matched these with his own compositions such as 'Give Me Your Love', the pop-influenced 'I've Got You', and 'Somebody Knows, Somebody Cares' directed at soft rock listeners. 'Angie Girl' (the B-side of 'For Once In My Life') was marginally superior to the aforementioned tracks, but, in all honesty, the album was saved from near death by its title track and Wonder's next single 'Yester-Me, Yester-You, Yesterday'. Nonetheless, *My Cherie Amour* peaked at number seventeen in the British album chart during August 1969. American sales faltered in the top forty.

Before the close of 1969, Stevie Wonder experienced a personal high when he was invited to the White House by President Nixon to be presented with the 'Distinguished Service Award' by the President's Committee on Employment of Handicapped People. Professionally speaking, the high continued, when the medium-paced, immediately catchy, love song 'Yester-Me, Yester-You, Yesterday', written by Bryan Wells and Ron Miller, shot into the American top ten, and to an incredible British number two in December, preventing fellow Motowners Junior Walker – with 'What Does It Take (To Win Your Love)' and Marv Johnson – with 'I Miss You Baby' – from climbing higher. Wonder confessed that 'Yester-Me, Yester-You, 'Yesterday' was an old song: 'I recorded that two years ago as an album track, at the same time as "My Cherie Amour". It should have been on the *Down To Earth* album but somehow it got missed.' A love song with a difference, the single related to feelings affecting two avenues: that of personal relationships and that of the closing decade, which had burst into life with a million ideas gravitating towards changing spirits and musical influences, but, most significantly, saw the breakthrough of black music into a white-dominated, mainstream record buying market. Black artists still had a long, hard struggle ahead, but with Motown's conviction to move with the tide and beyond, their signed artists were more fortunate than most. Progress was slow, but it was happening.

These were heady days, and Stevie Wonder, boy protégé, rode the changes and created some of his own. During the next decade his music broke free from Motown's strict guidelines and as a result, he, perhaps unwittingly, was instrumental in changing the face of black R&B music.

He also fell in love.

Chapter 5

SIGNED, SEALED, DELIVERED (I'M YOURS)

'Nobody expected anything to come out of Detroit – it was a car city'

Stevie Wonder

'Motown outside Detroit was unthinkable'

Martha Reeves

'It was only after I came to know [Stevie] that I realised how lonely he was'

Syreeta

By the mid-sixties Motown had grown beyond all expectation and Berry Gordy was richer than he could ever have imagined. Not only did the recording side of the company generate vast sums, but so too did the management company, Grapevine Advertising and Jobete, the in-house publishing arm. Gordy's writers signed the rights to their compositions over to the publishing house and, with few exceptions, all the early tunes were Jobete-owned. At one time artists were obliged to include Jobete-owned songs when recording an album, to generate even more royalties for Gordy. A prime example of re-recording was Stevie Wonder's 'For Once In My Life' which, to date, has been covered more than two hundred times.

As Motown roared into the seventies to celebrate its tenth anniversary, a musical era ended. Diana Ross left The Supremes for a solo career. Her replacement was the already groomed, experienced singer Jean Terrell, who was introduced at The Supremes' star-studded farewell concert at The Frontier Hotel, Las Vegas, on 14 January 1970. Stevie Wonder would later attempt to salvage The (new) Supremes' career, when it unexpectedly showed signs of flagging.

As one era ended, another began when Motown's new signing, The Jackson 5, with lead singer little Michael, released their debut single 'I Want You Back'. These five young brothers from Gary, Indiana, brought a welcome air of freshness and excitement to the charts in the early seventies, and scored a string of number one titles. Deke Richards, one of the writing/producing team (dubbed The Corporation) behind The Jackson 5, was so delighted with 'I Want You Back' that he played a test pressing to Wonder, 'because this was a guy I really respected. We were friends. Everyone else was too influenced by Berry to give me an objective opinion. He listened to it carefully, and he said, "Now, man, I don't like the drums!" I had to laugh.' Complete with drums, 'I Want You Back' shot to the top of the American chart, and laid the foundation for a multi-million selling run of blue-eyed sweet soul music, Jackson 5 style.

While the world welcomed the young brothers with open arms, Wonder was beavering away, preparing material for the coming months. However, he took time out to visit the Eye Institute of the Columbia Presbyterian Medical Center in New York, responsible for the treatment of thousands of children with eye disorders, regardless of race or religion. Wonder, who also received The Fight for Sight 1969 Show Business Inspiration Award for his 'compelling achievements in the world of enter-tainment', distributed his records to the children during his visit. The Fight for Sight organisation, which gained its initial impetus from the world of show business with support from personalities like Bob Hope and Sammy Davis Jr, said they had elected Wonder for the award as he was 'the most recent champion of its cause'. After the presentation, Wonder left the Center to prepare for his debut engagement at The Copacabana. Now twenty years old, he was able to follow in the footsteps of his Motown colleagues by performing at New York's most celebrated of nightspots. At Berry Gordy's insistence, he had a clutch of familiar mainstream songs to perform.

The singer issued his first single of the new decade, 'Never Had A Dream Come True', which was more positive than his dreamy offerings of late. This lurchingly paced song, composed by himself, Sylvia Moy and Hank Cosby, was backed by a plethora of strings, brass and percussion. Again, the single fared better in Britain by entering the top ten while in America it stalled in the top thirty. The British success was attributed to Wonder's two-week tour of the country, where he was joined by the mixed-race soul group The Foundations and the female trio The Flirtations. His relationship with The Flirtations' lead singer, Earnestine Pearce, attracted more publicity than his music, and when the media suggested the two were lovers, and due to marry, an annoyed Wonder admitted he had no one to blame but himself – he had, after all, told reporters, 'I'm gonna steal her and take her home.' On the other hand, twenty-year-old Pearce encouraged the attention, saying Wonder had dedicated 'My Cherie Amour' to her. When the two were first introduced she thought he was 'stuck up', but quickly added, 'after he started dating me every day and riding on the tour bus instead of in his own car I found out how sweet, kind and understanding he really is'. During the closing dates of the 22-day tour, Pearce confirmed, 'We definitely want to get married but it's too early to make any firm plans because of our careers.' Realising the relationship had been blown out of proportion, an embarrassed Stevie Wonder attempted to squash the rumours: 'That thing going around about Earnestine and me, where did that come from? She's a real nice girl but who said we were getting married?' Whether it was a joke that had backfired or a fact of life was never confirmed, but with the lady's parting shot that she expected to renew the romance when The Flirtations returned to America, fans expected a future marriage.

Meanwhile, before Motown's anniversary celebrations could take place, Marvin Gaye's 24-year-old singing partner Tammi Terrell died. Gaye and Terrell had enjoyed a wonderfully successful career together with singles like 'Ain't No Mountain High Enough', 'Ain't Nothing Like The Real Thing' and 'You're All I Need To Get By'. They were lovers on vinyl but not in real life. Terrell lost her two-year battle against a brain tumour despite seven attempts by surgeons to eradicate it. Fellow artists joined friends and family for a tearful farewell at the Jane Memorial Methodist Church, while outside an estimated three thousand people stood in the pouring rain. Before the end of 1970, one of the company's best-loved musicians, Benny Benjamin, died. A distraught Wonder told British journalist Lon Goddard:

> Benny's history goes back a long way in the Motown story. In the beginning there was no Musician's Union . . . and all the musicians were helping to build something. Nobody expected anything to come out of Detroit – it was a car city. Then all the musicians who lived there began to combine and a totally original approach to music was born. Nobody could play like him, nobody had his beat. It gives me a great feeling of loneliness as he has done so much without recognition. A lot of people have passed away since Motown started, but it really hits hard when someone's really close to you. Someone who was so original.

During 1970 Wonder released two live albums. The first, *Stevie Wonder Live*, was recorded at an unspecified American venue, as author Spencer Leigh reported, 'It's generous on playing time but the stage performances lack the excitement of his studio work . . . For UK buyers the most significant track is his harmonica solo 'Alfie' which wasn't released here.' Issued in March in America and during June in Britain, this insignificant project was followed by a more superior concert recording when, in July, Wonder became the third Motown act to perform at London's premier nightspot, The Talk Of The Town. (The Supremes and The Temptations had previously performed there in 1968 and 1969 respectively.)

While the *Stevie Wonder Live* front sleeve showed narrow pictures of the performing singer within the letters 'LIVE', the British-released *Live! At Talk Of The Town* front packaging was divided into four, each square holding a shot of Wonder in action. Production credits changed also: Hank Cosby and Clarence Paul produced the *Stevie Wonder Live* album, whereas EMI Records' in-house producer Norman Smith produced the October-released

British project, although the finished product was not what Wonder had intended . . .

> We had a bad start. On the first night we'd planned to do many new and less familiar numbers, not just my hits. Unfortunately, it seemed we'd made a wrong decision, and received some bad press. [So] we sat down and worked out a complete new act. The result was great. My only regret is that the press couldn't come back to review the new act.

With backing singers Pat Arnold, Madeline Bell and Syreeta, his future wife, the Motown star worked his way through a selection of his hits ('My Cherie Amour', 'I Was Made To Love Her', 'Yester-Me, Yester-You, Yesterday' and so on), his version of Simon and Garfunkel's 'Bridge Over Troubled Water' and the instrumental 'Alfie'.

It was during this visit that he once more faced public curiosity about his blindness. Annoyed at having to defend his disability in a country that was rapidly becoming his second home, Wonder barked:

> I don't want people to come and see me or buy my records because I'm blind. I want people to dig me for what I've got to offer, for the way I sing and play. If they don't then that's cool but I don't want to be treated differently from any other singer! . . . I just act the way I feel when I'm on stage. If I feel good, I jump around . . . If I knew I couldn't play well I wouldn't do it at all. No one would question the motives if any other performer did the same things on stage. People would credit that as versatility.

The singer never walked with a cane or dog, preferring to be escorted by his brother Calvin, his cousin John or a member of his entourage. On the rare occasions Wonder travelled alone, he carried cash in various denominations in different pockets to pay for, say, a cab ride or a meal in a restaurant.

Also during this British tour he fought unprovoked criticism about his music, when he was openly condemned for his choice of material, which many felt was 'whitewashed', denying fans his gutsy, R&B roots. In defence, Stevie Wonder once more reacted sharply, 'I don't want to be confined to one bag. People said "My Cherie Amour" wasn't really me because it was different from what they expected. That was written in 1966 and was what I was into then, so I don't know how people can say it's not me.' And so the battle raged on. When the singer had performed in Britain before, his shows were in theatres, but The Talk Of The Town was not a venue that attracted young diehard fans – the high ticket price and dress code meant it was more an audience of middle-of-the-roaders enjoying a night out. For these reasons Wonder vowed his next tour would concentrate on clubs and theatres, 'I enjoyed doing "Talk Of The Town" but next time I want to get to the kids who buy my records.'

The gutsy R&B roots returned and critics had to eat their words when 'Signed, Sealed Delivered (I'm Yours)', Stevie Wonder's second single of 1970, soared to number three in America, number fifteen in Britain. Dave Godin noted this as 'Stevie's best contribution to soul music in a long while'. It was true. The delivery was fast, furious, upbeat, exemplifying Wonder's unique ability to change tack. When the single peaked in Britain, his fellow Motowners were close behind – namely, Marvin Gaye and his poignant 'Abraham, Martin And John' and The (new) Supremes with their debut 'Up The Ladder To The Roof'.

Stevie Wonder worked with Lee Garrett and Syreeta on 'Signed, Sealed, Delivered (I'm Yours)' and also on 'It's A Shame' for The Spinners who had joined the company in 1963, following a spell with the Tri Phi label. Prior to hooking up with Wonder, the group had released a handful of mellow soul singles such as 'I'll Always Love You' and 'Truly Yours' and generated income from live shows, appearing with Marvin Gaye, The Supremes and others. The Spinners also played clubs, where they established a name as a singing comedy act: 'We had to come up with something different,' the group's Pervis Jackson said. 'So we started impersonating people like Smokey Robinson, The Beatles, The Marvelettes, but our best impersonation was of Diana Ross. That used to get a lot of laughs.'

It was while on tour with Wonder that The Spinners' career

changed. Group member Bobby Smith recalls, 'Stevie told us he had a song which he thought might suit us. We gave it a listen and decided to cut it right then and there. Stevie always carries a lot of equipment around with him so we cut it on the spot.' That track, 'It's A Shame', released late 1970, catapulted to number twenty, their first British hit. It had a marvellously high sound, solid hookline and strong melody. 'We'll Have It Made', written by Wonder and Syreeta, followed but bombed by comparison. Nonetheless the group had been elevated from ground zero and it was an elated Pervis Jackson who said, 'Since the records took off things have really happened for us. In a sense we're starting all over again.' The group later left Motown for Atlantic Records where, known as The Detroit Spinners, they enjoyed a wonderfully successful recording career from 1972 onwards with gems like 'I'll Be Around', 'Could It Be I'm Falling In Love', 'Ghetto Child' and 'Then Came You' with Dionne Warwick.

The Mississippi-born Lee Garrett, a radio DJ, singer and composer, first met Stevie Wonder in 1963 when their favourite nighttime pastime was to cruise nightclubs without the knowledge of their guardians. They then drifted apart until years later when Garrett moved to Detroit where, among other things, he earned a living impersonating his friend: 'To keep myself alive, I'd do little gigs passing myself off as Stevie Wonder.' Garrett then went on to record his own work, his most notable release being the 1976 album *Heat For The Feet*.

When Stevie Wonder went into the studio to record 'Signed, Sealed Delivered (I'm Yours)', Garrett opted not to join him, saying, 'I felt Motown didn't need another blind guy bouncing around', but once he'd heard the completed track he was convinced it was more suited to Stax recording artist Johnnie Taylor. Wonder disagreed, saying it was too good to give away, although admitted he had blatantly emulated the Stax sound, having tired of Motown's predictable presentations: 'I had the desire to move out of the one little thing that the musicians were in and that Motown was in,' he told David Breskin. 'And I wanted to do it . . . because I liked the groove.'

With Stevie Wonder sitting in a large cardboard box marked for posting, the *Signed Sealed, Delivered* album had many likeable qualities because for the first time Wonder had ignored record company regulations to take his own initiative. Of course, four singles helped its sales, namely, 'Signed, Sealed, Delivered (I'm Yours)', 'Heaven Help Us All', 'We Can Work It Out' and 'Never Had A Dream Come True'. Although the singer was credited album producer, he was only responsible for two tracks, with co-production on a further three. He also co-penned seven of the twelve tracks. In true Motown fashion, Wonder delivered 'Sugar', before re-moulding 'You Can't Judge A Book By Its Cover' from its traditional Blues/folk heritage into an updated love song. The ballads here were mature beyond his years, particularly the love-laced 'Don't Wonder Why' and 'Anything You Want Me To Do', while, critics believed, 'I Can't Let My Heaven Walk Away' penned by Pam Sawyer and Joe Hinton to be the album's highlight. Injecting funk into 'Joy (Takes Over Me)', he changed tack to insist music and love cured all in 'I Gotta Have A Song' (flipside of 'Heaven Help Us All') and 'Something To Say', the album's closing track. All things considered, this album was a positive musical move, giving Stevie Wonder credibility as a producer and stylist.

Another track culled from the album was Stevie Wonder's final single of the year. Written by Ron Miller, it was the intense 'Heaven Help Us All'. Not originally intended as a single, the track was greeted with such enthusiasm by American DJs that Motown clipped it for release. It was a pointed departure from Wonder's style, in that the lyrics were deliberately striking – 'heaven help the roses when the bomb falls' – which he acknowledged, saying, 'This is a part of me which I haven't been able to get into before.' He further explained his feelings to journalist Alan Smith:

I want peace. There's a lot of people want peace. I want peace for brothers and sisters everywhere. The trouble today is that the biggest handicap is lack of communication . . . Young people can do so much for understanding and peace, because they're not set in their ways. And music can be used as a great force for bringing people together.

'Heaven Help Us All' shot into the American top ten in November 1970, and was a British top thirty entry.

With his career on course, Stevie Wonder privately worked away studying voice techniques, learning Braille notations to assist with music arrangements, and of course, composing prolifically. This time, however, his lyrics of love were inspired by a young woman whom he intended to marry.

Syreeta Wright worked as a secretary-cum-singer at Motown, following an invitation from Holland/Dozier/Holland to join the company. As Rita Wright she recorded one single, 'I Can't Give Back The Love I Feel For You' in 1968. Although it sold poorly at the time, it went on to become an in-demand collector's item. She laughs, 'I guess the single wasn't followed up because the company had other ideas for me.' Syreeta and Stevie first met when Stevie traipsed through her office laden down with a pile of songs. This led to an impromptu recording session with Syreeta as his support vocalist. 'He walked over from the piano to where I was sitting and suggested that I try the backing in a different way,' she remembers, 'I must say I wasn't very impressed!'

On another occasion, Wonder strolled into her office and asked if she was free that particular evening. When she replied she had to visit the library, he didn't believe her: 'I thought it was a brush off but I found out she really did go to change her books . . . I felt that from Syreeta's voice she was a very warm and generous person, but obviously I didn't make much impression on her.' Syreeta, on the other hand, was wary of becoming involved with him, knowing his track record with women: 'It was only after I came to know him that I realised how lonely he was.'

The marriage took place on 14 September 1970 after a four-month engagement. The ceremony was, however, held up for forty minutes as the bridegroom battled with a nose bleed while dressing for his wedding. He was promptly rushed through the gathering crowds and into the side door of Detroit's Burnette Baptist Church where his bride, dressed in a white satin gown with a cowl-like satin veil, was waiting. Their respective parents had arrived earlier for the candle-lighting that signified the start of the ceremony, officiated by the Reverend Caldwell. Motown employees attended with friends and family, while Berry Gordy flew in from Los Angeles, joining Wonder's parents, his brother, Fuller, and sisters, Gwen and Esther. After the ceremony, the couple hosted a gala reception at

Detroit's Mauna Loa Restaurant for three hundred guests, before honeymooning in Bermuda.

A happy Syreeta told the press: 'Steve's a remarkable person and that's outside the fact I'm in love with him. He never shows he's sad to anyone. To me he'll show his grievances but when he steps out he never shows it if he's angry or depressed. He feels life is too short to upset other people.' On the matter of their future family, she revealed, 'We're going to have at least twelve children, that's no exaggeration because we both adore them.' She also stressed that her husband's blindness was not an issue because he didn't consider it a handicap: 'He doesn't like being babied and he likes people to forget he's blind and to treat him as any other human being.' Their marriage was short-lived and was the only one of Stevie Wonder's personal relationships that he publicly spoke about. However, at this stage the young couple were wrapped up in their love for each other, and unaware of the changes going on around them – changes that could result in their professional security being whipped from under them.

With the honeymoon over, the couple began working on Wonder's next (and last) album due under his 1960 recording contract, his first without any influence from Motown's creative control team. However, before the project could hit the streets, their record company shifted location. Motown may have taken the motor city's name, but the company had outgrown its roots. For some time, Berry Gordy had desperately wanted to expand into television and films, but unable to do so from Detroit he began transferring his offices to 6255 Sunset Boulevard in Los Angeles, where a new television wing, Motown Productions Inc, was opened, alongside a recording studio.

It was a time of transition for 'The Sound of Motown', which lost many fans as well as gaining new converts. For the Detroit-based artists the company's move was devastating. By 1972 a few of the bigger artists had also relocated, leaving the remainder to face the same situation they were in during the sixties – stranded in Detroit looking for a recording deal.

Martha Reeves said she was the last artist to be told of the move, and felt betrayed by Berry Gordy, 'When I first started at Motown, there was a game plan, a strategy and goals for my career. Now that I had recorded million-selling records, had headlined prestigious nightclubs and became an international star, Motown treated me like a poor stepchild . . . I felt lost in the shuffle.' She later recalled that the move led to further upheavals:

[Although] The Temptations still continued at the company, The Marvelettes disbanded. Gladys Knight and the Pips were soon to leave the label, as well as The Four Tops. Berry wanted to be near the movie world because he wanted to make Diane into a film star. Other than Marvin, Stevie and Smokey, who all wrote and produced their own material, the rest of us had to fend for ourselves.

Otis Williams recalls, 'The old friendliness and camaraderie that had supported all of us in the beginning was replaced by a general air of businesslike formality. By moving the operation off West Grand, Motown took the first step away from its roots, not only geographically but spiritually . . . Motown outside Detroit was unthinkable.'

Hank Cosby believed Motown lost its whole creative structure when it moved west, while Stevie Wonder said he supported Berry Gordy's decision. Transferring Motown to Los Angeles was, he considered, a long-awaited positive step: 'He had to change with the times. I think the move is a very good thing. There are other things to be said now. People who do not want to change ideas, who are safe, usually get left behind.'

Chapter 6

MUSIC OF MY MIND

'The contract Stevie finally agreed granted him the greatest freedom of any Motown artist'

Mary Wilson

'If my own records aren't getting accepted . . . then I'll drop the name Stevie Wonder and . . . become part of Wonderlove'

Stevie Wonder

'I don't want to hear any of that ecology bullshit'

Mick Jagger

During 1971 Stevie Wonder became a man in more ways than one. With his personal life on a high, he now had to sort out his career. However, while that was being discussed in private, he clipped as a double-A-sided single the John Lennon/Paul McCartney original 'We Can Work It Out' and 'Never Dreamed You'd Leave In Summer' from the *Signed, Sealed And Delivered* album. Fans were stumped by the reasoning behind this release, but general consensus was that it was the singer's tribute to The Beatles, who were an influential force in his music. The cover version gave Wonder an American top twenty hit. In May 1971 the British release of 'We Can Work It Out' was coupled with 'Don't Wonder Why' because it was felt 'Never Dreamed You'd Leave In Summer' was worthy of A-side status. In July it was duly released as a single, with 'If You Really Love Me' as the flipside. Not a good move, as the single bombed, while its predecessor reached the top thirty. In this instance maybe the Americans knew best.

Thankfully this hiccup did not typify the year. Stevie Wonder was to release his last album under the terms of his original Motown contract, a project that had taken a year to complete. Titled *Stevie Wonder The Man* and with Syreeta co-writing, the album was inspired by his growing musical influences, such as Eric Clapton, and Sly Stone, and his widening interest in American politics, particularly the dire situation in Vietnam. Social issues and his dissatisfaction with Motown also figured in this revolutionary enterprise, which to a certain extent would symbolise his future thinking. Wonder explained his wife's involvement: 'I'm no good at words so she helped me on the lyrics. She's a romanticist, so we find it easy right now. We're trying to touch on the social problems of the world today in many of our songs. We want them to be relevant, to mean something.' He also insisted the release wasn't simply a selection of songs: 'The project is based on world problems, with songs of war, anti-drugs and about the racial issue. I feel it's the most important thing I've done.' Realising the project was not a money-spinning Stevie Wonder album as such, Motown held back its release hoping to issue a 'greatest hits' package instead.

Not surprisingly, Stevie Wonder got his own way and, at this crucial stage in his career, would unfortunately pay the price. The album now known as *Where I'm Coming From*, Motown's first free-expression project, was released in April 1971 (June in Britain). 'I was kinda expressing the things I wanted to say,' Wonder later told author David Nathan. 'It was amazing at the time because Marvin was working on *What's Going On* which was the greater of the two albums. His album was just awesome, because it spoke so much of what was going on.' *Where I'm Coming From* stalled in the American top seventy. Wonder was devastated and blamed Motown: 'I don't think it was promoted properly. The album was premature perhaps but I wanted to express myself . . . People never got to hear it, so the singles that were pulled didn't really make sense.'

Just how premature was *Where I'm Coming From*? Perhaps Stevie Wonder was too ambitious with this work. Producing *Signed, Sealed, Delivered* had given him a confidence that was, some believed, overblown because, although this current album was the merging of his musical influences, the resulting melting pot of assorted styles was cumbersome and confusing. Nonetheless, all credit to him for having the guts to take the step, particularly as he had a new contract pending, something that Berry Gordy was also well aware of. In retrospect, Wonder's free rein taught him and Berry Gordy a great deal because both discovered the singer's inadequacies. But when critics maliciously dissected the project, Stevie Wonder's confidence took a hammering.

Pointing an accusing finger at the older generation for their ineffectiveness 'I Wanna Talk To You' was followed by the luxuriously balanced 'If You Really Love Me', which typified the mid-tempo flow of music at the time. Perfect for single release during August 1971, when it soared into the top ten, and five months later in Britain, when it peaked in the top twenty. 'Look Around' moved into 'Do Yourself A Favour', a slice of Wonder funk spanning six minutes of musical cacophony. With 'Think Of Me As Your Solider', Wonder joined others in condemning the horrors of the Vietnam War, to which he felt he should have contributed, before quickly returning to the subject he knew so well – love – with 'Something Out Of The Blue', the smoothest track on the album. But even this paled in comparison to the mighty first clipped single 'Never Dreamed You'd Leave In Summer'. The further love- slanted 'Take Up A Course In Happiness' clashed with 'Sunshine In Their Eyes', a deep-rooted look at social issues. Indeed, the album was a muddied project, which fans and critics felt dipped too heavily into past impressions, but which demonstrated the strength of Wonder's melodies when set against Syreeta's sensitive lyrics.

Even Motown's marketing department had been at a loss to find the most effective way of promoting the album. A Stevie Wonder mobile appeared to be the answer. Under the direction of Curtis McNair, the album's green front cover showed Wonder's name and album title in the top left-hand corner. Across the cover in large print was his surname, each letter holding a picture of either his face, torso (in battle fatigues) or legs. The letters could be pushed out to construct a mobile. This appeared to make a mockery of the music within.

Motown recouped any lost investment by promptly releasing

the previously planned *Greatest Hits Volume 2* package aimed at the pending Christmas market. Once again, the company was unable to restore Stevie Wonder's selling power as the compilation bounced in and out of the American top seventy. British sales were far superior, due to the surprising success of 'If You Really Love Me', which catapulted the compilation into the top thirty.

On 13 May 1971 Stevie Wonder turned 21. Having prepared for this day for some time now, his lawyers presented his demands to Ewart Abner, then president of Motown Records. Abner had been aware of the singer's frustrations but was shocked when he was instructed to dissolve Wonder's original contract. 'I decided to not sign with anybody for a while and just cool it,' Wonder stated. 'I was thinking of looking at other companies and talked to just about every company there was.' One of the demands was to release his unpaid earnings since he signed to Motown, which his trustees had invested for him and which he estimated to be in the region of $30 million. Wonder accepted $1 million. With the money he relocated to New York, lived at the Howard Johnson Motor Inn, Manhattan, and booked studio time at the Electric Lady Studios in Greenwich Village, where, with a pile of half-completed songs, he intended to reflect on his past career and experiment with new music. He recorded forty songs during his stay and told Constance Eisner, 'I wanted to do an album with the money I had accumulated. But this time it wasn't so much a question of where I was coming from but where I was going to. I had to find out what my direction and my destiny was.'

Malcolm Cecil and Bob Margouleff worked with Stevie Wonder at Manhattan's studios. British-born Cecil was an ex-member of the BBC Radio Orchestra, who had been working for some time at these studios as an engineer with Margouleff, a musician and photographer. Stevie Wonder was drawn to Margouleff not for his photographic talents but his Moog. Having heard this synthesiser on the album *Zero Time* by Tonto's Expanding Headband, who were, Wonder later discovered, actually Cecil and Margouleff, he wanted to be taught how to programme the Moog for his own use. Margouleff told Adam White and Fred Bronson: 'We never stopped working from that moment, night and day. He'd do the playing, we'd do the programming, and we started to accumulate a huge library of songs.'

Meantime, back at Motown Berry Gordy fully understood his artist's reluctance to re-sign at this time, and was aware that lawyers from Atlantic Records and CBS Records were waving open chequebooks in Stevie Wonder's direction. However, it wasn't this that upset Gordy but the fact that after he and Wonder had partied together at his 21st birthday bash, Gordy had returned to his West Coast offices to find a letter from Wonder's lawyer stating that there would be no future contract with Motown. Berry Gordy remembered, 'I was more upset about that than I was about his being able to do it. The attorney had jumped the gun. So [Stevie] fired that attorney and got another.' Johanan Vigoda, a tough yet sensitive man who cared for Wonder like a son, was hired to thrash out a new deal with Motown.

Stevie Wonder's demands weren't new. Marvin Gaye had made similar overtures for total creative control of his work. However, Gaye's fight was bitter and personal because he'd married Gordy's sister Anna. Berry Gordy was extremely reluctant to release *What's Going On* but agreed to lift its title track as a single. When that soared to the number two spot in America, he backed down and hastily released the mother album in May 1971. Gaye recalled, 'Stevie gained from that fight and the world gained from Stevie's genius,' while Gordy said, 'It's so hard to compare the two because they were so different. Marvin had a different kind of sex appeal than Stevie. Stevie was a technician, he would deal with contraptions and technology.' He further admitted that Stevie Wonder knew what he'd wanted before reaching adulthood: 'At first it was very rough (to accept), not because I didn't think Stevie could do it. He had proven that he could do things himself and that he had genius qualities.'

Two of Motown's top league artists had been working with Wonder prior to May 1971. He had produced material for Martha Reeves and David Ruffin, whose careers needed re-routing, but it was never issued because of the general disinterest in Wonder's work at this time. This was another item high on his list of demands, as he told *Rolling Stone* magazine: 'I was in the process of getting my thing together and deciding what I was going to do with my life, so a lot of things were left somewhat un-followed-up by me. I would get the product there and nobody would listen so I'd say "fuck it".'

Having stalled Motown for six months, Wonder and Johanan Vigoda (who had previously negotiated contracts for big rock names like Jimi Hendrix) negotiated with Motown's lawyers for six weeks before agreeing the 120-page contract. One of the major stumbling blocks was Wonder's demand to keep his own publishing. In the end, Motown conceded. 'It was a very important contract for Motown and a very important contract for Stevie, representing the artists of Motown,' Vigoda announced. 'He broke tradition with the deal, legally, professionally – in terms of how he could cut his records and where he could cut them – and in breaking tradition he opened up the future for Motown. That's what they understood.' The lawyer also insisted Motown now had a major artist, not simply someone who released hit singles, and that in itself would influence future company signings. With creative freedom, Stevie Wonder went on to form several companies, including Taurus Productions and the Black Bull Publishing Company (both associated with his birth sign), through which he would control his future career as a writer, singer and performer.

On hearing of the re-signing, Mary Wilson remarked:

> Motown had lost performers before, but never anyone it really wanted to keep. In addition to his long line of hit singles, Stevie was one of the few Motown acts to develop a broader audience. The contract Stevie finally agreed to granted him the greatest freedom of any Motown artist. Not only was he freed artistically, but financially. For once, Motown permitted an artist to control his own publishing, the key source of income for songwriters.

While lawyers completed the paperwork, Stevie Wonder joined mourners Cissy Houston, Aretha Franklin and others at the funeral of King Curtis, who was fatally stabbed following an argument outside his New York apartment in New York City. Born Curtis Oustey, he became a legendary soul saxman, quickly earning the title King Curtis. He was 37 years old.

As Motown moved into its second decade, songwriters and producers took on an even more vital role within the company's structure, as did the introduction of new labels. It seemed logical that when Berry Gordy moved to Los Angeles, a new label be introduced. Mowest – an abbreviation for Motown/West Coast – was opened to handle records emanating from the Los Angeles nerve-centre. Mowest's music was commercially slanted and introduced new acts like the Commodores, Devastating Affair and Tom Clay, with seasoned performers like Thelma Houston, Frankie Valli & the Four Seasons, Sisters Love, and Stevie Wonder's wife, Syreeta, whose first American Mowest single 'I Love Every Little Thing About You' was issued in September 1972, three months after Suzee Ikeda's version of her 1968 classic 'I Can't Give Back The Love I Feel For You'. Syreeta's single was extracted from her eponymous album, mostly comprising tracks written by her and Wonder, who also produced the release and played most of the instruments.

With contract negotiations and Syreeta's project behind him, Stevie Wonder toured Britain again, bringing Wonderlove with him for the first time – a group of four singers and eight musicians, some from The Butterfield Blues Band. It had taken Wonder three months to find the musicians and rehearse them to the standard required for the road and studio: 'I can do a lot more of the things I want to do musically with these people . . . the show is now funkier than it's ever been because the musicians know exactly what I want. It's like being part of a tremendous amount of energy.' He also introduced his Moog and ARP synthesisers to his British audiences. But it wasn't a happy start. Kicking in at London's Hammersmith Odeon on 13 January 1972, the tour ended on 2 February in Manchester's Odeon. Following his opening night, the singer conducted interviews in his Kensington hotel where he previewed tracks from his forthcoming album, *Music Of My Mind* from a portable tape player. During one interview, Motown/UK delivered gifts including cases of beer, which prompted him to tell the attending journalist, 'These guys are trying to get me blind and drunk!'

Poor audience reaction had proved a major setback for Wonder at his opening concert in London. Indeed, people had walked out, including radio DJ Tony Blackburn, because Wonder had concentrated on his new material, leaving his Motown stereotypes to his public's memory. Yet it was with an air of arrogance that he told Alan Lewis, 'You can't please everybody. I've spent ten years pleasing other people when sometimes I wasn't very happy. Now I just want to do what I feel. I'm tired of doing the same old things . . . This thing about people having preconceptions about what I should play, well, if that's gonna be, I doubt if I'll be here in 1973.' He further maintained, 'If my own records aren't getting accepted because of this categorisation thing, then I'll drop the name Stevie Wonder and just become a part of Wonderlove.' Whatever his real intentions at this time, the singer played a dangerous game. It's generally accepted that, in Britain in particular, audiences expect to hear familiar material for their ticket money, and not an artist experimenting with new songs. In fact, tour promoters and record companies usually advised visiting artists of their local hit songs which they suggested should be featured because audience toleration for unreleased material was generally low. It is then left to the artist to decide on a show's structure.

New Musical Express writer Roger St Pierre attempted to portray what happened at Wonder's debut performance: 'Fans were clapping . . . but there was a prevailing feeling of discontent in the theatre. He messed with the Moog (which never was loud enough anyway) and when that didn't work he'd slip his hands over to the Fender Rhodes electric piano. None of the improvision worked. Only the hits came across with any certainty.' Together with the Moog, Wonder had also introduced the Bag, which he explained was a tube-like device which he fitted inside his mouth: 'You don't actually make the sound with your voice, you just mouth the shape of the words and the air pressure acts on a resonator to produce the sound. I came across it in a studio in Detroit, and messed around with it until I found out how to get the sound I wanted.'

With the British tour completed, Stevie Wonder went on to perform in Germany. After the last date in Frankfurt, he returned to London to spend two days in the Olympic Studios, where he worked on twelve tracks which he'd written when he first arrived in London. He then rested for a day before transferring to the AIR

Studios, where he worked with a 22-piece string orchestra loaned from the BBC thanks to Malcolm Cecil's connections. Sitting on the stool in the control booth on the last day, the singer listened intently to the playback, swaying his head and tapping his fingers to the tempo. When he heard a slight flaw in the music, he stopped the tape to return to the studio to rectify the error which, of course, no one else heard. 'Stevie has an amazing ear,' Malcolm Cecil explained. 'He'll sit and listen to the musicians and if just one plays a wrong note he'll notice . . . We've already got 55 tunes in the can. Who can say when they're going to be issued, if ever. Stevie's only concern is getting the sounds he wants down on tape. He'd get very frustrated if he couldn't.'

While Stevie Wonder was in Britain, Motown in America worked towards releasing his debut album under the new contract. The first complaint came from the A&R department because they felt the project contained no single material, an unheard-of situation under his last contract. But the rules had changed because Wonder now personally chose his singles and his permission was also needed if Motown wanted to release other tracks as singles. Album compilations likewise needed his approval. One month after the tour finished, *Music Of My Mind* was released and became a media talking point; its importance was soon clear. When issued in Britain during May 1972, the album was the second release in the new STMA numbering system used for lavishly packaged albums sold at a higher price.

Music Of My Mind reputedly cost Stevie Wonder a quarter of a million dollars in studio time, and was a revolutionary departure from his familiar Motown sound that fans had supported so faithfully. He composed the entire album with Syreeta's help, and played most of the instruments, including piano, harmonica, drums and organ, with emphasis on his ARP synthesisers and the Moog. 'It was time for a change musically,' a satisfied artist said. 'Spiritually I had gone as far as I could have gone. I then asked the question again of where am I going, what am I going to do. I had to see and feel what I wanted to do, and feel what my destiny was. The direction of destiny anyway and we got into *Music Of My Mind*.' He also insisted he was happy to give Motown the album 'partly because of my new contract and partly from a verbal understanding. And because they don't understand what I'm doing, so they just let me get on with it.'

The Moog and ARP synthesiser allowed him, he explained, 'to do things I've wanted to do for a long time, but which weren't possible. They've added a whole new dimension to music. The Moog itself is a way to directly express what comes from your mind, hence the album's title . . . [but] I'm not trying to be different. I'm just trying to be myself.' While the synthesiser allowed Wonder to transform his musical visions into reality, he also believed it added a new dimension to music because 'after programming the sound, you're able to write or process the melody live immediately, and in as many different manners as you want'.

Released in the aftermath of the disappointing *Where I'm Coming From*, the new album was musically groundbreaking. The project's opener, 'Love Having You Around', with Wonder's Bag-warped voice, led into soft funk closeted in a carpet of electric piano, interrupted by Art Baron's trombone solo: a perfect start, which crept into 'Superwoman (Where Were You When I Needed You)', with Wonder pre-empting the breakdown of his marriage. 'I Love Every Little Thing About You' was attractively simplistic, although Syreeta's version on her eponymous album was that much sweeter. 'Happier Than The Morning Sun' followed in the same vein, its unpretentious construction typical of Wonder's sensitive pen. In retrospect, the high-octane performance of 'Keep On Running' was the highlight of the collection, while the closing track 'Evil' dealt with the darker side of human nature, haunting the listener with its direct lyrics. 'Girl Blue' and 'Seems So Long' were the other titles on this rather radical album, so reliant on the programming of Margouleff and Cecil, which Stevie Wonder meticulously and tirelessly manipulated to get the music he'd heard in his mind.

The packaging for *Music Of My Mind* carried Gaetano's profile photographs of the artist sporting a moustache and short beard, with his sunglasses reflecting extracts from the brightly coloured montage on the inside gatefold sleeve. Designed by Daniel Blumenau, this sleeve included pictures of the singer, eastern statues and dancers, a prancing bull, and a whole spectrum of mind images. Added to this interesting visual collection were profile-building notes about the developing Wonder, including: 'This album marks a milestone in the development of a great talent. A man who keeps his promise. Stevie in maturity shines with that same loving and brilliant light that has drawn people to him for a decade . . . This album is a gift to the spirit from one who really cares.'

The first extracted single 'Superwoman (Where Were You When I Needed You)', issued in May 1972 and in September in Britain, stalled in the American top forty. As an eight-minute album track, the song strolled through a musical maze without due regard for commerciality. As a single, the ploy failed but Stevie Wonder supported its release saying, 'Some people have said they don't see the connection between the two halves – but if you follow the song, it's saying the guy still needs her.' The second extracted American single, 'Keep On Running', was also a poor seller, indicating, perhaps, the public's indifference to his radical, changing style, as evidenced by David Nathan's comments: 'Judging by the reaction, it becomes apparent the change, as such, is the last thing a good proportion of soul fans want. But eventually even the most loyal of fans will tire of hearing the same old thing over and over, so I feel we shouldn't pre-judge anything our favourite artists do – as long as they continue to do it with soul.' Agreeing with Nathan, Stevie Wonder said, 'I had by this time got some new cult fans and they were into avant garde Stevie Wonder with synthesisers and that type of thing.'

Music Of My Mind and *What's Going On* pushed Motown into the seventies in a way that Berry Gordy could never have envisaged. The music was alarmingly different from Motown's rapidly stagnating late-sixties output when, some believed, the company became rather complacent and rested on its laurels. With these two albums to its credit, Motown had changed its musical policy and marketing ideas to keep abreast of changing musical tastes. It had to face the prospect of moving with the times or staying static; Gordy chose the former, although success wasn't as spontaneous as it had been in the sixties. Marvin Gaye recalled:

The seventies were rough for Berry because the artists' time had arrived. The old days when the producer ran the show was over. People like me, Stevie and Diana [Ross] knew that. There was no more 'Motown Sound' in the Seventies, just a string of separate singers doing their own thing. It wasn't easy for Berry. He always lived through his artists, and now all of a sudden his artists were running their own careers. He felt left out, and was nervous. We were nervous too. He wasn't there to take care of us like he used to.

It goes without saying that Berry Gordy was extremely wary of Stevie Wonder's new independence and when *Music Of My Mind* peaked at number 21 in the American chart perhaps he had good reason to be worried. However, the album did open the door to another type of audience: in June 1972, Wonder was support act to The Rolling Stones, opening shows on fifty dates spanning Vancouver to New York. Ironically, the last time the Motown star had played with the British rock 'n' roll band was in 1964, when he had had top billing! Stevie Wonder's act included tracks from his new album *Talking Book* and his most recent singles, backed by Wonderlove comprising eight musicians and four singers. Wonder declared, 'To me, the challenge in performing is to make an audience aware of everything that's within me now. People shouldn't expect a set thing from me because I love to grow.'

Despite being a sell-out tour, the participating acts clashed behind scenes, mostly at Wonder's expense. It transpired the aggravation was far more serious than the Motown star cared to admit. Mick Jagger and Keith Richards bad-mouthed him to the media, while he in turn desperately tried to respect a group that was living through their most decadent tour, awash with alcohol, drugs and sex. Jagger was particularly spiteful when Wonder refused to participate in these sessions as Wonder told author John Swenson in *Stevie Wonder*: 'Jagger said, "Stevie Wonder and his group came to jam with us, but they couldn't keep up." And they said something about we spent the night "fucking and sucking". I didn't hang out with those cats, man.' Another dispute arose when Wonder's drummer unexpectedly quit, forcing him to cancel a show in Texas. Wonder notified the Stones of his dilemma but assured them he would find a suitable replacement for the second performance. There appeared to be no problem until he was informed that Keith Richards had told the media 'Stevie Wonder was a c*nt'. 'If Keith did say that, he's just childish,' a shocked singer told *Rolling Stone* magazine's Ben Fong-Torres. 'I love people too much to fuck up and miss a show. And it's crazy the things he said. And if he didn't say them he should clarify them because I will always hold this against him . . . What really bugged me about the whole thing was that our drummer was in a very bad situation and that's why he left.' Then Jagger and Richards slammed his music: 'Mick and Keith said a couple of things in magazines I was surprised about. They didn't say them to me. Like Mick was quoted as saying "I don't want to hear any of that ecology bullshit." He never said that to me, maybe because he knew I'd challenge him.' As an afterthought, he laughed, 'I'd probably have had a better time with The Beatles!'

Whatever the differences, the tour ended on a high note when Wonder and the Stones performed on stage together, singing 'Uptight' and '(I Can't Get No) Satisfaction'. On the night Mick Jagger celebrated his birthday, the jamming session turned into a pie-throwing shambles with musicians caked in crushed pies, dangerously sliding around on stage, and between the assorted pieces of equipment. The performances were recorded but the proposed two-album set was never released. Wonder blamed record-industry machinations: 'The problem with being an artist and having managers is that, whenever money is involved, people want to get their share, so contractual hassles mean the album is probably doomed to stay in the can.' Keith Richards agreed as he told journalist Nick Kent in 1973: 'A whole live album with Stevie on it was scrapped because Decca [the group's then record company] ballsed it up.' The tour was also filmed by Robert Frank under the title *Cocksucker Blues*. It apparently included off-stage footage featuring young groupies, one of whom, author Gary Herman reported in *Rock 'N' Roll Babylon*, agreed to be filmed 'with her fresh face stuffed with the genitalia of Stones associates.' Once the tour finished, the same groupie admitted, '[I didn't] have to bother putting the make on anyone. [I was] there just to say yes.' Herman also conveyed to his readers Jagger's response, 'There's really no reason to have women on a tour unless they've got a job to do; the only other reason is to screw.'

In Stevie Wonder's absence, Motown acts were on the move. With a lack of regular hit material, The Four Tops' career nosedived. As their sales potential dropped, Motown lost interest, leaving the quartet with no option but to look elsewhere for a recording deal. It was with reluctance that The Four Tops signed with ABC Records in 1972.

The Supremes, with lead singer Jean Terrell, were also struggling with their new membership, following a pregnant Cindy Birdsong's retirement. Mary Wilson chanced to attend one of Stevie Wonder's concerts where she spotted Wonderlove member Sundray Tucker, an experienced singer with stage presence. Sundray and her sister Lynda Laurence had both provided support vocals during Wonder's *Signed, Sealed And Delivered* period, as Laurence remembered; 'Stevie was in the studio recording the album and he asked me to sing back-up. I was in shock. The singers were Syreeta, Venetta Fields and me. He then allowed me to travel with him alongside my sister Sundray and Terri Hendricks.' Lynda Laurence first met Stevie Wonder when she was sixteen years old at The Uptown Theater in Philadelphia:

He was celebrating his birthday, and there was a cake on stage. I couldn't believe I met him! That started a chain reaction that I had no idea would occur not many years later. After I left high school I moved to Detroit where Billy Henderson of The Spinners introduced me to Stevie again. Would you believe it, he remembered me!

Faced with the choice of two potential Supremes, Mary Wilson finally chose Laurence, who said, 'I wasn't going to leave but Stevie said, "Look, with me, you'll be a back-up singer. With The Supremes, you'll be a Supreme. It's a whole different thing. So, go at least try it." So I went because Stevie told me to.' While working with him, the new Supreme learnt much to help her in her later career: 'Stevie is much more than the consummate performer. He's also the most gifted musician, singer, writer, arranger. He has perfect pitch which in itself is a marvellous gift. He's so focused on his music that if you work for him you cannot help learning more and more every day. He literally exudes music!'

Stevie Wonder's quest for musical perfection rubbed off on his support singers and musicians. Indeed, Wonderlove was a launching pad for soloists. One such vocalist was Deniece Williams, born in Gary, Indiana, who replaced the departing Lynda Laurence to join the remaining Lani Groves and Gloria Barley. She went on to spend three years touring and recording with Wonder, and told John Abbey: 'I learned such a lot from working with Stevie. I guess it was really finance that prompted me to take the job when it was offered but I saw a whole lot of things that I would never have seen in Gary . . . I looked upon that era as my developing period. As an artist, Stevie encouraged me to grow in every way.' Williams further confided, 'It was my goal to keep the job for as long as I could, but you can't be that unattached to Stevie, he's too warm a person. It was he who encouraged me to start writing and I'll always look back on those years as the first exciting, well-paid years of my career.' Deniece Williams went on to enjoy success, which included the international number one single 'Free' in 1977, and a duet with Johnny Mathis titled 'Too Much, Too Little, Too Late' a year later. She also made guest studio appearances on Stevie Wonder's later work.

At the time, The Supremes' releases had become erratic and diverse. The group struggled for suitable material, often against their ex-lead singer Diana Ross, who had the choice of Motown's finest in-house staffers, as Lynda Laurence told author Susan Whitall: 'It appeared to us that [Motown] were putting most of their eggs in her basket, and we were left out in the cold.' However, before the trio hit rock bottom they worked with Stevie Wonder who, once again, influenced their musical style. Jean Terrell recalled, 'There's so much we wanted to do for a while but there was no one at Motown except Stevie who could interpret things the right way.' Having listened to her voice for some while, he believed her true potential was being suppressed: 'Basically, some of the writers were doing tunes that they thought might be good for her, but I listened to the way she did certain riffs and really she's something like Al Green in style.' By changing the double-time drums and strong bass rhythms to what Mary Wilson called 'a chugga-chugga beat', and with a musical backdrop that included shrill whistling, The Supremes released 'Bad Weather', their most innovative single to date. It was a remarkably refreshing, hypnotic sound, and Mary Wilson, for one, was delighted: 'Stevie was a dream to work with. He was very attentive, and he worked quickly and efficiently. As Stevie taught us the song, I thought, he really is a genius . . . Believing this style would put us back in good standing with the DJs, I encouraged Lynda and Jean to do some informal promotion, but they refused.' With this vital promotion ignored, Wilson was unable to fully support the release in America where it reached an abysmal top ninety placing in May 1973. In Britain, where The Supremes were revered as goddesses, 'Bad Weather' peaked at 37. '[This] was the last straw,' Wilson storms. 'Despite glowing reviews, the record went nowhere. Even Stevie was upset. He complained to Ewart Abner who promised the company would "get on it" [but] it was too late.' Subsquently, Wonder's plans to record an album with The Supremes were scrapped because he felt it was unfair to spend more of the trio's money on a project that wouldn't ride on a hit single. The Supremes then moved on to work with Jimmy Webb but that project also bombed. Eventually Jean Terrell left to be replaced by Scherrie Payne, and in 1974 Lynda Laurence departed. Cindy Birdsong replaced her! 'Stevie asked why I thought Lynda had left The Supremes . . . and remarked that in his opinion Cindy lacked something onstage,' Mary Wilson wrote in her autobiography. 'I found this last point interesting, considering Stevie couldn't see her. He just heard something in our show and suggested that we might think about replacing her. He added that he had written some new songs for us. Although he was very upset about what had happened with "Bad Weather", he said it didn't bother him that much anymore.' Wonder further told the Supreme of his concern about their own future, saying 'with the exception of Diana or Smokey, no one was happy with what Motown had become'.

In fact, Stevie Wonder's concerns for his own career were unfounded. He would go on to fulfil his new contract's stipulations by delivering breathtaking albums, enabling Motown to profitably balance its books but, unbeknown to him at this time, a brush with death would trigger the inspiration he needed to achieve such high standards.

A well-used Little Stevie Wonder publicity pose from 1963. It was, for instance, used on the 'Recorded Live – The 12 Year Old Genius' and 'With A Song In My Heart' albums.

above: Little Stevie Wonder is squashed between The Temptations' Melvin Franklin and The Supremes' Diana Ross at a photoshoot at EMI Records during 1965. The line-up also includes The Miracles (middle) and Martha and the Vandellas (dressed in white). **below: Stevie Wonder receives** The Fight for Sight 1969 Show Business Inspiration Award for his 'compelling achievements in the world of entertainment'.

above: A teenage Stevie has outgrown his adolescent awkwardness to become a confident young man. **below: Stevie was four years old** when he was given his first harmonica. The instrument, which was immediately recognisable on his early recordings, is still one of his favourites.

above: When the album 'Songs In The Key of Life' was further delayed, Stevie and Motown president Suzanne de Passe advertised the fact with specially made T-shirts.
below: Motown/EMI's preview of 'Songs In The Key of Life' may have been a low-keyed affair but the company's advertising was second to none. Not only did London buses advertise the album's network but also Motown's new label logo.

Stevie married Syreeta in September 1970. The ceremony was delayed while the groom battled with a nose bleed.

Stevie and Yolanda Simmons paid a surprise visit to London in 1977. During their stay, Stevie sang in Motown's offices, assisted Gullivers' DJ at the decks and appeared at Wembley Arena with Elton John.

A serious Wonder of the seventies. This picture was one of several snapped during a series of press interviews held in London.

A performing star during the eighties – a decade of great success with multi-million selling albums like 'Hotter Than July' and 'The Woman in Red' and two number one singles as a soloist and duettist.

Chapter 7

YOU ARE THE SUNSHINE
OF MY LIFE

'Here is my music. It is all I have to tell you how I feel'
Stevie Wonder

'[Stevie's] head was swollen up about five times normal size. And nobody could get through to him'
Ira Tucker

'Anyone who has had such an event happen to them never looks at life in quite the same way again'
Stevie Wonder

In the new year of 1973 Stevie Wonder flew to London to record 'Superstition' (his new single) and 'Alfie' for a Burt Bacharach television special. It was a lightning visit but he spent one day in his hotel suite conducting interviews. At hand was his tape recorder with a selection of unreleased tracks including a rough version of Syreeta's forthcoming 'Your Kiss Is Sweet' single. When he returned to America 'Superstition', swiped from his pending album, had soared to the pole position, nine years and five months since he had last topped the same chart with 'Fingertips Part 2'. The single also returned him to the British top eleven in February. The track, Wonder's debut in hard funk, was in fact written for Jeff Beck, as the composer explained at the time: 'I did a show with Jeff in Detroit and he told me he'd like to record something funky, so I said I'd cut it too and maybe include it on my next album. He said he didn't want my track to sound like his and I assured him it wouldn't. I played on his session, then finished off my own version and put it on my album *Talking Book*.'

However, according to Malcolm Cecil the story was slightly different. During a trip to London, Stevie Wonder had played Jeff Beck the 'Maybe Your Baby' track, which he said Beck could have. The two met up in June 1972 in New York's Electric Lady Studios where Bob Margouleff and Malcolm Cecil were finalising production on Jeff Beck's album due to be released by Columbia Records. By this time, Wonder had changed his mind about 'Maybe Your Baby': he wanted to keep it but offered Beck another song. He wrote the melody of 'Superstition', and dictated the lyrics to a studio secretary, telling Beck he could have the song but not his musical arrangement. When Wonder finally heard Beck's version of 'Superstition', he changed his mind again. According to Malcolm Cecil: 'Stevie said . . . "I'm going to keep it, it's too good." No one argued with him . . . We never got paid, the studio never got paid and it broke up my relationship with Jeff.'

Motown went against Wonder's dictate and scheduled his album track version of 'Superstition' as a single. Wonder remembers, 'In fact, they really insisted because I hadn't put out a single to coincide with my last album.' However, he'd previously advised Motown that he had earmarked another track for single release titled 'Big Brother', which was, he thought, a more commercial slice of personal funk. But when Motown requested the masters, he couldn't deliver, so 'Superstition' stayed on the release schedules irrespective of any arrangement made with Jeff Beck, whose own version was now put on hold.

Naturally, Jeff Beck was angry at Stevie Wonder for going back on his word because he believed 'Superstition' was exclusively his. Wonder attempted to rectify the situation by offering him another song but the damage had been done. The two artists did, however, later patch up their differences and went on to work together in the studio.

While Stevie Wonder topped the American singles chart Marvin Gaye was working on his next album, which the media called 'the most incredible collection of screwing music available'. *Let's Get It On* was brilliantly conceived with all aspects of love set against moody music, which made some tracks more erotic than soulful. The album eventually passed gold status in the USA, earning its creator the title 'Love Man'.

If the public believed *Music Of My Mind* was a throwaway album then *Talking Book* more than compensated for its predecessor's inadequacies. While criticism was levelled at Wonder's new project for his overindulgence in ballads – a short-sighted remark perhaps when considering that one such track was 'You Are The Sunshine Of My Life', one of his more beguiling and, later, most re-recorded of titles – *Talking Book* blended a variety of sounds and styles that he would take to the limit on future releases. For example, the track once earmarked as a single, 'Big Brother', was a personal interpretation of George Orwell's novel *1984*, while Wonder touched on God's enduring love during 'I Believe (When I Fall In Love It Will Be Forever)', with its anthemic melody and wonderful chorus. 'Maybe Your Baby', with Ray Parker Jr on guitar, was a seven-minute laid-back rocker, later recorded by the group Rufus. Syreeta co-penned 'Blame It On The Sun' which, if diagnosed, perhaps suggested the reasons for the breakdown of their marriage. Jeff Beck contributed towards 'Lookin' For Another Pure Love', and on 'Tuesday Heartbreak' David Sanborne played alto sax. Once again, Wonder used the ARP and Moog synthesisers, and recorded the album in the AIR Studios, London, Electric Lady Studios, New York, and the Los Angeles-based Crystal Studios and Record Plant. *Talking Book* was such a wonderful insight into its creator's talent; the easy-flowing melodies, the poignant and often stinging lyrics that Wonder found so easy to put to music. Many felt he had reached the turning point in his career, and despite the shaky start, his creative freedom promised a wealth of music in the future.

The front gatefold sleeve showed Bob Margouleff's picture of a seated reflective artist, dressed in a full-length copper-tinged gown, complemented by necklace and bracelets, with corn-row hair. Inside, a silhouetted Wonder sat against a backdrop of a darkened mountainous range, lit only by the descending sun. On the American sleeve, Wonder had written in Braille: 'Here is my music. It is all I have to tell you how I feel. Know that your love keeps my love strong.' Released in October 1972 in America, and in January 1973 in Britain, soaring to numbers three and sixteen respectively, *Talking Book* let no one down and surely convinced his sceptics that his earlier tag of the twelve-year-old genius was rightly awarded.

Releasing a follow-up to a number one single is usually difficult, but Stevie Wonder succeeded by selecting the obvious 'You Are The Sunshine Of My Life'. The title returned him to the American pole position and the British top ten. The compulsive ballad, which featured the voices of Jim Gilstrap and Gloria Barley in the introduction, broadened the singer's appeal into the lucrative middle-of-the-road market, as evidenced by later cover versions from artists like Liza Minnelli, Johnny Mathis and Frank Sinatra.

As the single dominated the US chart, selling in excess of one million copies, the singer attended the funeral of a ten-year-old black child Cloephus Glover, who had been killed by a New York City policeman. Deeply affected by the death, Wonder believed it to have had an extremely damaging effect on the already volatile black community: 'It brings America down another notch in my book,' he sighed. 'I hope that black people realise how serious things are and do something serious about it'. Just what he had in mind he didn't elaborate, but by mentioning the goals of Malcolm X and condemning the practices of the American president, Richard M Nixon, for slashing financing that had benefited black communities, he enabled journalists to use their imagination in print. He then lent his by now considerable weight to support John Lennon's Detroit benefit for John Sinclair, the incarcerated White Panther party leader. Yet, despite the unfair treatment of his race, Wonder saw fit to attend a White House ceremony hosted by President Nixon.

Prior to the official release of Marvin Gaye's *Let's Get It On*, Stevie Wonder, with a catalogue of one thousand unreleased songs, was able to schedule his next project *Innervisions*, a personal statement of social issues: 'I was going to call it "Last Days Of Easter" but I've scrapped that idea now. People would only relate it to Easter and not the other things I'll be saying.' The album's artwork was also planned, he revealed: 'It was going to be the picture of a very old man who's been through it all and can now rest and look back at the confusion. He would have the wisdom and the contentment.'

However, in August 1973, three days before *Innervisions* was simultaneously released in America and Britain, Wonder was nearly killed in a car accident. His cousin John Harris, was driving him from Greenville, South Carolina after a concert, to Durham, North Carolina. The singer was wearing a seatbelt and was sitting in the front seat when Harris attempted to overtake a timber truck, which was swaying across the road. The truck stopped suddenly, sending logs crashing on to the car. Wonder was rushed to the Rowan Memorial Hospital in Salisbury, and later moved to the intensive care unit of the North Carolina Baptist Hospital where a bruise on his brain and suspected broken skull were diagnosed. Although no surgery was immediately contemplated, first reports suggested Wonder was dying, as he was comatose for over a week. Indeed, the media believed him to be dead and hinted as much in print. Berry Gordy was woken at three in the morning by a phone call advising that his protégé was not expected to live, and later wrote: 'I was groggy, numb and hoping I was having a nightmare. I was, but I wasn't asleep. All of a sudden nothing else was important.'

Wonder's road manager, Ira Tucker, says, 'When I got to the hospital I couldn't even recognise him. His head was swollen up about five times normal size. And nobody could get through to him.' As Wonder listened to his music louder than most Tucker shouted regularly into the singer's ear. At first there was no response, but eventually, after Tucker had sung 'Higher Ground' for a day, Wonder started tapping his fingers to the beat. Although there remained cause for concern, Wonder slowly recovered sufficiently to make passes at his nurses; but, more seriously, with consciousness came the temporary loss of his sense of taste and smell.

Another anxiety for him was possible damage to his co-ordination and rhythm which, of course, would affect his ability to play instruments. This was tested by Ira Tucker: 'When [I] brought the clavinet to the hospital . . . you could tell he was afraid to touch it. He didn't know if he'd lost his musical gift. You could actually see the relief and happiness all over his face when he finally started playing it.'

Thankfully, Stevie Wonder made a complete physical recovery; doctors were unable to measure the side effects of his brain injury but were convinced there was no permanent neurological damage. To this day he still bears facial scars, including one above one eye, but as he said at the time, 'What's a few scars here and there, I've got my life.' He was flown back to California for further treatment at the UCLA and at the airport he was greeted by a relieved crowd of Motown artists, staff and friends. Obviously, due to the severity of his injuries, the singer's convalescence was slow. Recurring headaches, tiredness and constant care meant his career was put on hold. 'Anyone who has had such an event happen to them never looks at life in quite the same way again,' Wonder says. 'I felt it was a second chance at life and I felt it was time for a different awareness of other people's problems.' Press conferences and full-length tours (including a proposed British visit) were ruled out until 1974 at least, allowing Wonder time to rethink his future life, which now included Yolanda Simmons, a secretary and bookkeeper at Black Bull, his publishing company, whom he met during his convalescence and who would become the mother of his children. While recuperating the singer had spent time at Black Bull where one particular day he chanced to be on phone duty, as he told John Swenson: 'and we met on the phone. I liked the way she sounded and we became friends. Then it turned into other feelings which made our friendship more beautiful.' The couple later became engaged but would never marry.

'For the first time I believe I have a much better conception or understanding of how important time is,' the recovering singer explained.

I guess it's made me more sensitive about people I've always loved, meaning fans, and just people – period. It has made me check out myself and the people around me, made me realise that although I have such a great love for music, it shouldn't be so important to me that I don't do the very important and basic things of life. I think somehow when we get involved in a profession like this we take for granted or don't even think about the basics. I'm going to take some time to just relax.

In Stevie Wonder's absence the music played on. 'Higher Ground' was the first single to be lifted from *Innervisions* to become a top four American hit and British top thirty entrant. The singer later explained the song's sinister connotations:

I wrote the song before the accident but something must have been telling me that something was going to happen to make me aware of a lot of things and to get myself together. This is like my second chance for life to do something more, and to value the fact that I'm alive. And if I felt that not living would be better, to conclude it.

His first public appearance following his accident was with Elton John at the Boston Gardens on 25 September 1973. Midway through his show, the British singer announced to his capacity audience that a friend who had been recently been hurt in an accident was backstage. The two stars stood on stage for fifteen minutes while the audience wildly greeted Wonder's return, before kicking into an impromptu jam session featuring 'Superstition' and 'Honky Tonk Women'. 'That was the start of things really getting back to normal,' Wonder smiled.

What Elton John omitted to tell his audience was that the two had actually travelled together to Boston but John had been unaware of it. As he boarded the plane in New York, a member of his staff had arranged to surprise him with Stevie Wonder sitting at his portable piano in the rear cabin, singing 'Crocodile Rock'. 'But when Elton came out to get on the plane, he was in a terrible mood,' Sharon Lawrence (who travelled with John) remembered in Philip Norman's book *Elton – The Definitive Biography*:

He hadn't got his chart placings that morning or something. He didn't even see or hear Stevie. He just went straight into the front cabin and sat there, fuming. Stevie carried on playing and singing, and still Elton had no idea. In the end I had to go to him and say, 'For God's sake Stevie Wonder's back there.' He and Stevie played together that night, and were wonderful together.

An edited version of 'Living For The City' was the second single from *Innervisions*, returning Wonder to the American top ten and the British top fifteen. This starkly vivid, and, many felt, authentic view of Black America was very distressing in part: it told a complete story in the groove of a singer arriving in New York, where he inadvertantly becomes involved in a street crime, is arrested and later incarcerated. To inject credence and life into Wonder's lyrics, Bob Margouleff taped a real street incident as it happened, to which he added extra vocal drama by using Johanan Vigoda as the judge, brother Calvin playing the singer, and Ira Tucker as the street hustler. As the song was being created in the studio, it occurred to Margouleff that Wonder's vocals seemed too tame for the aggressive musical background: 'To get the anger, we would do things purposely to make Stevie mad . . . One of the things he hates the most is in the middle of a [vocal] phrase, you stop the tape. So we did this purposely to get him riled up.' The plan worked and as Wonder shouted until he was hoarse, they completed a track that, when presented to the public, was a powerful short film without visuals. Wonder's verdict is, 'I was able to show the hurt and anger.'

The salsa-styled 'Don't Worry 'Bout A Thing' followed in March 1974 to peak at number sixteen in America, while EMI Records opted to release the ten top entrant 'He's Misstra Know-It-All'. This was followed by 'Don't Worry 'Bout A Thing' in October. It bombed.

Innervisions sold in excess of one million copies, to reach the top five in the US and top ten in Britain. It was launched to the media at a New York reception, which included a tour of the city. Guests met in Times Square, Manhattan, where they were blindfolded as they boarded an awaiting coach. They toured the city in a haphazard fashion, before stopping at a recording studio. Wonder told Fred Bronson: 'The idea of the blindfolds was to try to give people an idea of what's happening in my mind. When you look at something, your hearing is distracted by your eyes.'

One attending journalist considered *Innervisions* to be boring with 'arrangements only lapsing from the predictable when they rely on gimmick-surprises'. A lone voice, because the majority of critics and fans felt this album verged on perfection. High on the list of favourites were, naturally, the singles, followed by the personal ballad 'All In Love Is Fair', dealing intimately with his failed relationship with Syreeta. The tranquility of 'Visions' melted across the grooves as it pleaded for world peace ('I hope it will be the song I'm remembered for,' Wonder once said), while the remaining tracks, 'Too High' (the album's opener), 'Golden Lady' and 'Jesus Children Of America' were individually distinguished. Admitting *Innervisions* carried an overriding theme of impending tragedy, Wonder believed the project actually held a warning of his near fatal accident in August 1973. Subsequently, many listeners spent hours sifting through the lyrics for indications of this.

The album's double gatefold sleeve, credited to Efram Wolff, was dull yet strangely attractive. The front cover showed a drawing of the peering singer in a left-hand corner oblong, while mashed green, brown, yellow and white depicted what appeared to be a mountain range and rocks in the foreground. Lyrics were included on the inner sleeve, next to which three painted characters sang and pranced, while the back cover showed a composite of colours and shapes. The assumed African theme added to the seriousness of the music within, indicating Stevie Wonder was not messing about this time.

Entirely produced and composed by the singer, *Innervisions* was recorded at the Record Plant, Los Angeles, and at Media Sound, New York. Malcolm Cecil and Bob Margouleff programmed the synthesisers he used and were credited as associate producers. They set up the studio in such a way that Wonder had room to move easily from one instrument to another. These included synthesiser, grand piano, Fender Rhodes, drums and other specialised instruments. Margouleff recalled, 'They would all be in a big circle and they'd all be switched on at the same time. Stevie could walk from one to the other.' Using his tried-and-tested method and with his tape running, Wonder would tape the melodies he had in his head and work on them, using the clavinet. Often lyrics would come to him, particularly if he'd been playing around with a phrase or actual song title. Other times, he'd hum or 'la la' where the lyrics should be, ensuring no idea was lost.

While Stevie Wonder was basking in the album's success, a fellow Motown artist was changing musical key. In October 1973, four weeks after her British stage debut since leaving The Supremes, Diana Ross's album of duets with Marvin Gaye was released, despite his vow when Tammi Terrell died that he would never record with another partner. *Diana & Marvin* was a commercial success, and sales from the album and spin-off singles ran into millions. Both artists, however, agreed the project was a one-off, vowing never to work together again!

American taste in popular music diversified widely during the early seventies. For example, the British were making their presence felt with artists such as Elton John, and solo Beatles George Harrison, Paul McCartney and Ringo Starr, who competed against Cher, Carly Simon and Helen Reddy. Nonetheless, Motown survived to secure five number one singles in 1973 – two from Stevie Wonder: 'Superstition' and 'You Are The Sunshine Of My Life'; Diana Ross's 'Touch Me In The Morning'; Marvin Gaye's 'Let's Get It On' and solo Temptation Eddie Kendricks with his in-vogue single 'Keep On Truckin''. However, it was generally felt that Berry Gordy's music had lost direction following his move to Los Angeles. No longer could a Motown single be recognised from its opening bars or chorus. Although established names were still able to deliver hit singles, newly signed artists were difficult to launch. America no longer led the way in music.

It was an interesting time.

FULFILLINGNESS' FIRST FINALE

'A relationship just doesn't end with a piece of paper being signed'
Syreeta

'[Stevie's] always been real close to me'
Minnie Riperton

'[Motown is] the only viable surviving black-owned company in the record industry'
Stevie Wonder

Following his near-fatal accident, Stevie Wonder was determined to change the way he lived. He realised how mortal he was, and that he wasn't prepared for death because there was still so much he wanted to achieve in his personal and public life. The runaway success of *Innervisions* and its singles had rallied overwhelming public support which, in turn, carried an obligation to be with his fans. Wonder, however, was determined to take the opposite approach to his future, as Ira Tucker explained to John Swenson: 'The accident changed him more than anything. It's really cooled him out. There was a time when if he wasn't playing the piano, singing or listening to tapes, he'd get restless and have to go out and do something. He never used to sleep.' Adopting a calmer pace of life, Wonder discovered an inner peace. He prioritised his work, and avoided becoming embroiled in record-company demands which, he felt, had previously plagued him. On that front, Motown wasn't worried: *Innervisions* could be rifled for singles for at least a year, which it ultimately was. In a bid to feed his inner peace, the singer toyed with relocating to the Republic of Senegal, Africa, and went as far as discussing this with Michael Jackson, who, with his brothers, had recently returned from a ten-day African tour. Jackson told author J Randy Taraborrelli: 'Before Stevie told the public about moving there he told me. I asked him why and he said he would feel safe there because that was his home.' Wonder later changed his mind, although, it was reported, he intended to purchase property there.

So, for the first part of 1974 the semi-retired singer played where and when he wanted. First amusing himself with guest spots in America and Britain, he also flew to France, where he performed a twenty-minute set at the Midem music festival in Cannes, during February. An attending *Melody Maker* journalist wrote in the weekly newspaper that the singer, dressed in a gown 'provided a breath of sanity after two hours of bland Euro-pop. He played like he'd never been away.' Returning to the US, Wonder jammed with Johnny Winter and Dr John at the opening reception of New York's Bottom Line, before a jubilant return to touring with a number of American and British dates.

A month after his Midem performance and with support from Wonderlove (now including Shirley Brewer, Deniece Williams and Lori Groves), a hand-picked group of tight musicians, and a show finale that boasted Eddie Kendricks, Sly Stone and Roberta Flack, Stevie Wonder played his first major sold-out date for one and a half years at New York's Madison Square Garden. It was, quite rightly, dubbed the concert of the year. He then switched to London to perform at the Rainbow Theatre, where his British fans welcomed the return of their musical hero with a genuine, heart-warming, wildly estatic reception, which both shocked and pleased the Motown star who had thought he'd lost much of their support following the rejection of *Where I'm Coming From* and *Music Of My Mind*.

Unashamed fan worship rubbed off on to the American record industry when in March 1974 Stevie Wonder scooped five Grammy awards at the 16th annual awards ceremony. They were: Best Pop Vocal Performance – Male for 'You Are The Sunshine Of

My Life'; Best R&B Vocal Performance – Male and Best R&B Song for 'Superstition', and Best Album of the Year and Best Engineered Album of the Year for *Innervisions*. In his acceptance speech for 'You Are The Sunshine Of My Life' the recipient proudly told his audience: 'I would like to thank all of you for making this night the sunshine of my life.' However, the success of the single went on to have a downside when it attracted a second major award that Wonder refused to accept. The National Association of Record Merchandisers (NARM) voted it the Best Soul Song of the Year, whereupon he told journalists, 'I feel that after writing songs like "All In Love Is Fair" (a version of which was Barbra Streisand's current single) and others, that it's wrong to say I'm just a soul singer because all those songs are typical ballads of America. I am a black man but music is music.' Many felt Wonder reacted badly to this award, believing that as the single had been honoured by both black and white music associations he was in the novel position of being a major artist in both buying markets. Needless to say, the American press milked the story for all it was worth.

Meanwhile, Wonder had another ace up his sleeve. Prior to his accident he had been working with Syreeta, and the project was now completed. Released in June 1974 and aptly titled *Stevie Wonder Presents Syreeta*, the album reflected the failure of their marriage, with each track telling a story. Syreeta explained further:

What I can't make people understand is a relationship just doesn't end with a piece of paper being signed. The love and feelings don't end. It's just that that particular phase is dissolved. We were divorced, yet the track 'Cause We've Ended Now As Lovers' was to make people understand why two people split up. When I wrote 'Blame It On The Sun' people reckoned it must have reflected Steve and I having gone through a bad time, but we never had bad times and I actually wrote that song when we were first married. The whole album is very special. Steve and I will carry on creating and fantasising through music because we work well together.

They also remained close friends, which Wonder believes some people found strange:

I'm always a friend and it's hard for friends to understand it. Women think 'I know you guys are here, so I know you're gonna get back together.' But if your head is really cool, like I used to always worry about when I used to go with someone, about them doing something with somebody else. I wasn't really the jealous type, I wouldn't show it. This is one thing I've tried to do and I think successfully. When you realise that nothing really belongs to you, you begin to appreciate having an understanding of just where your head is at, and you feel so much better.

Two of Syreeta's extracted singles, 'Spinnin' And Spinnin'' and 'Your Kiss Is Sweet', were her first British hits (numbers forty-nine and twelve respectively). She flew to London to promote the rising 'Your Kiss Is Sweet', her first visit since backing her ex-husband at the Talk of the Town as a member of Wonderlove. The only criticism of this beautifully conceived joint project was that Syreeta sounded like a female Stevie Wonder, which, in retrospect, was not surprising. For her future releases, however, she had more creative input.

Stevie Wonder was spreading his musical wings. Among his various projects at this time, he penned 'Tell Me Something Good' for Rufus's lead singer, the mighty Chaka Khan, and he produced and contributed to his dear friend Minnie Riperton's masterpiece *Perfect Angel*. And proving yet again that Wonderlove was a training ground for future soloists, Jim Gilstrap found success in his own right with his 'Swing Your Daddy' single in March 1975. Of his time with Wonder, he said, 'He sets the perfect example and I can say he has taught me much of what I know about the business and making music.'

While these artists are most commendable in a writer's logbook, Stevie Wonder must have glowed with pride when his life-long friend Aretha Franklin recorded one of his compositions. She wrote in her autobiography *From These Roots* – 'I always wanted to work with Stevie. However, Motown and Atlantic [her record company] seemed to keep us at arm's length. A little later though, Stevie sent me a song he wrote, "Until You Come Back To Me (That's What I'm Gonna Do)" that became one of my biggest hits.' It was included on Franklin's *Let Me In Your Life* which marked her first studio album for Atlantic Records which credited her as co-producer, and her last hit record with the Wexler, Mardin, Dowd team. Ironically, Franklin's 'Until You Come Back To Me (That's What I'm Gonna Do)' ousted Wonder's own 'Living For The City' from the top of the American R&B chart.

Stevie Wonder had first recorded this song in 1967, as Clarence Paul remembered: 'First, I recorded it on Stevie. Later, four or five years later, Stevie played it to [Aretha]. I love Aretha's version. I always figured it was a good song.' During the nineties, further light was shed on the song when Wonder presented Gladys Knight and the Pips with a Lifetime Achievement Award from the Rhythm & Blues Foundation. In her acceptance speech, Gladys Knight said, 'I remember when we were on the road and Stevie would keep messing around with this song. He kept telling us he was writing it for us.' Many believe it was this that caused the rift between Ms Knight and Ms Franklin. Wonder's own version was eventually included on his *Anthology* album released in 1977.

This decade of rapidly changing musical tastes, in which a fickle public swung from one style to another, rubbed off on Stevie Wonder's next project which shipped gold in July 1974, establishing it as one of the music industry's largest advance orders, and elevating it to the pole position in the American chart within three weeks of sale, his first number one album since *The 12 Year Old Genius*. Titled *Fulfillingness' First Finale*, written and produced by Wonder (with the exception of 'They Won't Go When I Go' co-penned with Syreeta), it was recorded in studios in Los Angeles and New York. In preparation, Wonder dug into his hoard of songs for suitable material. Rejecting most, he decided to concentrate on new tracks that he felt reflected his current frame of mind irrespective of what his fans wanted. 'I know everyone was expecting another *Innervisions*,' he told the press, 'but I hate categorisation, and people must get used to change.'

Wonder planned it as a double album set but abandoned the idea when Motown insisted he stick to their planned worldwide release date of July 1974. Promising that volume two of *Fulfillingness' First Finale* (the title came to him in a dream) would follow, Wonder made it clear that this first project was his most personal to date; it also confirmed he had lost none of his creative juices since his accident. If anything, the accident had heightened his awareness and strengthened his ability to enter any musical sphere with conviction, reinforcing the music business's belief that Berry Gordy's precarious signing in 1961 was blossoming into an international leader of music.

Kicking off with the blissfully relaxing 'Smile Please', the album took the listener on a journey through Wonder's feelings on love, spiritual leanings and current politics. With 'Heaven Is 10 Zillion Light Years Away', Wonder-the-preacher-man, demonstrated his belief in God, with lashings of keyboards and Moog bass, allowing a gospel-swaying chorus of Syreeta, Shirley Brewer and Paul Anka to build into a crescendo, highlighting the song. Wonder explains, 'I did the basic track of the song in 1972. I even talked about it in print. I said look for this song on the *Talking Book* album, but it didn't come out in that album because it wasn't ready.' With synthesiser and steel guitar support, he weaved through the touching love song 'Too Shy To Say', breaking the momentum with the funky hard-grooved 'Boogie On Reggae Woman' which, when released as a single in its edited version, peaked in the American top three and British top twelve early in 1975. Stevie Wonder worked on this track at the same time as 'Jesus Children Of America' in 1973, with both tracks originally destined for *Innervisions*. Only one made it. The spontaneous melody of 'Creepin'', made delightfully memorable with Minnie Riperton's assistance, gave way to the rock-inspired, Jackson 5-backed 'You Haven't Done Nothin'', which resonated with Wonder's political views. Swiped as the project's first single, it returned the singer to the top of the American chart in November 1974 (his first number one since 'You Are The Sunshine Of My Life' eighteen months earlier) and to the British top thirty. Released shortly before Richard Nixon resigned as America's president, this politically slanted track prompted its creator to tell the media that he was tired of politicians promising changes that never happened:

I don't vote for anybody until after they have really done something that I know about. I want to see them do something first. The only trouble is that you always hear the President or people say that they are doing all they can. And they feed you with hopes for years. But that is probably typical of most people in very important positions who have a lot of power. I'm sick and tired of listening to all their lies.

His strong lyrics were naturally coated in a commercial musical backdrop – 'wrapping it up nicely' was how he described it. Wonder's love affair continued through *'Fulfillingness' First Finale'* to 'It Ain't No Use', while the synthesiser was used to its fullest on 'They Won't Go When I Go', leaving the mysteries of nature to be explored with 'Bird Of Beauty', for which Sergio Mendes translated lyrics to enable Wonder to speak to his fans in Mozambique and Brazil. The closing track, 'Please Don't Go', a lover's plea, was highlighted by The Persuasions' vocal support. Certainly a capacious collection of ideas and thoughts, amply complemented by Wonder's increasing musicianship.

Once again the gatefold packaging was busy. Designed by Bob Gleason and Ira Tucker, it was a montage effect of the singer's life (from Little Stevie and Motown's touring bus), his awards, influential people in his life, his various musical instruments, his tiny bull (denoting his birth sign and the name of his production company), all fused into a soft cameo of reds and brown, reminiscent of an African carpet.

To celebrate and capitalise on his runaway success at the time, the happy star, still on medication following his accident, embarked upon a two-month American trek dubbed 'Stevie Wonder's Fall Festival Tour – Wonder Loves You', his first since he shared billing with The Rolling Stones. Starting at the Nassau Veterans' Memorial Coliseum in Uniondale in September 1974, he played to standing-room only audiences in 35 cities and ended victoriously with a Christmas performance at Madison Square Garden, with the proceeds benefiting several New York-based charities. He then toured Japan, one of Motown's biggest markets.

As expected, Stevie Wonder once again dominated the 1975 Grammy awards at a gala staged in March at the Civic Auditorium, Santa Monica. Winning Album of the Year – Artist and Producer for *Fulfillingness' First Finale* and Best Pop Vocalist – Male, Wonder scooped Best R&B Vocal Performance – Male, for 'Boogie On Reggae Woman' and Best R&B Song for 'Living For The City'.

Also at this time, he received the NARM Presidential Award 'in tribute to a man who embodies every facet of the complete musical artist'. Reeling from his earlier rejection, the Association carefully worded their award citation, to prevent another refusal.

Chicago-born Minnie Riperton joined Wonderlove in 1973. She had left the music business having recorded as a soloist and as a member of Rotary Connection, an R&B/psychedelic rock group, then married writer/producer Richard Rudolph and raised their family. Persuaded to join Stevie Wonder's vocalists, Minnie Riperton toured with him and later contributed to *Fulfillingness' First Finale*. When she signed as a soloist to Epic Records during 1974, Stevie Wonder agreed to produce her debut album for the label. Titled *Perfect Angel*, the project spawned the US number one 'Lovin' You' written by Riperton and Rudolph, which demonstrated her amazing five-and-a-half octave soprano voice. A year later, when Riperton was basking in her first taste of recorded success, she was diagnosed with breast cancer, and underwent a mastectomy. 'Aside from my family, only Stevie knew what was happening to me in terms of the operations,' she explained at the time. 'He's always been real close to me and really sensitive.'

Minnie Riperton went on to become spokeswoman for the American Cancer Society, which led to President Carter honouring her with a citation for the 'Most Courageous Woman Of The Year'. Continuing to be treated for the disease, Minnie remained active as a performer, singer and promoter of cancer awareness. She switched from Epic to Capitol Records, and while working on the *Minnie* album was devastated to learn she had lymph cancer. Stevie Wonder also contributed to this album, as Minnie recalled: 'Stevie was eating dinner at my house, he loves my cooking, and I played him a tape of a tune we were working on to use for the album. He said he'd like to work on it and within a few days, he'd done the whole rhythm track himself. The only things he didn't do were the strings, horns and vocals.'

Minnie was released in February 1979; five months later the perfect angel died at the age of 31. Stevie Wonder visited her the night before her death and she whispered to him, 'The final person I was waiting for has arrived, so everything will be all right now.'

Among the awards and honours showered on Stevie Wonder during this spectacularly successful period in 1975, Washington DC named him special honoree at the city's fourth annual Human Kindness Day, for his 'humanitarian efforts and artistic brilliance'. As in previous years, the main event of Human Kindness Day was a free concert in the Washington Monument grounds, where previous artists including Roberta Flack and Nina Simone had been the star performers. The all-day events were sponsored by several city organisations, and were community celebrations involving the entire DC metropolitan area. Kwame Braithwaite reported the 1975 bash in *Blues & Soul* magazine: 'Human Kindness Day was, in the vernacular of the streets, "The Monster". It started with a community leaders' breakfast and award presentation to Stevie at the new Kennedy Center. Although Stevie wasn't scheduled to perform at the breakfast, he insisted on doing a number to say "thank you" for the morning's tribute.' Then, following a day packed with tributes, celebrations and performances, it was time for the evening's star concert:

> The Wonderlove band . . . set it up for the master to appear and spin his magic on the admiring masses who seemed as much a part of the music as were the musicians themselves. Stevie enjoyed the show as much as the 200,000-strong audience as he played, sang and bumped with the Wonderlove girls and really got into it . . . He partied through hit after hit, which seemed to thoroughly satisfy the crowd. By the time the hour or so was up, there was truly a feeling of 'Fulfillingness' among the audience, who by now was worn out applauding Stevie's offerings. A job well done.

As Stevie Wonder's career went from strength to strength, others suffered, notably those of The Jackson 5, whose success at Motown nosedived as quickly as it had peaked in 1970. When the brothers' recording contract was due for renewal, their father, Joe Jackson, declared himself unwilling to sign over his sons' publishing rights to Jobete, and instead negotiated a multi-million-dollar deal with CBS/Epic Records. As Motown continued to own the name 'Jackson 5', the group was renamed The Jacksons.

Brother Jermaine, who married Berry Gordy's daughter Hazel, remained with the company to pursue his solo career. Randy Jackson replaced him.

Stevie Wonder became a father for the first time on 7 April 1975. Yolanda Simmons gave birth to an 8lb daughter named Aisha Zakiya, meaning strength and intelligence. With Aisha's birth Wonder was obliged to provide a permanent home for his family, although he had no intention of marrying again. To this end, he purchased a townhouse on the east side of Manhattan, with the intention of spending more time at home. His previous nomadic lifestyle was over; he now had the responsibility of fatherhood. However good his intentions though, he soon drifted back to spending long periods of quality time in the studios as he became engrossed in his next project – not the expected second volume of *Fulfillingness' First Finale*, but the formidable *We Are Seeing A Lot*.

He also became involved in charity events such as performing for The National Newspaper Publishers Scholarship Fund in San Francisco during June, before returning to New York where he guested on Geraldo Rivera's annual 'One To One' telethon for youngsters with special needs. He performed, answered the phones and donated $10,000 to the cause. Following this, he flew to the Shaw University in Raleigh, North Carolina, to discuss establishing a new scholarship with the board of trustees, because he had been told by students that the university had financial problems and was due to be closed. The performance earned $10,000 whereupon he arranged for other acts to stage similar benefits to help the university. In addition, an ongoing programme was financed by Wonder when he allocated the interest accruing from one of his personal bank accounts. Also during this period Wonder had donated $34,000 to a needy boys' charity and during a trip to Jamaica had pledged $40,000 to a school for the blind, and was considering financing a student exchange project. He also attended the opening of the long-awaited Stevie Wonder Home for Blind and Retarded Children.

'When you hear about Stevie it's basically about his music,' Ira Tucker told *Soul* magazine's Lee Underwood, 'but there are so many things we do to bring people together outside of music that you don't hear about.' With the singer's wealthy status publicly announced via contract negotiations and concert ticket sales, he is an easy target, as Tucker explains: 'People figure the way to get him to do something is to make him feel bad about what he's achieved.' When Wonder is on tour he is often approached by people unknown to him requesting his presence at a function. Rather than fobbing them off, Wonder directs them to the appropriate person in his entourage. Tucker says 'Instead of coming to us, we'll get a letter from them saying Stevie committed himself to their thing. A lot of people come at Stevie with "you forgot us". Well, the point is, you can't remember everybody.'

It's no secret that Stevie Wonder refuses to talk publicly about his charity work. Even when pressed in interviews he will invariably change the subject or give a vague answer. Ira Tucker explained that Wonder is an extremely private and modest man who loathes talking about any subject that could be interpreted as self-glorification. So nobody outside his immediate staff really knows the full extent of the singer's immense generosity.

Meanwhile on the music front, a dedicated listener could hear Stevie Wonder's voice in the short reprise on 'Give Peace A Chance', a track from John Lennon's *Shaved Fish* album released during October 1975. This reprise was recorded on 30 August 1972 at New York's Madison Square Garden when he joined Lennon, his wife Yoko Ono and others on stage for their 'One To One' benefit concert to raise funds for one of their charities.

The Motown star's relatively low public profile during 1975 and 1976 afforded him the time to visit South Africa to soak up its culture and again consider whether to relocate on a permanent basis. Once more he opted not to move, believing his involvement in the country's racial issues would be best served by being based in America with the heavyweight influence that his home country carried.

At this time he indulged his growing interest in reggae by hitching up with Bob Marley and the Wailers in Jamaica. Being tutored by Marley was an experience that would have a lasting effect on Stevie Wonder and would be heard in a diluted form in his later recordings.

This period was also used to finish what most fans later believed to be his most significant and probably most adventurous album of the decade: *Songs In The Key Of Life*, the re-titled *We Are Seeing A Lot*. Wonder had been pressurised by Motown to complete and release the new album in good time for the 1976 Grammy nominations but as Ira Tucker pointed out to Lee Underwood: 'The only concern is to get the album out sounding the way Stevie wants it to sound. When he feels that it's ready to present to the public that's when it goes out. If you just do what you do best, like Stevie does, then you aren't participating in any competition!'

A more accurate reason for the album's delay was the departure of Malcolm Cecil and Bob Margouleff, who left behind them a music catalogue in total disarray. They were forced to quit for a variety of reasons, they said, including their inability to converse directly with Wonder, as Cecil told *Newsweek*'s Maureen Orth:

> Unless he's prepared not to worry so much about his allegiance to the drones they are going to pull him down and isolate him from the very things that made him good. He has to deal with many levels of his reality through the eyes and trust of many other people. I wouldn't put up with for one minute the crap his organisation puts me through if I didn't believe Stevie has the power to be a very, very important figure, and not just musically. His product does more than sell millions of records. It reaches people and breaks down ethnic barriers.

There was also another contributing factor to the album's lateness – Stevie Wonder's recording contract was once again due for renewal. After what Berry Gordy called 'the most gruelling and nerve-racking [negotiations] we had ever had, mainly because Stevie was still represented by our old friend, Johanan Vigoda', details were agreed. These included the singer having the right to approve the purchaser of Motown should Gordy ever wish to sell it. Stevie Wonder was guaranteed approximately $13 million over seven years, a sum more than the recent deals of Neil Diamond and Elton John combined. Motown president Ewart Abner reported that he expected at least one album per year from Wonder and anticipated that both artist and company would make money on the deal. With a reputed 20 per cent royalty rate on records sold, the delighted singer said the money wasn't the key issue: 'It really isn't important to me as much as it is important for my children, family and loved ones. I want them to be taken care of and to be well off.' He was staying with Motown because:

> It's the only viable surviving black-owned company in the record industry. Motown represents hope and opportunity for new as well as established black performers and producers. If it wasn't for Motown many of us just wouldn't have had the shot we've had at success and fulfilment. In the record industry we've seen many cases where the big companies eat up the little ones and I don't want this to happen to Motown. I feel young black children should have something to look up to. It's vital that people in our business, particularly the black creative community, make sure that Motown stays economically healthy.

He admitted the company had its faults but none that couldn't be corrected. Besides, he continued:

> If I went somewhere else there'd be other problems, possibly a lot worse ones. I feel comfortable here and I've known the people for a long time. They've let me get away with things that other companies may not have allowed. My reason also was the fact that I'm a black man. I'm not a black man who's a racist and I have no hang-up about anybody. I love people for what they are. We can get along and communicate as long as we respect each other.

Berry Gordy too felt the new deal was a bargain, despite the hard negotiations:

> I knew what Stevie could do, what he was as a human being, and I know how he spends his money and time on making records. In other words, it's impossible for Stevie to put out a bad record

because of his fortitude, his insight. It doesn't matter what it costs, I felt I couldn't get hurt by Stevie. With some other artists who are motivated by money, or who had not grown as much as a human being as Stevie, I'd be very sceptical of doing something like that.

Unfortunately for Stevie Wonder he was destined to release 'bad' records forcing Berry Gordy to debate their commercial viability, but before that unthinkable situation arose, both would enjoy the overwhelming success of *Songs In The Key Of Life*.

Chapter   9

SONGS IN THE KEY OF LIFE

'Stevie can you see us?'
Andy Williams

'My daughter and son have changed my life for the better'
Stevie Wonder

'. . . My spirit is married to many and my love belongs to all'
Stevie Wonder

As 1976 dawned, Diana Ross topped the American singles chart with 'Theme From Mahogany (Do You Know Where You're Going To?)', the title track from her second film *Mahogany* (her debut in major acting was as Billie Holiday in *Lady Sings The Blues* for which she was nominated an Oscar. Liza Minnelli won it for her role in *Cabaret*). Ex-Temptation David Ruffin was also in the top ten with 'Walk Away From Love', a single that would become an international hit. And news filtered through from Motown that their top league acts, including Diana Ross, Eddie Kendricks, Jermaine Jackson, Marvin Gaye and Stevie Wonder, were scheduled to release albums this year. The company was riding high, but not so the memory of The Supremes.

In February ex-Supreme Florence Ballard was found dead on the floor at her home by her sister Maxine. Ballard, 32 years old, later died from a cardiac arrest at Detroit's Mount Carmel Hospital. It was a tragic ending for the founder of The Supremes, who had been sacked from the trio by Berry Gordy during August 1967, and had, in the ensuing years, attempted to carve out a solo career for herself. Ballard's funeral, held at the New Bethnal Baptist Church on 27 February, was conducted by the Reverend Franklin, and in tribute a nearby record store blasted 'Where Did Our Love Go?' as thousands lined the streets to see celebrities arrive, including Stevie Wonder, Diana Ross, Mary Wilson, and The Four Tops. Wonder was particularly devastated by Flo Ballard's sudden death because The Supremes had taken him to their hearts from his first day at Motown. It was a sad day for those who loved Florence Ballard, the true Supreme.

From the summer of 1975 advertisements for *Songs In The Key Of Life* graced the largest billboard in America. Spanning one city block, overlooking 46th and Broadway in New York City, nobody could miss the news that Stevie Wonder's album was due to be released. Unfortunately, the advertisement was rather premature. Berry Gordy realised the delay would mean lost revenue and, of course, the inevitable string of dissatisfied record dealers. But he could do nothing about it.

Stevie Wonder's first album under his new $13 million Motown contract and without Cecil and Margouleff, was compiled in confusion. The double-album package, with a four-track single insert ('Saturn', 'Ebony Eyes', 'All Day Sucker' and 'Easy Goin' Evening (My Mama's Call)') and a 24-page lyric and credits booklet showing the singer's thumbprint, was eventually delivered after a two-year wait. At one stage, with the singer's assurance that the completed work would be available, Motown arranged a media preview for March 1976. It didn't happen. Although the completion date was October 1975, Wonder withdrew his work at the last minute, insisting it needed further remixing. Instead of complaining at the delay, Motown's marketing department cashed in on the wait by distributing 'We're Almost Finished' tee shirts. Wonder recalled, 'I knew when we did "I Wish" I'd almost finished, so we did the tee shirts. My brother had another idea later and we started wearing tee shirts with tracks titles on them, like, we had one with "Isn't She Lovely" on it.'

Having been put on standby for six months, Motown/EMI was alerted of the project's master tapes arriving in time for a 30 September release, with the artwork following. EMI Records' factory in Hayes, Middlesex, worked non-stop to ensure simultaneous release with America, thereby stemming import sales, which severely stung the record industry in Britain on a regular basis.

Songs In The Key Of Life did make its scheduled release date of September 1976 in America and Britain, but set a precedent for Wonder's inability to deliver product on time. He shrugged off the 1976 delay, saying,

> It's all about pleasing myself, not everybody and anybody, but myself. I'm the hardest person for me to please, and when I finally please myself, I know I have made something good. I also know that people expect great music from me, that doesn't bother me, but they don't understand that you can't make good music overnight. I do the best I can no matter how long it takes.

Participating bassist Nathan Watts recalls, 'There were times when Stevie stayed in the studio forty-eight hours straight. You couldn't even get him to stop to eat.'

The double package passed platinum status in America with over one million advance orders, prompting Bob Jones, Motown's publicity director to brag:

> It's one of the biggest albums in music history and the first album in Motown's history to enter the Billboard and Cashbox trade charts as number one with a bullet. The original advance orders were in excess of 1,300,000 units in the United States alone, which means it shipped platinum before buyers even heard it played. It went on every major pop and R&B station across the country the day it was released. Stevie is the first American artist to do this, black or white. He is undoubtedly in a class by himself.

Songs In The Key Of Life remained at the American pole position for fifteen weeks. In Britain, where it shot to number two, the release marked a double celebration, by introducing Motown's new label logo – a large 'M' placed against a pale-blue background, encircled in a dark blue edge.

Songs In The Key Of Life was presented to the media by its creator at a rustic farmhouse set in 145 acres in Massachusetts. The rental for the day was $1,000, added to which were the following expenses: journalists were transported by jet to a small airport near the farm, where champagne and food delicacies were served all day; *Songs In The Key Of Life* was played continuously throughout the ranch house and in the studio where Wonder spent much of his time. Dressed in a cream-coloured cowboy suit with matching ten-gallon hat, he wore two cardboard album covers suspended from a gun belt around his waist. In describing the project to the attending press, Wonder said it was a conglomeration of thoughts from his subconscious: 'An idea to me is a farmed thought in the subconscious, the unknown and sometimes sought for impossibilities, but when believed strong enough, can become a reality . . . So let it be that I shall live the idea of the song and use its words as my sight into the unknown.' He also believed that God had given him the key in which to sing, and if it was a key that others could enjoy then so be it. He further remarked:

I hope you enjoy this but it really doesn't matter. I gave my all, and all is the best I can do. I've never considered myself an orator nor a politician, only a person who is fortunate enough, thanks to all of you, to become an artist given a chance to express the way I feel and hopefully the feelings of many other people.

By comparison, the British preview was a low-key affair at the Abbey Road Studios, where attending journalists listened to the album while drinking wine, eating from laden plates of finger food and watching a slideshow featuring Stevie Wonder. The only consolation here was that they were privileged to sit in the most famous of all recording studios.

The artwork for *Songs In The Key Of Life* was subdued, and the (uncredited) design was devoid of pictures of the singer, except for a tiny sketch of his face surrounded by spiralling circles of yellow, orange and brown. This dominated the front cover, while the inner packaging was a play on it, with a series of face sketches growing in size.

So what of the music? Stevie Wonder was at pains to explain

that it related to experiences of people all over the world and to his own life: 'It involves taking a look at the problems we experience in life and giving them the kind of constructive criticism and assistance that will make life better. It's for those who believe in a positive idea of tomorrow and is an album we hope everyone can enjoy because we gave a good deal in it.' Dedicated to Yolanda Simmons and their daughter Aisha, 'Isn't She Lovely' features not his new baby's gurgles – as was widely thought at the time – but those of a nearby infant in the same hospital ward. The father also gave specific instructions that the track should never be released as a single because it was too personal and because it couldn't be edited. Pye Records signing David Parton thought otherwise and re-recorded an edited version to enjoy a British number four hit in January 1977. Motown/EMI was furious because they knew the original version (which attracted more radio play than other album tracks) would have given Wonder the number one single they felt he had deserved for some years, but acknowledged that as an album track it sold more albums.

Written by Stevie Wonder following a Saturday Motown picnic during the summer of 1976, 'I Wish', the album's first single in December 1976, topped the American chart, replacing British artist Leo Sayer's 'You Make Me Feel Like Dancing', and holding off Rose Royce's 'Car Wash' from the movie of the same name. 'I Wish' peaked in the British top five. While fans grumbled when 'Isn't She Lovely' was bypassed as a single, reviewers felt 'I Wish' was a good choice: a cross between 'Living For The City' and 'Boogie On Reggae Woman'. The singer's tribute to Duke Ellington, Count Basie, Louis Armstrong and others, 'Sir Duke' was the second extracted title and his second American number one in May 1977. It was reported that Stevie Wonder advised attendees at *Billboard* magazine's UCLA conference that he had had the song's title for some while 'but wanted it to be about the musicians who did something for us. I wanted to show my appreciation.' He went on to say: 'It's no problem with me to say that there have been many people who've influenced my music. Music is a world within itself with a language as we all understand, with an equal opportunity for all to sing, dance and clap their hands.' With its crisp bass lines, this pop-flavoured slice of peer dedication rose to number two in the British chart, prevented from reaching pole position by ex-Wonderlove member, Deniece Williams with 'Free'.

The mediocre yet compulsive track 'Another Star', with George Benson on support vocals, followed during August 1977. This title broke Wonder's chart-topping run by, astonishingly, struggling into the American top forty, and the British top thirty. This wasn't what the artist or Motown had expected.

With a Yamaha synthesiser at hand, Stevie Wonder and his studio family created virtually every musical sound; familiar rhythms joined a kaleidoscope of arrangements through tracks that were both delicate and hard-edged. For instance, 'Pastime Paradise' with its 'segregation, dispensation, mutilation' set against an uncomfortably eerie, spine-curdling chant and wail sequence from the West Angeles Church of God Choir and Hare Krishna vocalists, contrasted vividly with the desperate appeal of 'Love's In Need Of Love Today'. 'Have A Talk With God' was not an option when life was tough, Wonder sang, and 'Joy Inside My Tears', with support vocals from ex-Supreme Susaye Green, was typical of his tenderness. Caught between the two strongest emotions, love and hate, the Syreeta-influenced 'Knocks Me Off My Feet' attempted to present a balance against a strong melody, while the prominent harp in 'If It's Magic' continued the underlying love theme found in most of the tracks. 'Ordinary Pain', tipped by many as the album's highlight, told of a broken relationship from the viewpoint of the man and the woman (Shirley Brewer). Ex-Wonderlove singers Lynda Laurence, Deniece Williams, Syreeta, Sundray Tucker and Minnie Riperton added their voices to this most extraordinary slice of music.

Top New York DJ Gary Byrd provided the lyrics for two blindingly innovative songs: 'Village Ghetto Land' and 'Black Man'. Wonder and Byrd had first met in 1971 when they intended to work on three of Byrd's songs, and years later when Wonder needed a lyricist he knew who to contact, as Gary Byrd remembers:

He called me and had me listen to a track over the phone. It was to be 'Village Ghetto Land' and it sounded more like a composition by Bach or Beethoven. Stevie told me he wanted it to be about all kinds of ghettos. I kept on working on it and then, the day I finished I let him hear it over the phone and he told me he needed another verse and would call back in another fifteen minutes for it!

Of 'Black Man' Byrd said, 'It wasn't just about a black man, but more, about the contributions that people have made to the world we live in, a documentary.' It took four weeks of research using the staff of his GB company, EXP Corporation, and the help of Harlem's Al Fann Theatrical Ensemble in the teacher/student vocal sequences on the completed track.

With a Zulu translation, 'Ngiculela' leading into 'Es Una Historia – I Am Singing', Stevie Wonder signified the international flavour of an album that held no barriers. Indeed, *Songs In The Key Of Life* was the musical marathon promised in the advertising: a comfortable, unprecedented monument that was certainly worth the wait.

Being such an awesome musical package it came as no surprise when, a year later in 1977, it scooped five Grammy awards: for Best Album of the Year; Best Producer of the Year; Best Pop Vocal Performance – Male; and for the tracks 'I Wish' and '*Songs In The Key Of Life*', Best R&B Vocal Performance – Male. These awards were followed by those won at the fourth annual American Music Awards ceremony for Favourite Album and Favourite Soul Vocalist.

At the time of the Grammy presentation Stevie Wonder was performing at FESTAC '77, the second international black and African cultural festival in Lagos, Nigeria. His performance with fifteen American musicians (including three members of the Duke Ellington band), and the George Faison Dance Troupe, was due to be linked by satelitte to the Grammy ceremony. When the transmission failed through technical difficulties, host Andy Williams thoughtlessly asked, 'Stevie, can you see us?' Later Wonder presented his *Songs In The Key Of Life* awards posthumously to Minnie Riperton and Donny Hathaway (who died in January 1979 after throwing himself from the fifteenth floor of The Essex House Hotel in New York) during an Image Awards gala staged in Los Angeles.

In 1994, when Guinness published Colin Larkin's book *All Time Top 1000 Albums*, *Songs In The Key Of Life* came third in the Top Fifty Soul Albums category. Marvin Gaye's *What's Going On* topped the chart, with Otis Redding's *Otis Blue* at number two. Other Stevie Wonder albums to be placed were *Talking Book* (four) and *Innervisions* (eighteen). Interestingly, the only other Motown artist in the top ten was Lionel Richie with *Can't Slow Down*, while the only British placing was Dusty Springfield's *Dusty In Memphis*.

Stevie Wonder was also featured in a very different type of publication in 1977. When Jackie Collins published her *Lovers & Gamblers*, a book many believed to have been influenced by the flamboyant lifestyle of British superstar Tom Jones, Wonder and his music received several mentions. For instance, Collins' fictional star Al King sang 'You Are The Sunshine Of My Life' in his stage act, while other mentions referred to Wonder's songs being played as romantic background music. The author is well known for her love of black/soul music and this invariably permeates her writing in much the same way that actor Eddie Murphy's passion for thoroughbred soul can be heard in the soundtracks of his movies.

In his personal life Stevie Wonder was also celebrating: he became a father for the second time in April 1977, when Yolanda gave birth to a boy Keita Sawandi (a combination of South and West African words meaning 'worshipper' and 'founder') in New York. A thrilled father told the media: 'My daughter and my son have changed my life for the better. They're the one thing that I have needed in my life and my music for so long.' Both children used Morris as their surname.

And his music played on. An edited version of 'As' was issued simultaneously in America and Britain, representing the final track to be extracted as a single from the award-winning album. The gospel-flavoured, easy mid-tempo ballad struggled into the American top forty, and bombed in Britain, suggesting the hit run might be ending. As the single reached the stores, during November 1977, one of Wonder's fellow Motown artists visited Britain. Since leaving The Miracles in 1972 (a departure that attracted minimal attention in the wake of Diana Ross' tide of publicity as she began her own solo career in earnest and married

Robert Silberstein) Smokey Robinson had seen his solo career fail in Britain. He attempted to rectify the sitation by touring the country, where he delighted audiences with this laid-back, no-nonsense stage presentation. 'A living legend' one music critic enthused. Unexpected visitors to Robinson's London concert were Stevie Wonder and Yolanda Simmons, who flew to the city from Paris as part of their European holiday. Motown/EMI were unaware of their arrival until they appeared in their offices, where, during one visit, they met Robinson to sing an impromptu 'Happy Birthday' to secretary Noreen Allen, before presenting her with a bouquet of flowers. During their six-day stay, Wonder spent his evenings in the city's top nightclubs including Gullivers, in Mayfair, where his friend DJ Graham 'Fatman' Canter hosted the evening, with the Motown star assisting. The fun was hot; so much so, the club's opening hours were extended to accommodate Wonder, who had no intention of leaving until the sun had risen. On another evening, he joined Elton John on the Wembley Arena stage to play keyboards on John's finale 'Bite Your Lip'.

Being re-established as a heavyweight artist of the decade, Stevie Wonder was in the somewhat unenviable position of being on a pedestal – and liable to be knocked off. American journalists in particular were fearsome in their attempts to compare his work with others who, they claimed, threatened to replace him. One such comparison was between Wonder and Elton John, and angered the Motown star sufficiently that he told journalist Lee Underwood:

> Neither of us are competition to each other. We both have something to say in our own way, and we're saying it. For us to stoop as low in our minds to compete, or to think of ourselves as each other's competitors, is relating to the level of many people who are doing that, but who only show their insecurities. Basically, I have a great admiration for Elton's music.

The British star said later, 'Stevie Wonder can eat me for breakfast as far as musicianship goes, but that doesn't make me angry or jealous or uptight. I'd give anything to have his talent but that doesn't make me paranoid.'

Believing this to be the media's attempt at a racially motivated game, Wonder also pointed out: 'It's like a poor white man and the poor black man. The poor white man is told, basically, that because you're white, you're better, and someday you're gonna be better than now, and you can do it all. The black man is told, you're black and because you're black, you may as well forget it.' He was probably remembering his own childhood, when he was told by his teacher that blind black kids had no useful purpose in the real world. Hence his determination to do all he could to ensure that in future his race was treated equally, with the same opportunities afforded to everyone, irrespective of colour. And it was this thinking that encouraged him never to take his privileged position for granted:

> I do believe that Stevie Wonder is the necessary vehicle on which Stevland Morris must be carried on his mission to spread love mentalism. In every album that I have and shall do, it's not my goal for that to be better than that and the next to succeed others, but only that I do and give the best I can at the time of my doing and giving, and that only happens because of the dis- or satisfaction that made me want to be a better someone. My mind's heart must be polygamous and my spirit is married to many and my love belongs to all.

As to the financial side of things, Motown, and in particular Berry Gordy, shared Stevie Wonder's success, and for the fifth year running Motown Industries was the top black-owned company in America. Sales rose from $43.5 million in 1975 to $50 million in 1977, putting it $2.4 million ahead of its closest competitor, Johnson Publishing. Indeed, Motown was now an extremely powerful entity, but with expansion and development came personal and professional upheavals. The Supremes, for example, who had been without Motown's support for some time had no choice but to disband in 1977. Motown had also suffered the departure of artists such as The Temptations, The Four Tops and The Jackson 5, yet the losses seemed to make little difference to the company's financial situation. Otis Williams explained why The Temptations left the Motown family: 'We just didn't get any freedom. We always got the feeling that they didn't want us to learn that much.' When the group produced their 1976 *The Temptations Do The Temptations* album, they wanted to become involved in other production work: 'We always felt that the album never got the sales it should have got. It was a political thing because the company knew we were unsettled and thinking about moving, and so they didn't promote us getting into writing and producing. At the time, I remember Stevie telling us that he'd gone through exactly the same problems when he first wanted to produce himself.' The group signed with Atlantic Records but in time would, with help from Smokey Robinson, return to Motown.

With the loss of these acts, Motown concentrated on pushing its new signings. Many failed to develop into major stars because, they claimed, the company was too involved in promoting Diana Ross, Stevie Wonder, The Commodores and Marvin Gaye. However, to be fair, the established artists were not a serious threat because new acts were afforded healthy marketing campaigns in the hope they would keep Motown financially stable. On the one hand, some artists were signed to cash in on the latest music craze and survived as long as the musical trend, while others with a history in the business joined expecting to reach Motown's top league, and when it was clear this wasn't to be, left to find another company bursting with promises. One such artist was Tata Vega, who had worked with Dobie Gray and Pollution before joining the group Earthquire. The group auditioned for Motown but only Vega was signed as a fully fledged artist. With a debut album *Full Speed Ahead* containing compositions from Stevie Wonder and Ashford & Simpson, among others, critics were quick to compare Vega to Wonder because her diction and phrasing were similar. Naturally, the flattered songstress was thrilled: 'It's a nice compliment to be compared to such a great singer. But when you think about it, nobody is really original and when you are a new name people have to try to make comparisons.' Although the talented and instantly likeable Tata Vega failed to reach Motown's top shelf as a soloist she went on to work regularly with her soundalike, notably on his next album, which was a horticultural nightmare . . .

The poor-selling 'As' marked the end of *Songs In The Key Of Life*, and Stevie Wonder spent the next year away from the public spotlight, using the time to be with his family and work on his next project. He continued his public guesting, and turned up unannounced at concerts by Earth, Wind And Fire, the Commodores, Billy Preston, Ella Fitzgerald, and others, and worked with artists like The Chi-Lites, Tavares and Bobbi Humphrey. Among his charitable activities at this time was sponsoring a high-school talent scholarship in his name and lecturing in a handful of universities.

Stevie was also responsible for another, rather more private act of charity around this time. He was alerted by the Suicide Hotline that a friend – composer Lee Garrett, with whom he had previously worked – had locked himself in his bathroom with a gun. Wonder was escorted to Garrett's house where, after several hours he was successful in dissuading his friend from killing himself.

Meantime, in Stevie Wonder's musical absence, the scene had shifted alarmingly: The Bee Gees had created their musical monster *Saturday Night Fever*, which spawned innovative disco singles, commercialising the dance sound that had been popular in nightclubs for some time. With singles like 'Stayin' Alive' and 'Night Fever', The Bee Gees' success unleashed a flood of disco music from established artists who should have known better, and new acts who cashed in on the lucrative market. Not to be left behind, Motown joined the fray but first paid tribute to a man who had been the guiding force behind Berry Gordy's ambitions. On 21 November Berry's ninety-year-old father 'Pops' died. When Motown was formed he became a vital figurehead in the organisation and soon earned the respect of the artists he worked with. And four of these artists paid tribute to him, when Stevie Wonder joined Diana Ross, Marvin Gaye and Smokey Robinson to record the Pam Sawyer/Marilyn McLeod song 'Pops, We Love You', which later became the American 'Father's Day Song Of The Year'. The tribute single peaked in the American top sixty and British top seventy, and was followed in June 1979 by the *Pops, We Love You* album, featuring tracks by the aforementioned quartet and others.

To bridge the gap until his next album was available, Stevie

Wonder authorised the resurrection of a 1974 project titled *Anthology*, a triple album compilation of his most popular tracks to date. The singer had strongly objected to its original release whereupon it was abandoned, with most of the 200,000 pressed copies filtering into record stores as deleted items, while others were imported into Europe. Re-naming the compilation *Looking Back*, and now with Stevie Wonder's approval, the triple set was issued as a limited edition. When Motown/EMI scheduled the project for release after *Songs In The Key Of Life*, the company imported copies from America to sell, stickering the front covers to indicate their place of origin. Those fans who hastily purchased the pricey American copies doubtless cursed their impatience because the British sale price was considerably less.

It became obvious that during the unpredictable seventies the wonderful 'Motown Sound' that had launched the company in the late fifties was all but a memory. Motown had become another record outlet fighting for hits in an industry that had, with the disco explosion, reached saturation point. Through its new labels Motown was able to pad out its release schedules with re-issued material and 'greatest hits' compilations, but with a new decade looming, priority had to be given to the new faces if the company was to remain successful.

So with a new policy of dollars, sophistication, supply and demand, Motown would stride confidently into the eighties. However, with a few exceptions, it was a policy that would fail to take account of the variable quality of the music itself.

Chapter 10

BLACK ORCHID

'I hadn't ever given much thought to writing a score before . . . but this film interested me, being about plants'

Stevie Wonder

'This was a tough picture to score because it deals with things that people have rarely seen'

Michael Braun

'If you want an uneventful one-way ticket to Dullsville USA *Plants* should suffice'

Blues & Soul

Stevie Wonder's name was linked to several acts during the late seventies. Some projects were completed, others not, like the album with his backing vocalists Wonderlove. He had at least one thousand half-finished songs to work with, and was still composing on a daily basis. 'He turns out five songs some days, others he writes one or two,' his ex-wife Syreeta said. 'He has to write at least one a day because he feels incomplete if by the evening he hasn't written a tune and got it down on tape.' Wonder explains, 'I usually come up with the music first and then come up with an idea about the song. I sing the lyric out loud and then change it right away if it sounds like too many words. I also practise piano every day and sing other people's songs when I do.'

One project that was accomplished was with the soul/blues songstress Jean Carn, as she excitedly told David Nathan: 'It was incredible. Before he's finished one song, he's already got another one lined up for you. It's real informal too. He'll usually play you a rhythm track over the phone and get your feedback. Naturally, he usually does all the instrumentation himself, but he allows a lot of input, at least that's how I found him to be.' Wonder then swapped the recording studio for a radio studio when his Taxi Productions purchased the Los Angeles radio station KJLH for $2.2 million. Negotiations for the sale were conducted by Ewart Abner, now Wonder's manager. With radio playing such a vital role in his early life, buying his own station seemed the most natural of moves, but it was a costly venture.

During 1979 Stevie Wonder spent as much time as he could performing on a casual basis, making impromptu appearances at various benefits including a Duke Ellington memorial concert in Los Angeles when he played 'Sir Duke'. And he didn't think twice when Dr Martin Luther King's widow, Coretta, contacted him to appear at a special benefit concert in Atlanta to commemorate what would have been her late husband's fiftieth birthday. The concert was part of an event held annually to observe King's birthday, where all proceeds were donated in his name to a Center for Social Change. In less than two years the singer was to lobby the American government to make King's birthday a public holiday, but for the meantime, this concert geared Wonder for future tours. He also guested at several shows benefiting the charities he supports, such as sickle cell anemia: 'It's good to do something for sickle cell anemia or for the Black Panther Party if they want to give clothes to kids or food to the community. If it's really a sincere move on one's behalf to do something for people and I can contribute my services I will do so.' From charity to surprise when he gave Jan Gaye a hand, by performing for thirty minutes at a surprise birthday thrown for her husband Marvin.

Stevie Wonder also didn't miss the opportunity of meeting up with Bob Marley and the Wailers when reggae came to Philadelphia. He joined them on stage at the Black Music Association Convention where Marley had been invited to perform as Jamaica's ambassador of reggae. By the time the Motown star joined in with Marley's 'Stand Up For Your Rights' the audience of leading black musicians and record producers were climbing on chairs and tables in an enthusiastic demonstration of reggae fervour. This was, in fact, the second time the two artists had performed together on stage. The first had been three years previously, at the National Stadium in Jamaica, when the audience response was pretty much the same. In typical Stevie Wonder fashion, he switched from reggae to country and western, arriving unannounced at Nashville's Grand Ole Opry, where Skeeter Davis was performing. Wonder amazed the audience with his versatility by singing a version of the country standard 'Behind Closed Doors'. He had been attending an executive meeting of the Black Music Association and the Country Music Foundation when he decided a spot of entertainment Ole Opry style was a good idea!

Midway through 1979, Motown's marketing department rumbled with pre-promotion for their upcoming major event, by producing tee shirts announcing 'Stevie Wonder's secret is almost out'. However, the media was unkind to Motown's British licensee in its attempt to sustain public interest, when, for example, *Music Week*, the industry's weekly trade paper, moaned 'Wonder's secret has been almost out since last Christmas and the on-off, on-off saga of the album is fast approaching the ridiculous with Motown still unable to confirm a release date.'

For some months, Motown/USA had worked closely with all its overseas licensees, particularly Britain, to achieve the simultaneous release of its star's new project – titled *Stevie Wonder's Journey Through The Secret Life Of Plants* in October 1979, three years after its conception. Recorded in numerous studios including Sigma Sound Studios, Philadelphia, and Motown's own Hollywood studio, the work, composed, produced and arranged by Stevie Wonder, was the soundtrack to an Infinite Enterprises Film, distributed by Paramount Pictures. The album's release was planned to coincide with the film's première but when Paramount announced the project was temporarily shelved, Wonder had no choice but to add a commercial element to his work by including three unrelated extra titles. A further postponement occurred when he felt some tracks would benefit from what he called 'sounds of nature'. Then, of course, these revised songs had to be digitally remixed. Berry Gordy said that when he heard the work for the first time, he knew it wouldn't be the hit that Stevie Wonder so desperately wanted: 'And I wanted to be wrong real bad.' Motown intended to press two million copies of the album to cater for advance orders, as was the practice with the singer's most recent releases, but Gordy followed his gut instinct and halved the run: '[And that was] around nine hundred thousand too many,' he sighed.

American author Peter Tompkins and biologist Christopher Bird wrote the book on which the movie was based, an investigation of all the information available concerning plants and their sense and feelings, which had involved researching hundreds of documents written by scientists during the last century. American film producer Michael Braun, who worked on the screenplay of the movie, approached Wonder to pen the soundtrack after seeing him perform at London's Rainbow Theatre in 1974. Braun didn't class himself a Wonder fan but following the concert he admitted, 'I knew that if any contemporary musician possessed the qualities necessary for creating a meaningful soundtrack it was Stevie.' The fact that the artist was blind and had never previously scored a film was irrelevant to Braun. The idea also appealed to Stevie Wonder, but he stressed he had first to complete his then-pending album *Songs In The Key Of Life*. 'It was such a great challenge for me and I enjoy challenges,' Wonder said at the time. 'I hadn't ever given much thought to writing a score before Michael approached me, but I'd always figured if I ever did one it would be for a film that would raise society's consciousness about black people. But this film interested me, being about plants, and it seemed a good place to start.'

Michael Braun was also instrumental in assisting Wonder by explaining the contents of each movie sequence in meticulous detail and how much music was needed per sequence, as he explained:

There were times when he first played some music before it was put with the picture when I thought, 'Oh hell, it's going to be terrible.' But when it was put with the picture it somehow always worked perfectly. And this was a tough picture to score because it deals with things that people have rarely seen on the screen before, so there are no standard ways of composing music for those things, like seeds sprouting or the Venus flytrap catching a bug. I'll bet a lot of veteran composers wouldn't know what to do with some of those sequences – except in the most mundane literalistic way. But Stevie did. He's uncanny.

In reply, Wonder also hoped that his scoring a movie soundtrack would give encouragement to others:

It shows that a blind person can come up with music that can work in a film. You don't have to see a film to do a good score and it's important for people to realise this. I can 'see' there are certain shapes and colours that I am able to perceive because at some point I have been given a verbal understanding of what they're about. I get a certain feeling in my head when a person says red, blue, green and so on.

He added that he'd been told some people can actually 'see' in their dreams but that hadn't happened to him: 'Blind people have certain pictures that I believe they are able to draw. We can perceive the same as another person can visually perceive, but there is no possible way for someone like me, blind from birth, to "see" in their dreams.'

The 98-minute documentary dwelt on the looks rather than the thoughts of plants, with Stevie Wonder appearing in the final frames of the film. But despite the innovation of the movie, *Variety* magazine summed up most people's feelings:

The use of microscopic lenses and time lapse photography is extensively employed and on a certain level there's not much difference between this pic and numerous National Geographic TV specials except the Dolby sound. There are several scenes, both historical and current, of experiments proving plants say their own equivalent of 'ouch' when pinched, but nary a word from the opposition, in this case the majority of scientists

The film's narrators, author Tompkins, Elizabeth Vreeland and Ruby Crystal, also came in for criticism, with their precise, clipped quotes such as 'the touchstone to the universal consciousness' – and with references to the comradeship of plants in Russia, all of which were ridiculous more than educational. The review closed: '*The Secret Life Of Plants* may find its greatest audience ironically from those who don't converse with plants, but smoke them!' Ultimately, Stevie Wonder's music struggled to inject life into a film that was doomed to die.

Critics sharpened their venomous pens, while Stevie Wonder himself justified the work, although he didn't sound that convincing:

> It's about the emotional, physical and mental relationship between plants and between men and plants. It's a musical way to help people understand and appreciate the film, even though I cannot see it. I achieved what I wanted to do. I appreciate it may throw some people because it's not what they expect from me. When people are basically hearing the kind of music they expect, they can tolerate a few songs that are out of the ordinary. But the songs on this album are in an unusual context for me and I think my fans will accept it, but I'm not totally sure.

The double album, digitally recorded on his newly purchased Sony PCM 1600, featured Tata Vega and Syreeta's vocals and the latter's lyrics on the track 'Come Back As A Flower'. Syreeta intervened when her ex-husband was searching for a lyricist: 'He gave me a tape of the music but at first I couldn't come up with anything either. One day I got all these mental images of gardens, flowers, dawn and dusk, and the lyrics just came.' She also felt the movie failed to live up to the soundtrack: 'It's Stevie's most creative piece of music yet and if the film had been more up to par, it would have done better. [His] fans had waited so long for anything from him, so they felt disappointed that it wasn't like the albums before.'

As soon as Motown took delivery of the album lacquers, copies were flown to its various overseas licensees. Three hours after the plane carrying the tapes and masters landed at London's Heathrow from Los Angeles, Motown/UK's general manager, David Hughes, had delivered them to the EMI Records factory in Hayes, Middlesex, where production began immediately. It was then, and only then, that the London-based office announced the project was finally complete. Now, pre-promotion was put into action: Motown on both sides of the Atlantic distributed copies of the paperback that had inspired the movie, and packets of sunflower seeds to record retailers with the message that the album would be delivered when the seeds had sprouted. However, fully grown flowers actually graced record stores by the time the records arrived! A scent was created by an American chemist intended to perfume the records' packaging and a phial was flown to Motown in London for analysis by EMI's technical department, where they discovered that one of the ingredients attacked the vinyl, causing surface damage. It was the record company's practice to test any unfamiliar or unusual chemicals planned for inclusion on record sleeves by heating both sleeves and vinyl in ovens to test reactions in different climatic conditions. Needless to say, unlike the American release, the pale green, triple gatefold packaging remained scent-free upon British release, but did carry a Braille message at the bottom of the front packaging: 'Inside the embossed square is the outline of a flower with veined leaves. Stevie Wonder, Journey Through The Secret Life Of Plants.' With the album's title in raised lettering above the boxed flower, the only picture of the singer was inside the gatefold. With braided hair and no glasses, the smiling Stevie Wonder was surrounded by Margo Nahas' flora illustrations and song lyrics.

Stevie Wonder unveiled his unusual project in the backyard of a Malibu property during November to which he invited five hundred guests. In keeping with the 'journey' aspect of the release, his guests were ushered through six giant tents to hear different sides of the records. In the final tent, Indian, African, Oriental, American and Middle Eastern food was served. A further reception was held at New York's Bronx Botanical Gardens. And a month later, when *Stevie Wonder's Journey Through The Secret Life Of Plants* peaked at number four in the American chart, he premièred the work in New York's Metropolitan Opera House, where he devoted the first hour to the new album accompanied by the National Afro-American Philharmonic Orchestra with scenes from the movie projected above the stage. After the interval Wonderlove joined him on stage for a selection from his past repertoire. In all, the performance contained forty songs and lasted three hours.

'What was originally anticipated to be a reviewer's dream has turned out to be a reviewer's nightmare! After listening very carefully to this new album project from Stevie, I am still not sure just what exactly the purpose of the LP is,' wrote *Blues & Soul*'s Bob Killbourn in his balanced review.

The original concept was soundtrack music for the movie, and to be perfectly frank, I believe the soundtrack loses considerable impact and validity without the visual aspect to act as a guide. It remains, nonetheless, an extremely brave and courageous effort, and despite the lack of any apparent course, it most certainly has his inimitable stamp of genius all over – but the question remains, is it enough?

Noting that the release lacked instant appeal, he also found certain aspects puzzling:

The significance of the Japanese song titles and cast of thousands (there are seventeen Japanese credits on the track 'Ai No Sono') totally escapes me, while 'Race Babbling' – the leading contender for disco action – has lyrics, but so far laid back as to be quite pointless. Some of the lyric content I found a trifle odd too, and almost alien to the usual Wonder style. 'Venus Fly Trap And The Bug', for instance, is straight out of a George Clinton project, whilst other song lyrics, particularly 'Come Back As A Flower' and 'Power Flower' seem almost laughable in their content, but then maybe I'm missing something.

Pointing out the project's few high spots, Killbourn felt 'Same Old Story' was unquestionably a lovely and melodic outing, while 'Outside My Window' was an outstanding candidate for single honours. 'Send One Your Love' he observed should have little difficulty in charting, and 'Black Orchid' could be ranked as the album's 'standard'. His final analysis summed up the feelings of most reviewers: 'The release remains an enigma, and one which only time will answer. As for me? I'm still an ardent Stevie fan, but I trust the next LP will not take another three years to materialise.'

'Send One Your Love', 'Black Orchid' (British release only) and 'Outside My Window' were all extracted as singles during 1979 and 1980. Only 'Send One Your Love' hit the American top five, while all floundered in the British top one hundred. Compared to his previous outings, *Stevie Wonder's Journey Through The Secret Life Of Plants* was considered a commercial failure, and as a Motown/EMI staffer snapped, 'The album shipped silver and returned plantinum [platinum].'

Over in Britain, Syreeta was smiling as her ex-husband scowled because she was enjoying an unexpected high profile with her duettist Billy Preston. Their single 'With You I'm Born Again', a ballad of endearing qualities, clipped from the *Fast Break* album and Preston's solo *Late At Night* album, was climbing the chart. Released first as a British single in August 1979, 'With You I'm Born Again' caught the imagination of Motown's record promoter Chris Marshall. He believed it held hit potential and continued plugging it at radio stations until it peaked at number two during December, earning the duo a silver disc. American release followed, where the single shot into the top four in April 1980. 'I didn't expect the single stood a chance of success because everyone is into disco and not love songs,' an excited Syreeta said at the time. 'The people in England worked super hard to break it and we owe our success in America to that British breakthrough.' The follow-up single, 'It Will Come In Time', faltered in the British top fifty and marked the end of her recording career with Billy Preston who, following an uninspiring *Pressin' On* album in 1982, left Motown to sign a deal with the Hi-NRG label Megatone, based in San Francisco. Six years later he returned to Motown to release one single 'Since I Held You Close'.

Also at this time and nearer home, Stevie Wonder, having fended off the media's adverse reaction to his work with claims that his album hadn't been properly promoted, appeared on Smokey Robinson's album *Where There's Smoke*. A milestone in the ex-Miracle's career, it spawned his biggest American solo hit in years. Titled 'Cruisin'' it soared to number four and was typical of Robinson's relaxed genius; yet despite its American success, the title bombed in Britain. However, he was due to enjoy a British hit in 1981 when 'Being With You' captured the pole position for two weeks. And as Smokey Robinson enjoyed his rejuvenated career, Marvin Gaye floundered when his proposed *Love Man* album was rejected as inferior by Berry Gordy. The embittered artist would eventually re-work the rejected tracks for the 1981 release *In Our Lifetime*, his final album for Motown, which, alas, was also considered to be sub-standard. Indeed, when *Blues & Soul* magazine printed its 'Hall Of Shame (The Best Of The Worst)' in 2000, *In Our Lifetime* dominated the listing, with, not surprisingly, *Stevie Wonder's Journey Through The Secret Life Of Plants* at number ten. The printed comment implied that the only plants most soul fans were concerned about smelt funny, were smoked and grew in the loft under floodlit conditions: 'Maybe Stevie was "too high" on the stuff himself when he concocted this soporific double album . . . If you want an uneventful one-way ticket to Dullsville USA *Plants* should suffice.'

Marvin Gaye took Berry Gordy's rejection to heart and it was probably this that marked the start of his rapid deterioration. He fled to Hawaii as his marriage to Jan collapsed and his property was confiscated by the IRS in lieu of unpaid taxes. Now penniless and with an increasing drug intake, he turned to friends like Smokey Robinson and Stevie Wonder for financial help. When they refused, Marvin Gaye approached his first mentor Harvey Fuqua who bailed him out until the singer could arrange to flee America for Britain where, with help from tour promoter Jeffrey Krugar, Gaye based himself in London to rethink his shattered life. His immediate future was bleak.

C h a p t e r   1 1

MASTER BLASTER
(JAMMIN')

'I don't tell him how to write his songs'
a pressman about Stevie Wonder

'When [Stevie] wanted to be DJ, segue-ing the records was a bit of
a problem'
Graham 'Fatman' Canter

'Like no other American, Martin Luther King . . . died for American
Democratic principles'
Stevie Wonder

During 1980 Motown and Jobete celebrated their twentieth
anniversary (even though the celebration was a year short) and
records and merchandising carried a specially designed logo to
mark the fact. More artists visited Britain, its second most
important selling market, during this year than ever before and
due to the high quality of music the company enjoyed its best year
since the sixties.

A struggling 'Black Orchid' heralded the new year for Stevie
Wonder. When the single stopped selling at number 63 in the
British chart, Motown tried again with 'Outside My Window',
which one reviewer cited as the most successful cut from *Stevie
Wonder's Journey Through The Secret Life Of Plants* before
adding, 'I presume Motown are praying it'll meet with success
here. It's another typically Wonder-styled ballad of the kind that

sounds superb on an album but not as good as a single.' Once again, it did little for the mother project, stalling in the top sixty, so Motown conceded defeat and left the flora to die a natural death.

With his own work struggling Stevie Wonder must have derived much pleasure when his song 'You Are My Heaven', written with Eric Clapton, was released by Atlantic Records. The duet by Roberta Flack and Donny Hathaway was issued almost a year after Hathaway's death. And in Britain, ex-Wonderlove member Lynda Laurence issued 'Living With A Married Man' on Motorcity Records, where she recorded as a soloist and as one third of The Former Ladies of the Supremes. (Without Motown's support Mary Wilson had no choice but to disband The Supremes in 1977. Laurence was the vital link in forming The Former Ladies of The Supremes in 1985 with Jean Terrell and Scherrie Payne, who together reflected the spirit of The Supremes. When Terrell retired in 1992, she was replaced by Sundray Tucker, another Wonderlove vocalist.)

One of Stevie Wonder's first public appearances that year was joining the ranks of roller disco devotees at Xenon's in New York, where he zoomed around the dancefloor at the club assisted by crew members of the Good Skates team. Pictures of the happy singer were splashed across music magazines. He took advantage of this photo call to speak of his music plans, indicating he was working on tracks for a forthcoming Syreeta album, planning to record an album with Mary Lee Whitney, currently a member of Wonderlove, and intended completing his own project for 1980 release. He had also been a featured musician on albums by B B King, The Pointer Sisters, Buddy Miles, James Taylor, Peter Frampton, Maria Muldaur, Don Hartman, Quincy Jones and others.

Motown's anniversary coincided with The Temptations' surprise return to the company; a move, according to Otis Williams, instigated by Smokey Robinson: 'Smokey was the revolving door, as we called him because he helped us leave Motown and then he helped us come back.' Williams admitted that Motown was the last company they had considered approaching, although they were curious to see if Robinson could negotiate a deal on their behalf. 'Berry Gordy had co-written a song called "Power" and he felt it was perfect for us . . . . We met [him] at an impromptu meeting in Smokey's office and before we knew where we were, we were gathered around a piano rehearsing "Power".' The Temptations are still signed to Motown to this day.

Jermaine Jackson, the only remaining Jackson brother at Motown, had his first taste of major success with his runaway hit 'Let's Get Serious' during February 1980, a month later in Britain. Taken from the album of the same name, the single had been written by Stevie Wonder and Lee Garrett, with Wonder intending to record it himself. However, when Berry Gordy heard the demo, he earmarked it for his son-in-law, as Jackson recalls:

> As well as Stevie writing and producing three songs for the album he also involved himself in the songs I did for myself. So much so he wanted his songs to fit my concept. He said that my songs inspired him to write two completely new songs 'Let's Get Serious' and 'Where Are You Now?' (with Renee Hardaway) and the third 'You're Supposed To Keep Your Love For Me' which I recorded years ago with The Jackson 5, and sang lead on.

The *Let's Get Serious* album was dance-orientated as dictated by the current music trend, much against Jackson's wishes because he felt disco music had damaged the industry, with record companies saturating the market with a basic four/four beat at the expense of other types of music. However, Jackson conceded when he realised this could be his most successful album to date following a two-year absence from the recording studio: 'I decided to stop what I was doing and go over my past to make sure *Let's Get Serious* was the best . . . The lack of my [previous] success forced me into searching for the right ingredients and I believe that's what has made this new album so acceptable.'

The 'Let's Get Serious' single was a typical Wonder composition – he even sang the middle chorus – so when Jermaine Jackson flew to London in May 1980 to promote it on British television he was forbidden by Wonder to sing the song 'live', causing untold problems with many of the music programmes. However, that was resolved when a Continental video featuring Jackson singing Wonder's part was used, unbeknown, of course, to the song's composer. With Jackson on hand for promotion, the single catapulted into the top ten. The American follow-up 'You're Supposed To Keep Your Love For Me' and the British release 'Burnin' Hot' failed to repeat their predecessor's success, thereby cutting short Jermaine Jackson's hit run. He did return to London in December 1980 to host Motown's Twentieth Anniversary champagne party held at the EMI Records headquarters in Manchester Square.

Back in America, Stevie Wonder took time out from the studios during June to join 97-year-old Eubie Blake, and others, to receive an honorary degree from Fisk University in Los Angeles. Both artists were established in the music business but this was the first time they had met. Wonder openly acknowledged the influence Blake had had on generations of American musicians, including himself, whilst Blake returned the compliment, adding, 'I like your voice. I like the way you play and I like your music.' The two went on to perform together at the university.

Also during this time, the British press reported that the singer had been booked by tour promoters Marshall Arts for September 1980 concerts at London's Wembley Arena. Motown, on behalf of Music Abroad, Wonder's company handling his foreign tours, denied the story, stating that although suggestions had been made to him that he might visit Britain during this anniversary year, no commitment had been received from the artist. However, the evasive singer was spotted in New York, where he performed an unrehearsed concert at Bogard's restaurant owned by The Best Of Friends. He surprised a capacity audience when he located the piano and began singing. A chance remark from Wonder suggested he was in training for forthcoming London concerts.

Before the ink had dried on his concert denial, Motown/EMI released the news that a new album was scheduled for July 1980 release. Aptly titled '*Hotter Than July*', the story seemed credible, but, in view of the series of postponements of *Stevie Wonder's Journey Through The Secret Life Of Plant*, no one took much notice. However, the media did take note when, attending the annual Black Music Association convention, Wonder took journalists to task, advising them how to do their jobs properly.

One annoyed pressman was heard to comment, 'I don't tell him how to write his songs!'

In truth, the media were fed up with half-cocked press releases about the singer, and those items that were published were usually tinged with sarcasm. So when Marshall Arts confirmed that the rumoured visit to Britain was indeed a reality, his first European concerts for six years, fans waited for a retraction. It didn't happen. The show, dubbed 'Stevie Wonder's Hotter Than July Music Picnic', would span 1–7 (excluding the 4th) September 1980, and would feature old repertoire and tracks from a new album. To coincide with the visit Motown scheduled the release of 'Master Blaster (Jammin')', the only track available from *Hotter Than July*, with the hope that the album would shortly follow. It didn't materialise, but the tapes did enabling a playback reception, attended by Wonder, to be held at Studio No 2 in EMI Records' Abbey Road Studios on 2 September. Attending journalists and celebrities were searched for tape recorders before admission, and when a European hack was later discovered with a machine hidden on his person he was instantly ejected in a most undignified manner, with the tape snatched from his recorder.

Diana Ross was also in London on a private holiday with her boyfriend, Gene Simmons (a member of the rock group Kiss). Currently riding on her Chic-inspired album *Diana* which revived her flagging career, she agreed to participate in Motown's anniversary celebrations by hosting a press reception at the Inn On The Park hotel. During the reception she was presented with numerous awards for British record sales held by Motown on her behalf. *Diana* was crammed with hit singles – 'Upside Down', 'I'm Coming Out', 'My Old Piano' – and went on to sell one million units in Britain alone following its June release.

Needless to say, Stevie Wonder's London dates were instantly sold out, and critics glowed with enthusiasm including *Melody Maker*'s Geoff Brown:

Material came from as far back as 1963, when he was hailed as the twelve-year-old genius, and from as recently as his next album. Many black American artists do scant justice to their past hits, preferring to plug new and usually inferior songs and dismissing old times in a flippant medley. Wonder's catalogue is too rich, and he too mindful of its rare quality for it to be so treated. He did full justice to the old hits played, and in fact took them to greater heights by frequently adding vamps and allowing himself and his excellent band, Wonderlove, to stretch out. After a particularly memorable and torrid 'Higher Ground', I recall, he was moved to laugh, 'Phew, we really got carried away on that one.' And they do. He started with 'For Once In My Life' and never let up for the next hour and a quarter. It was one of the best played sets I've ever heard. A warm romantic 'My Cherie Amour', an exuberant 'Signed, Sealed, Delivered', a lovely 'If You Really Love Me', and a truly beautiful 'Superwoman' (although much of the deft guitar work was sadly inaudible) into a grand piano backing for 'You And I', 'Too Shy To Say' and, re-joined by the rhythm section, 'All In Love Is Fair'. After 'Lately', he gradually increased the pace through 'Don't Worry 'Bout A Thing' which kicked along powerfully into the burbling funk of the exciting 'Higher Ground' and built to a thrilling climax with 'Golden Lady', 'Boogie On Reggae Woman', during which he danced lasciviously with each of his four background singers, led into a steaming version of 'Let's Get Serious', and a mightily tough 'Living For The City' finished the first half.

Thirty minutes later one of the sax players introduced, with a moderate bellow, 'Little Stevie Wonder'. Dressed now in an old style blue tuxedo jacket, white shirt and bow tie, Little Stevie did homage to his very first hit 'Fingertips'. Honest, amusing, nostalgic fun. Wonderlove took a solo spot while the boss changed togs and returned for a thumping 'Sir Duke', a rolling, tumbling 'I Wish', a rich 'You Are The Sunshine Of My Life', and a thrilling 'Superstition'. The final half of his second set led him deeper into the philosophical areas which much of his seventies work has predominantly inhabited. The beauty of his melodies is such that the messages don't suffer from the sanctimonious air that often infests other artists' attempts at cosmic thoughts. Even when Wonder plays no music and just speaks from his heart, there is such an obviously unrehearsed feeling in his thoughts that he wins full attention. Finally, two new songs

'Master Blaster' and 'Did I Hear You Say You Loved Me', more communal signing, then his band left the stage one by one until the drummer was left to thunderously bring this wholly memorable event to a close. It was marvellous, thoroughly involving entertainment. I shall play nothing but Stevie Wonder records for the next fortnight in an all too vain effort to recapture the night's magic.

On the singer's free day (4 September) he allowed a promotion video to be filmed of him singing 'Master Blaster (Jammin')' at Wembley Arena, provided it was completed in two takes. And on the last night of his Wembley concerts he was joined on stage by Diana Ross and Marvin Gaye, who was still exiled in London. Diana Ross and Gene Simmons were already seated in an exclusive enclosure situated at the side of the stage when Stevie Wonder began his show. Marvin Gaye arrived later, driven to the venue in a pale-coloured mini which was later parked in the vast hangar-type area immediately behind the newly designed stage. Gaye did not go into the auditorium, preferring to wander around backstage. A member of Wonder's entourage went on-stage to tell him that the two Motown artists had arrived, whereupon at his earliest convenient break he invited them both to join him. When Ross was told of Wonder's intention she immediately resisted, claiming she wasn't suitably dressed for an appearance, yet she looked stunning in a simply cut outfit, a make-up-free face and her long hair pulled back. Dressed in a striped, light-coloured shirt and suit, Marvin Gaye was unsure what to do. Both were escorted to the stage to face a disbelieving audience of eight thousand. The reception the three stars basked in was extraordinary. Hysterical fans rushed to the stage, causing pandemonium. Within seconds stage security was trebled while hand-picked photographers hidden in the stage pit climbed over themselves to point their lenses at one of music's historic events. When the thunderous reception had finally died down, Marvin Gaye sat at the piano to play 'What's Going On': he improvised the lyrics on the first verse before leaving it to his co-stars to pick up the song. After ten or so minutes two happy stars departed the stage, leaving Stevie Wonder to somehow retrieve the remainder of his musical programme. The three artists were later reunited backstage, where people gathered requesting autographs, and security men stood shoulder to shoulder.

On Monday, 8 September Wonder performed a charity show at London's Hammersmith Odeon. He announced this additional date during his last Wembley show, whereupon Marshall Arts' personnel worked through the night to transfer stage equipment to the new venue because Kiss were due to follow the Motown star at Wembley. After the Monday night performance, Marshall Arts hosted a party at Mayfair's Gullivers Club for Wonder, his musicians, crew, Motown personnel and others involved in the tour. Wonder left the nightclub at 5 a.m. after a weary Graham 'Fatman' Canter had played every dance record in his collection. 'Stevie really enjoyed himself but when he wanted to be DJ, segue-ing the records was a bit of a problem,' recounted Canter who was the first London DJ to hear 'Master Blaster (Jammin')' when Motown's publicity manager snuck him a tape of the song to play in his night's programme. The cassette was worn out within a week!

Stevie Wonder drew inspiration from Bob Marley and in particular their friendship, which they renewed in 1979 at the Black Music Association in Philadelphia. In fact, following their performance, Wonder wrote the skeleton of 'Master Blaster (Jammin')'. Keith Harris, Stevie Wonder's British manager, had for some time fed the singer's growing interest in reggae by shipping records to him from Britain, including Lee Perry's *Revolution Dub*, and the innovative scratching styles greatly impressed him. These combined influences allowed Wonder's own form of reggae to be born, a sound that crossed over into mainstream music when 'Master Blaster (Jammin')' shot into the American top five and to number two in Britain. Soon after the release of this single, Bob Marley collapsed while jogging in Central Park, New York, He was admitted to the Sloan-Kettering Hospital, where cancer was diagnosed. In November Marley was baptised as a Christian Rastafarian, and a month later flew to the Dr Josef Issels Clinic in Bavaria for treatment. He died on 11 May 1981, from lung cancer and a brain tumour, at The Cedars of Lebanon Hospital. On 13 May 1981, while performing in Stockholm, Stevie Wonder dedicated his birthday show to his friend.

Although the British tour bore the name of his new album, *Hotter Than July*, the actual record was not released until October 1980. Written, produced and arranged by Stevie Wonder and recorded and mixed at his own recently purchased Los Angeles Wonderland Studios, it was once again reviewed by Bob Killbourn:

The album's opening track 'Did I Hear You Say You Love Me' is an uptempo, lively and spirited number combining a pleasing bass/percussion mixture augmenting Stevie's synth lines and vocod-ed vocals which cuts into 'All I Do' which slows the tempo down, with Stevie's sweet/sour, but always melodic, vocals hitting home with back-up vocal assistance from Michael Jackson, Betty Wright and O'Jays' Eddie Levert and Walter Williams, plus a short sax break courtesy of Hank Redd. 'Rocket Love' finds Stevie in a reflective mood, over a haunting Paul Riser string arrangement . . . 'I Ain't Gonna Stand For It' and Stevie cuts a hard vocal edge on this essentially acoustic offering . . . Another sharp cut and straight into 'As If You Read My Mind' (with vocal support from Syreeta) which closes side one. 'Master Blaster (Jammin'); opens side two . . . a totally refreshing slice of reggae/soul. 'Do Like You' and the uptempo mood continues unabated with Stevie using 'baby talk' to introduce and close this saga. 'Cash In Your Face' is his social comment, and then the gem 'Lately' is a sad, but compelling lament with [him] solo-ing on piano and bass synth. 'Happy Birthday' closes side two, and it's Stevie's tribute to Martin Luther King whose birthday is being submitted by Stevie as a national holiday. A fine, joyous salute . . . and a fine joyous farewell from Mr Wonder . . . for the time being.'

The music was packaged in a colourful gatefold sleeve with a painting by Al Harper of the singer's head and shoulders, braided hair, sweat pouring down his face, looking every inch a religious icon in sunglasses. The inner sleeves were used as lyric sheets, while the back cover showed his burning piano. The disc's cover was dedicated to the memory of Dr Martin Luther King, with notes from the singer signed with his thumbprint. Certainly, when compared to previous packaging, this was attractively compelling.

Once again Motown/EMI embarked on an expensive marketing campaign as the album was Wonder's first contribution to the eighties. To enhance the advertising programme, approximately 600 display pieces and 3,500 full-colour posters were made available for in-store displays. *Hotter Than July* shipped gold with advance orders in excess of 100,000 copies, while Motown/USA's promotional activities were equally impressive, as were the initial album sales.

Upon his return to America following the tour, Stevie Wonder announced his intention to 'respectfully demand' that the American Congress declare Dr Martin Luther King's birthday, 15 January, an American national public holiday. At a press conference held in Berry Gordy's office in October, he said he planned to appeal 'to the highest and best principles of the American people' and to express his concern at the re-emergence of the Ku Klux Klan, who had resumed their atrocious activities, including lynching blacks in the southern states. Wonder, who had been planning this move for three years, said he would not rest until he'd achieved his dream. 'Like no other American, Martin Luther King stood for, fought for and died for American democratic principles,' Wonder pointed out. 'The holiday would be the first commemorating the enormous contributions of black people in the United States.' He also added that he intended to head a rally in Washington DC during 1981.

Before the close of 1980, 'I Ain't Gonna Stand For It' followed 'Master Blaster (Jammin')'; the single's packaging featured photographs of solo Wonder, and Wonder with Diana Ross and Marvin Gaye at Wembley Arena. As his career was on the rise once more, Syreeta attempted to regain the momentum of 'With You I'm Born Again' with 'Please Stay', one of two duets with Billy Preston included on her solo 1980 *Syreeta* album. The Commodores released their tenth album, *Heroes*, and struggled for hits amidst speculation that their lead singer Lionel Richie was due to embark upon a solo career. Richie had recently composed 'Lady' for the country and western singer Kenny Rogers which sold an estimated sixteen million copies. The Commodores felt Richie should have given them the song to rejuvenate their stagnating career.

Towards the end of their anniversary year, as Gill Scott-Heron supported Stevie Wonder during a seven-city American tour, Motown/EMI announced the year's record sales as the best ever. The company sold three million singles and one and a half million albums. Artists who contributed to the figures included Jermaine Jackson, Teena Marie, Diana Ross, Billy Preston and Syreeta, and, of course, Stevie Wonder. The magnitude of the success was surprising but obviously gratifying in a climate dominated by spiralling costs within the record industry. It also gave a boost of confidence to Motown and its staff, who were determined this anniversary year would be remembered for its hits. Motown had weathered twenty years and there was no reason to suspect the success and acclaim would not continue. However, it was not to be.

Chapter   1 2

HAPPY BIRTHDAY

'. . . I love everything about my personal life because it is personal'
Stevie Wonder

'["Happy Birthday"] means a lot to me and I had to be sure the intention to release it was right'
Stevie Wonder

'[Stevie] wants everything done his way'
Jermaine Jackson

As Stevie Wonder's 'I Ain't Gonna Stand For It' held on to the number ten spot in Britain, its mother album *Hotter Than July* passed platinum status in America. Meanwhile, the singer headlined his rally in Washington to celebrate the birthday of Dr Martin Luther King. A BBC-TV film crew joined him for the rally and travelled with him, gaining his confidence on and off stage, for an 'Omnibus' programme to be screened in Britain on 17 March 1981. Also during January 1981 Motown released two movie title tunes. The first was Diana Ross' 'It's My Turn' from the film of the same name, followed by The Temptations' 'Take Me Away' from the film *Loving Couples*. Diana Ross was the most successful. Meanwhile her ex-group, The Supremes, were providing the storyline for the Broadway musical *Dreamgirls*. When she saw the show, she angrily retorted, 'This is my life. This is not a fucking story!' Mary Wilson, on the other hand, attempted to reform the famous trio but she failed.

Motown's marketing department desperately wanted to issue

'Lately' as the follow-up to 'I Ain't Gonna Stand For It' but Stevie Wonder flatly refused to give permission. However, that was to change when a cover version of the song was rush released in Britain by Ensign Records artist, Rudy Grant, and reached the top sixty. Released in February 1981 and a month later in America, Wonder's original was commercially available in both vinyl and cassette form, the latter being fashionable in Britain at the time. The cassette sold in excess of fifteen thousand copies, which helped catapult the single to number three in the chart. In America it crawled into the top seventy.

Smokey Robinson began his silver anniversary celebrations this year with the release of his 'Being With You' single, the title track from his 33rd album. The single topped the American chart, marking Motown's 88th title to achieve this in the R&B chart, and Robinson's sixth R&B number one, four of which had been recorded with his group The Miracles ('Shop Around', 1960; 'You've Really Got A Hold On Me', 1962; 'I Second That Emotion', 1967; 'The Tears Of A Clown', 1970 and the solo release 'Baby That's Backatcha', 1975). 'Being With You' became an international seller and topped the British chart. Flushed with the success of this title – which had been the fastest selling single since The Commodores' 'Three Times A Lady' – Motown grabbed a second chart-topper in 1981 with a 1975 Michael Jackson track, 'One Day In Your Life', which was re-released in March. This was the first time in Motown's British history that one artist had followed another to the pole position.

In America, Motown's celebrations were highlighted by a concert held in Smokey Robinson's honour at the Los Angeles Shrine Auditorium, where performers included Stevie Wonder, Natalie Cole, Teena Marie and Aretha Franklin. 'It was a very special occasion for me and one that I will never forget', an emotional Robinson said. 'It was a magnificent gesture by everyone who came and I have to confess that I was totally choked-up inside by their show of affection.'

Stevie Wonder then left his colleague's celebrations behind to fly with a girlfriend, Stephanie, to Montserrat, the tiny volcanic island off the West Indies, to record 'Ebony And Ivory' with Paul McCartney. A jumbo jet carrying several tons of recording equipment landed at Antigua airport shortly before McCartney and his family flew in from New York. Ringo Starr and his wife also joined them. The day following Wonder's arrival, rehearsals began with him playing drums and synthesiser, and McCartney on bass and piano. It took them a day to complete 'Ebony And Ivory', a track for the ex-Beatle's forthcoming *Tug Of War* album. McCartney recalls, 'I dearly wanted to work with someone like Stevie because the song's about harmony between black and white. The idea is that ebony and ivory live together on a piano keyboard so why can't we as humans live together too.' Record sales were boosted by one of the most expensive videos ever made up to that time. Wonder's contribution was filmed in America (because he was unable to fit in a visit to Britain) and superimposed on the final copy in London to show the two artists singing together. Wonder remembers:

> Even though I did not write the song, I'm in total agreement with what the lyric was saying and because of that I felt it would be right for Paul and me to do the song together. I felt that for whatever significance we both have in a multi-racial society, we're all many different colours and cultures, it would be good for us to sing something like that. And so when I was approached to do it, I said it would be really good to do it. It was my pleasure outside of being a fan of his, the fact that we had mutual respect for each other throughout the years. It was a good time and a good song to get that message across about ebony and ivory.

John Abbey wrote in *Blues & Soul*: 'The fact that Stevie Wonder duets with the former Beatle makes it of interest to soul people, though the lyric content of McCartney's composition makes the song valid anyway. The song naturally has that McCartney feel to it but Stevie's distinctive vocals do come through in their own right.' These combined record-buying markets – soul and mainstream – bounced the single to the top of the British chart in April 1982, Wonder's first number one.

While the Motown star basked in his duet success, his friend Diana Ross was clawing for survival. To save her career, she announced her intention to leave Motown to sign a seven-year contract with RCA Records for North America and Canada, and Capitol Records for the rest of the world. Berry Gordy was devastated. In retrospect, it was the best move the star could have made at this time because the change of record company ignited renewed enthusiasm in her career, with an extremely promising future. Author J Randy Taraborrelli noted in his book *Call Her Miss Ross* that at 52 years old Berry Gordy was a changed man once Ross left Motown: 'As far as many of Motown's fans were concerned Diana's leaving Motown closed the final chapter in Berry Gordy's book of dreams-come-true. Stevie Wonder was still with the label, so was Smokey and a few other stalwarts. But without Diana as queen, the kingdom just didn't matter much anymore. Motown would never be the same again.' Also, later that year, after an eighteen-year association, Motown would switch its British outlet from EMI Records to RCA Records. The move resulted in Motown's dedicated working team being made redundant.

Meanwhile, Marvin Gaye consented to work with Motown's London staff to assist the promotion of his back catalogue although several activities were marred by his irrational behaviour. The commitments he did honour were conducted in controversial Gaye fashion resulting in tabloid headlines, which, in turn, sold his music. This stood him in good stead when Motown released the 1981 single 'Praise' from the album *In Our Lifetime*, which, to all intents and purposes, was a re-working of the rejected *Love Man* project with additional tracks. In the single, Marvin Gaye made reference to his love for Stevie Wonder, who later told Paolo Hewitt he was more amused than upset at Gaye's infringement of his music: 'He stole a riff from me. I don't know what it's from. I think it might be a little thing from "Summer Soft" . . . He was bad . . . it was ridiculous.'

In the Wonder camp plans were finalised for him to tour outside America once again; due to his high profile, he was in great demand. Before kicking off in Rotterdam during May 1981, he made a surprise appearance on London's Apollo Theatre stage during the final Teddy Pendergrass and Stephanie Mills concert. Wonder remembers, 'Teddy is a nice person and lots of fun. He's also a talented artist and must have been delighted with the response he got from the people in London, particularly the ladies.' When asked why he had this compulsion to appear at other artists' concerts, he laughed, 'I'm likely to pop up at all sorts of events, anytime, any place . . . !' This particular unrehearsed appearance prompted rumours of him adding British dates to the end of his European tour. However, he declined requests from Marshall Arts by saying further dates would follow too closely to his Wembley Arena performances. Interestingly, the singer also refused permission for any of his European shows to be filmed for television or video use, claiming his public wouldn't attend future shows if they could be seen elsewhere. From the Apollo Theatre, Stevie Wonder flew to Amsterdam, where he hosted a press conference on 5 May prior to the start of his tour.

With members of his immediate entourage, he flew to Sofitel airport where they boarded his touring coach, a modified vehicle to accommodate the singer, with its rear turned into a 'listening' studio complete with stereo system and lounge chairs. The press conference was Stevie Wonder's first in almost ten years, and was dogged with the usual banal questions from the journalists who packed into the small reception room. One female scribe attempted to break the singer's silence regarding his personal life, with a string of questions. Laughingly, he answered all in a negative fashion but did state, 'I love my children. And when I get the chance I love to bowl and go swimming. I also love everything about my personal life because it is personal. Anything that makes me feel good I love.' And still she persisted: 'What's your birth sign?' 'Taurus. What's yours?' 'Virgo.' 'Ah, now I can see why you wanted to know about my personal habits.'

The general mayhem of a press conference gradually subsided when Wonder rose to leave. 'Before I go,' he said, 'I want to thank the people who have followed me and given me a great deal of support in this career of mine. I've been performing for twenty years and I'll be 31 on the thirteenth of this month. It's a funny thing but I love doing everything . . . producing, writing . . . and I have come to the point where I am comfortable.' Although he insisted he enjoyed touring, he thought this current tour would be his last: 'Whenever I do perform it's my desire to make people feel as good as they make me feel. What I call my musical celebration. If people want me to come again, then I will come again.' He then retired to an adjoining room to give private interviews, leaving the remaining journalists to eat platters of raw fish and vegetables.

The tour ended in Paris at the Palais de Sport on 2 June 1981, following dates across Europe, New Zealand and Australia. Two members of Motown's London staff took Graham 'Fatman' Canter, a tabloid journalist and photographer to see the show. They stayed at the Sofitel Severes Paris, where Wonder was also booked because the hotel was close to the stadium. While in their rooms, relaxing after the journey, they were alerted by the hotel's tannoy system to a fire in the hotel. Clutching passports and money, and dressed in bathrobes, or clothes that were easy to grab, the company staffers went in search of Stevie Wonder, passing escaping guests as they shouted his name. Not having had time to check the exact location of his suites, they searched until firefighters confirmed that all the guests were safe, and led them to the outside fire escape where they climbed down the many flights to ground level. Dodging around the attending fire engines and general mayhem of panic, they enquired after Stevie Wonder in the hotel's reception area, only to be told he had transferred to another hotel earlier in the day. Anger followed relief: if the fire had been worse (it had been caused by a fault in the heating ducts), these Motown employees and their guests could have been injured. The incident was later reported to Motown/EMI's executive Gordon Frewin in London who was furious at not being informed of Wonder's change of hotel and that the lives of his staff had consequently been at risk, but who, when calmer, paid for their lavish evening meal with vintage champagne. It's unclear whether Stevie Wonder was told of the incident.

In the humid heat and pouring rain Wonder's evening concert at the Palais de Sport was as heady as those at Wembley Arena. The massive French venue was packed with six thousand over-excited fans, and within a short space of time it resembled an enormous sauna. Wonder and Wonderlove moved from R&B/soul, into country and western through to classic Wonder singles and Motown medleys. Unlike British audiences, when a song ends the French simply clap, maybe cheer, then ignite lighters or candles

'**Stevie is much more than the consummate performer.** He's also the most gifted musician, singer, writer, arranger. He has perfect pitch which in itself is a marvellous gift' – Lynda Laurence.

previous spread: A detail taken from the largest billboard in America advertising the pending release of 'The Songs In The Key Of Life'. above: During 1981 Stevie led a Washington rally to celebrate the late Dr Martin Luther King's birthday. He addressed the multi-thousand crowd before singing 'Happy Birthday'. below: On the final night of his 'Hotter Than July' concerts, Stevie was joined on stage by Diana Ross and Marvin Gaye to sing Gaye's immortal 'What's Going On'. It was a spectacular night which neither the audience nor the promoter had expected.

'**...I shall play nothing but Stevie Wonder records** for the next fortnight in an all too vain attempt to recapture the night's magic' – raved journalist Geoff Brown after attending one of the most talked about performances of the decade.

above: Sitting in his office at Black Bull Publishing, where one of his tasks was answering phones, Stevie was photographed by a British soul reporter who had travelled to America in the hope of being granted an interview. The hope was realised. **below: During the playback of 'Hotter Than July'** at London's Abbey Road Studios in 1980, Sharon Davis (middle) talks to the singer while Motown's club promotion manager, Noreen Allen, holds his hand. *Blues & Soul* magazine's editor, Bob Killbourn, can be seen in the background.

Caught in action during one of his 1980 concerts in London, Stevie Wonder performed to standing room only audiences and rocked the city with his music.

'**Stevie Wonder, through his musical development and innovation,** earned himself a place in musical history both as a teenage phenomenon and as a grown-up, fully-matured musical wonder' – Dave Godin.

and hold them head-high. Hopefully, Stevie Wonder had been appraised of this before the performance. 'The show started at nine o'clock and was still going strong at midnight,' one ecstatic reviwer noted. 'On stepping outside for a breather it was obvious Stevie was rocking Paris. No one in the immediate vicinity would sleep until he had finished. It was a marvellous feeling but I was utterly drained.' With the show's finale in full swing, Berry Gordy strode on stage, once again spurring the audience to rise as one in welcome. Then it was all over, whereupon a proud Motowner was heard to say, 'Stevie has now taken the world to his heart and given his heart to the world.'

What the speaker didn't know was that Berry Gordy's appearance in Paris was business-based. Motown Records was facing bankruptcy and he felt he had no option but to put his publishing company Jobete on the market. He had to save his record operation at all costs, but as Stevie Wonder's compositions were, of course, part of the deal, Berry Gordy couldn't complete a sale without his artist's agreement. Wonder was shocked when Gordy spelled out his plans, especially when the Motown founder also suggested that if he'd delivered his albums on time, Motown Records might not be in such a precarious financial position. Wonder refused to allow his compositions to be part of the Jobete package, whereupon the proposed buyer demanded a lower asking price. Berry Gordy rejected the offer, and thought again.

While in Paris, Stevie Wonder conceded to Motown's pressure to return to London to re-mix 'Happy Birthday' for British release in July 1981. The single featured a digital version of the song on the topside and a singalong version on the flip. 'I do not want the meaning of the record to be overshadowed by any commercial consideration,' he said. 'This song means a lot to me and I had to be sure the intention to release it was right.' Whatever his reasons, Motown recognised a money-spinner when they heard it. As the re-mixing took place, Marvin Gaye was part-way through a British tour that he dubbed 'A Heavy Love Affair Tour 1981'. During a low-key Apollo Theatre performance on 17 June, Stevie Wonder joined him on stage to sing 'I Heard It Through The Grapevine'. At the close of this tour Berry Gordy agreed to free Gaye from his Motown contract. Losing him in the wake of Diana Ross's departure was a huge blow to Motown's public image, yet the company continued to survive. Gaye went on to sign a new deal with Columbia/CBS Records, where in 1982 his *Midnight Love* album and, more importantly, the extracted single 'Sexual Healing', returned the singer to the high-ranking status that had been lost to him for so long.

With 'Happy Birthday' dominating the British soul singles chart and peaking at number two in the mainstream listing, held off the top by Shakin' Stevens' version of 'Green Door', it was announced that highlights from the fourth International 'Reggae Sunsplash' Festival, held at Montego Bay, Jamaica, during August, would be captured in a full-length feature film titled *Reggae Tribute*. The festival, co-sponsored by the Jamaican government, featured top reggae acts including The Wailers, The I-Threes, Black Uhuru, Third World and a surprise appearance by Stevie Wonder, who was certainly enjoying himself that year with impromptu guestings.

The 1980 collaboration between Stevie Wonder and Jermaine Jackson gave the latter confidence to release an album of his own work (except one track) titled *I Like Your Style*. That one exception was 'Signed, Sealed, Delivered (I'm Yours)', a song which he believed to be one of Wonder's best:

> I have always liked Stevie's writing and I wanted to see how I could do that particular song. Working with him is very different. He wants everything done his way. He's a very powerful producer. But sometimes you can go for that and miss the whole boat. However, I stress that in Stevie's case, it works. I just prefer to go with what feels good rather than what I am supposed to do.

In 1983 Jackson produced Syreeta's *The Spell* album which was a comfortable working relationship according to Syreeta because both Jackson and Wonder were perfectionists but, 'Jermaine is far more organised. If he says he'll be there at noon, he'll be there at eleven thirty getting things ready. With Stevie, noon could easily be six o'clock that evening.' Regrettably, *The Spell* was a poor seller despite encouraging reviews and radio play.

Towards the end of 1981, Stevie Wonder wrote a song as a

personal tribute to the slain Egyptian leader Anwar Sadat. As he was unable to attend the funeral due to family commitments, he intended the song 'The Day World Peace Began' to be a collective tribute to Sadat, John Lennon and Martin Luther King, and included on a future album. The singer also planned to instigate the building of a memorial in the Egyptian leader's memory in Washington DC. And in his determination to sustain public interest in Dr Martin Luther King, and following the march and rally organised and led by him earlier in the year, Stevie Wonder called a press conference in Los Angeles to announce plans for a second similar event to take place in January 1982. Having attracted between 150,000 and 200,000 people and collected two million signatures supporting the drive in January 1981, the next march was being organised in association with the Martin Luther King Centre for Non-Violent Social Change based in Atlanta. He proclaimed:

> To increase the effectiveness of our efforts next year, I contacted Mrs King, Congressman Fauntroy and Congressman Conyers with a view toward developing a national mobilisation strategy and developing a legislative plan that would be compatible with Mrs King's efforts in Atlanta and the Congressmen's efforts on Capitol Hill. I'm pleased that Mrs King, the black leadership and I have come together to mutually plan how we will be supportive of each other's efforts.

Stevie Wonder's next album was scheduled for release, and the surprise welcome for 1982 was the first clipped single 'That Girl'. 'Without attempting to sound too excited, [the single] is probably the best individual piece of music Wonder has come up with since the days of *Songs In The Key Of Life*. Gone are the feint punches at the dancefloor ("Master Blaster"),' wrote Mick Clark in *Blues & Soul* magazine. 'The pace is deceiving at first, the slumbering beat builds throughout the production to (ultimately) a pounding finish. If this is an example of what he feels like at the moment, someone for chrissake lock him in the studio!' Despite the enthusiasm, 'That Girl' floundered in the British top forty but became an American top four hit in March.

It was reported that the single's surprise appearance was the result of an unusual deal between Stevie Wonder and Motown. Having never concerned himself with money, Wonder's personal finances were dwindling, and his business interests, including his KJLH radio station, were draining his resources. With his erratic delivery dates, Motown was unable confidently to include his projects in release schedules, which, in turn, meant Wonder wasn't paid. Berry Gordy was aware of his financial predicament in late 1981 and reputedly offered him $2 million to release a 'greatest hits' compilation. Wonder wanted $3 million but for that he would compile a double album and include four new tracks; 'That Girl' was one of them.

The single's American success was timely because Stevie Wonder was the nineth recepient to be presented with a Special Award of Merit at the annual American Music Awards ceremony for his 'extraordinary contribution to the music of America and the world and for his exceptional courage and spirit'. Attending artists who paid tribute to his achievement included Diana Ross, Ray Charles, Lionel Richie and Paul McCartney. Wonder also collected the Best Male Soul Vocalist award.

The success of 'That Girl' helped warm the singer's heart when icy conditions froze a crowd of 50,000 gathered at the Capitol Mall in January 1982. The biting wind didn't deter the patient fans waiting for Stevie Wonder to address them. When he eventually took the stage, there was a minute's silence for those who had recently perished in an Air Florida jet that had crashed into the Fourteenth Street bridge between the state of Virginia and Washington DC. Wonder broke the silence with the words: 'Many things happen and we question God why? These are not easy times, yet they're not hopeless times either. We must refresh our souls and uplift our spirits and harmonize with our brothers and sisters.' He also thanked the crowd for standing so long in the bitter weather to support his call: 'I hope your spirits are warm, are "Hotter Than July",' he told them. Diana Ross, Gladys Knight and Jesse Jackson also attended.

Once more Motown's publicity machine rolled into a delirous pre-promotion flurry to announce the new album, due in May 1982. Titled *Stevie Wonder's Original Musiquarium I*, it was a two-album compilation of his best-known post-1972 material borrowed from seven different albums. Tracks included 'Isn't She Lovely', 'Living For The City', 'Send One Your Love', 'You Are The Sunshine Of My Life', 'Higher Ground' and 'Superstition' plus four new compositions – 'Do I Do', with Dizzy Gillespie on trumpet, 'Ribbon In The Sky', 'Front Line' and 'That Girl'. The double album, the first to fall under Motown's newly negotiated licensing deal with RCA Records (later to become BMG Records), and one that, perhaps, they had wished Wonder had given Motown/EMI as a parting shot, was originally scheduled to cash in on the 1981 Christmas period. However, it was delayed because Motown rejected three sides of the release as being technically unusable. The album was not without its merits or sales appeal, as Bob Killbourn wrote:

> The best of the four new songs is 'Do I Do' – Stevie's musical comment on the pursuit of true love: insidious rhythms interspersed with those familiar Wonder-horn lines; short, sharp, staccato bursts of brass cutting through the bitter-sweet Wonder vocals augmented by effectively-arranged strings . . . That little touch of magic is just not there on three of the four new tracks but Stevie is a most surprising man; his *Plants* album was knocked by the majority of critics and he answered them in the best possible way – with the magnificent *Hotter Than July* album. I believe this may well be the situation with his next production.

Stevie Wonder's Original Musiquarium I went on to become an American top four and British top eight hit.

The open double-fold sleeve was devoted to embossed, brightly coloured fish swimming in an aquarium; the inner sleeves advertised the albums rifled for tracks, though the track listings and sleeve notes were barely readable against the black background. Oddly, while the record labels read *Stevie Wonder's Original Musiquarium I*, the album's front sleeve read *Stevie Wonder. The Original Musiquarium I*.

To launch the album's British release a media reception was held in London's Regent's Park Zoo, where a pre-planned telephone link with the singer in New York was to be the highlight. The link never materialised and 'modern technology' was blamed.

Stevie Wonder's Original Musiquarium I was the first project to be issued under Wonder's new contract with Motown signed during May 1982. Unlike his last re-signing, the financial details of the new contract remained undisclosed during a hastily arranged press conference in Berry Gordy's eighteen-floor office in Motown's Los Angeles offices. The reason for the secrecy this time was, the singer explains, 'People thought I was walking around with $13 million in my pocket!' More seriously he said it was a remarkable deal, particularly in America's then-unsteady financial climate, and it was important for him to have continuing happiness with Motown because, 'Only when I'm happy can I give the best I have to give. I don't think there's anywhere else in the world where I could get the kind of creative control I have with Motown.' Berry Gordy, also at the reception, stated that money was not, as many believed, the most important factor of the deal:

> Most people don't understand that there are also relationships. Honesty, loyalty and a lot of things that make up one's life. Stevie is not only a genius in his music but also a human being. I am extremely grateful that a man of his calibre, who has become a legend for many years now realises at a time when we are in a recession, that money is only part of the value.

Wonder also used the conference as a publicity platform for his recent compilation, by saying, 'There are many songs that I write, many songs that could have gone on, say, *Innervisions* or *Talking Book* which are in the can, and I had to make a decision about those songs . . . I've never done an album consisting of all the songs I've done over the last two years, a kind of review, so I decided it was best to do that now.' This type of album was to become popular with high-profile artists who were either unable to record an album of totally new songs to meet record-company schedules, or who simply wanted to fulfil a recording contract before switching to another company. It was the fans who suffered because they either had to purchase the album for the new tracks, or wait to see if the record company released them as singles. Either way, it was a shoddy practice.

The final announcement at the conference concerned the opening of the singer's own record label, Wondirection, whose signed acts included Grease, Wonderlove, Little Willie John's sons Kevin and Keith, and Boots Rising. Wonder said, 'We basically have as much variety as possible but this doesn't mean to say I'm going to produce every artist that I have and write a song for each album.' Despite his enthusiasm, Wondirection appeared to be a half-hearted venture as evidenced by his next musical collaboration with the established reggae fusion group Third World, who were not a Wondirection signing. The two acts recorded a pair of songs at Wonderland for the group's forthcoming album *You've Got The Power* on Epic Records. One track, titled 'Try Jah Love', issued as a taster, bombed in America but peaked in the British top fifty. This collaboration attracted much media interest. Third World member Stephen 'Cat' Moore explained that they had first met in 1969 in Kingston, Jamaica, before performing together in the 1982 Sunsplash Festival:

> Then Stevie suggested we go into the studio together. He wanted to get into reggae and from there our relationship grew into a strong friendship. He wrote the single and 'You're Playing Us Too Close' practically on the spot in the studio. We offered suggestions and it eventually turned out to be a two-way thing. The songs are kicking hard against certain people and informing people as to what 'jah love' is, and to look towards certain directions. The song is also meaningful because it is the first time a black American has written a song that really involves the Rastafarian movement as such. We got the feeling that when Stevie wrote those songs, he had listened to what we'd done before and just brought an extension of concept.

Working with the Motown star was a 'natural' experience, he pointed out, although Wonder insisted on strict working conditions: 'He was very tight although relaxing, but we all felt extremely confident. It took us three days to lay down the rhythm track on the two songs he wrote, then another five weeks for us to do the whole album.'

Meanwhile, two women who had touched Wonder's life hit the headlines for totally different reasons. The first was Susaye Green who filed a lawsuit against Motown Records, Stone Diamond Music, Black Bull Music and Jobete, seeking $1 million in damages and lack of financial accounting. Part of her action stemmed from unpaid royalties for sales from the track 'I Can't Help It', which she wrote with Stevie Wonder for inclusion on Michael Jackson's *Off The Wall* album. Green said she was extremely upset that Wonder was involved, 'But because his publishing house is involved, it couldn't be helped. Business is business.'

And Syreeta attracted publicity of a far more palatable nature when her new solo album *Set My Love In Motion* was released. She worked on it with Berry Gordy. Now married to Curtis Robinson (bass player with Gladys Knight and the Pips) and mother of two boys, Syreeta was visiting Britain to promote her debut album for Motown's new British outlet. During interviews she spoke for the first time about twelve-year-old Tina, explaining that she was the child's legal guardian: 'She's the godchild of Stevie and myself. She's from Detroit and we brought her out to Los Angeles to live with us because we thought it would give her a better start in life.'

While Syreeta promoted, her first husband consoled himself with 'Do I Do', the second colourful fish to escape from the aquarium, which raced upstream into the American top twenty and the British top ten during July 1982. He followed this with 'Ribbon In The Sky' in September, which swam downstream to the American top sixty and the British top fifty – a huge disappointment for both the singer and Motown. A lack of interest among radio DJs was to blame.

Of the last three Motown artists to hit the pole position in Britain, Michael Jackson was the only one to have left the company. (Smokey Robinson and Stevie Wonder were the others.) Now another ex-artist followed suit. Originally released in 1977, Charlene's 'I've Never Been To Me' was re-released after concentrated radio play. Motown's first number one single under its new deal with BMG Records, it later climbed the American chart convincing the company to re-sign her. Charlene (Duncan) was actually living in Britain at this time but soon relocated to California to re-start her career. The chart-topper's follow-up 'It

Ain't Easy Comin' Down', a 1976 single, died after its release in June 1982. However, Charlene was the first white Motown artist to top the British chart, although R Dean Taylor came close in 1971 when he peaked at number two with 'Indiana Wants Me'.

In an attempt to inject life into Charlene's career, Stevie Wonder joined her on disc to record 'Used To Be', produced by Ken Hirsh with Ron Miller as lyricist and arranger. Released in October 1982 (a month later in Britain), its controversial lyrics which bitterly condemned the atrocities and uncaring attitudes of modern life prompted John Abbey to write: 'The actual tune is very simple, very basic, but the depth of the vocal performance by both artists adds a special dimension to the whole record. A veritable classic and I only hope that the lyric doesn't get lost on the world.' With the lyrics in mind, an edited single was pressed for British radio play while the full-length version was commercially available in America. It failed miserably probably due to its content, but Charlene released the *Used To Be* album anyway.

A further track was lifted from *Stevie Wonder's Original Musiquarium I* for British release only. A limited number of copies of 'Front Line' was made available to a select number of radio and club DJs, who had requested the track due to audience demand. The 12″ single included an instrumental version of 'Front Line' on the flip which meant that a DJ with two singles could maintain his dancefloor all night if he wished!

Stevie Wonder's own career thus far had been a series of stylistic peaks and troughs. Which direction would the Motown star take next? It came as a great surprise, or shock, to many when he set side his R&B roots to record a thoroughbred pop song that would, in time, become as popular as any standard tune of the century.

Chapter   1 3

I JUST CALLED TO SAY
I LOVE YOU

'Martin Luther King showed us, non-violently, a better way of life'
Stevie Wonder

'Marvin . . . encouraged me that the music I had within me I must feel free to let out'
Stevie Wonder

'Bastard, I bet he can see'
Boy George

In 1983 Motown celebrated its 25th anniversary and in honour of this achievement a five-hour spectacular, 'Motown 25: Yesterday, Today, Forever' was staged at the Pasadena Civic Auditorium, Los Angeles on 25 March. The proceeds from this gala event were donated to the National Association for Sickle Cell Disease. Past and present Motown acts flocked to honour Berry Gordy's achievement, and as Smokey Robinson announced early on in the show, 'Once a Motowner, always a Motowner.' The artists returned with style irrespective of hit record status, to re-live the company's memories, even though many were allocated only a few minutes of stage time to do so. Hit makers like Smokey Robinson and the Miracles, Martha Reeves, The Four Tops (who rejoined Motown following their performance), The Temptations, Marvin Gaye, The Jacksons, Diana Ross and the Supremes, and Stevie Wonder. He sang 'I Wish' before delivering an emotional tribute 'to all of you who have made it possible for a man from a black culture to have a dream fulfilled. The moments of magic that I've experienced because of you, the artists, management and staff of Motown, encouraged me to create music.' He then closed his set with 'My Cherie Amour' and 'You Are The Sunshine Of My Life' to a thunderous reception. Wonder was originally slotted in to close the first half of the gala, but, to the surprise of no one, he arrived late at the venue. Despite his sensational performance, it was a cool and reflective Marvin Gaye, sitting alone at his piano, recalling the roots of black music before moving into 'What's Going On' who attracted the most attention. After the show, Diana Ross glowed: 'It was amazing. There were some people there I hadn't seen in thirteen years. Like Michael and Stevie, they were all backstage with me . . . it was just wonderful.' Berry Gordy too was delighted with the gala: 'It means a great deal, the culmination of 25 years of success that has been even greater than we realised.' By 1986 Motown was up for sale for the first time.

Prior to his appearance in 'Motown 25: Yesterday, Today, Forever' Stevie Wonder was inducted into the Songwriters Hall Of Fame during a ceremony held at New York's Waldorf Astoria Ballroom. His two children, Keita and Aisha, collected the award on his behalf.

Leaving his music aside, Stevie Wonder rose to the challenge of comedy by appearing on American television in *Saturday Night Live*, the comedy series that had elevated Eddie Murphy, Chevy Chase and Dan Aykroyd, among others, to stardom. Some thought this a bad move for Wonder, but he went ahead regardless. Complete with a British accent, the singer portrayed Rodney Rhythm, a rock music critic, and assisted by Eddie Murphy and other show regulars, skitted through a burlesque imitation of television commercials and the sordid side of music business management, and revealed his pleasure in artists who had abandoned songs of social comment to concentrate on sex (i.e. Marvin Gaye). Wonder's sharp wit offended some viewers, but as he told author John Swenson: 'My feeling was that the whole show was such an obvious joke in the first place, that if you're going to participate, you have to be that. And it was fun. I'd like to do it again.' Also during the show he previewed 'Overjoyed', a new track, and played 'Superstition' before announcing he'd tell the truth about himself. 'I was adopted. I'm from Brixton, in London,' he teased. 'My real name is Trevor Smith. I hate R&B because it's just a noise!' He then sang 'You Are The Sunshine Of My Life' to the melody of the British Music Hall favourite 'You Are My Sunshine'. The American viewing public seemed to enjoy the joke.

Eddie Murphy, too, had upset viewers during one of the shows, with his impersonation of Stevie Wonder. In reply to the complaints received, Murphy included the following in his act:

Stevie 'n I are in the car and I just say, 'Shut the fuck up, Stevie. You're a genius 'n all that shit 'n we hang out 'n it's nice 'n all that shit but I don't appreciate all the flak. Personally, you know how I feel about the piano 'n the singing. I ain't that impressed. You wanna impress me? Take the wheel for a while

Author Frank Sanello wrote in *Eddie Murphy: The Life And Times Of A Comic On The Edge*:

'[Murphy's] grotesque impression of Stevie Wonder's Tourette-like tics offended handicapped people of all colours. Murphy assumed his usual pugnaciousness when people complained. 'Stevie says he listens to the show, and he loves it. So the critics can kiss my ass!' His sense of humour quickly replaced his anger, and he added that if Wonder did object 'I'll kiss his ass!'

Following the announcement of Stevie's new label Wondirection during a contract re-signing reception in 1982, rumours of pending releases were all that appeared to be on offer. However, in July 1983, one rumour turned fact when the first Wondirection single was released on 12" only – Gary Byrd and the GB Experience's rap '(You Wear) The Crown'. The 10-minute-56-second track, marketed and distributed by Motown, was also available in Britain on chrome cassette (aptly dubbed 'the chrome dioxide blaster'). Teena Marie, Syreeta and gospel star Andre Crouch were featured backing vocalists, while Wonder played piano, drums, synthesisers, tambourines and wood blocks!

Byrd began writing '(You Wear) The Crown' in 1979 but it

wasn't until 1981 that Stevie Wonder heard his completed lyrics and insisted he write the music. Byrd recalls, 'I played it to Stevie over the phone and he told me to fly to Los Angeles to record it with him. Stevie laid down the backing track quickly and I did the vocals and the company were excited about releasing it. I couldn't believe Stevie was so satisfied because all his songs go through a long evolutionary process.'

Gary Byrd's rapping lyrics ran through two successive dimensions: his interest in African history and knowledge gained from motivational literature. A British reviewer glowed with enthusiasm: 'tight pumping rhythm, dominant flowing rap from Gary, a typically sparkling vocal passage from Stevie, and a decidedly catchy chorus from the vocal choir'. The rap single took Britain by storm, racing to number six in the chart during July 1983, quite an achievement for a 12" single. 'It was a totally different story in America 'cos nothing happened of any consequence,' sighs Byrd. Despite plans to record a follow-up, this was his only Wondirection release, however, as a DJ he has gone from strength to strength.

Also around this time Diana Ross, inspired by fellow artists including Stevie Wonder, decided to add her weight to charitable causes by performing a free open-air concert before an audience estimated at 300,000–400,000 on the Great Lawn, close to the centre of Central Park, New York. Ross intended to raise money for a children's park on West 81st Street and Central Park West. J Randy Taraborrelli reported: 'One concert was called off due to a terrible storm, the next day Diana Ross performed. When she injected the thoughts and meditations of Kahlil Gibran into the show, she was armed with a large book of readings from *The Prophet*. Now she was ready to follow the lead of Stevie Wonder and become a visionary artist.' Ross said, 'I want people to think of me like they do Stevie. I want to be an artist who is appreciated.'

As 1983 drew to a close, Motown began hinting that a new Stevie Wonder album was due, and promised a new year slot. The record company also refuted suggestions that pirate test pressings of the album had been smuggled out of the studio for distribution in Britain; they claimed that at the time of the alleged abduction, the album was far from finished. The media adopted its usual policy with Wonder's release dates and filed them under 'fantasy'. While Motown hinted, so the artist worked on a project he knew would probably need defending:

> I just want to do what I feel because I'm tired of doing the same old material . . . People have always had a pre-conception of what my music should be, but if it doesn't feel right I won't do it. Some of my albums didn't do so good because people expected me to do a particular thing but that's a chance I took. There are still things I want to express musically and that takes time.

However, he did perform two intended album tracks, 'Overjoyed' and 'Go Home' at New York's Rock City Music Hall, where he kicked off an American 'You And Me' tour destined to take him to Atlantic City, New Jersey, Boston, New York and San Carlos. He also paid tribute to fellow Motown artist, Lionel Richie, by singing an extract from Richie's 'All Night Long (All Night)', telling the audience it was his favourite single of the moment. Now a soloist, Lionel Richie could do no wrong. 'All Night Long (All Night)' topped the American chart; it was culled from his second solo album *Can't Slow Down*, which went on to sell in excess of ten million copies in America alone. At Wonder's same Rock City Music Hall concert, Eddie Murphy, who had recently sung 'Super Freak' with Motown's funkster Rick James at his Madison Square Garden concert, joined Wonder on stage to do his famous Stevie Wonder impersonation during 'Ebony And Ivory'. Critics suggested Murphy never knew when to quit!

Before Stevie Wonder could finish his 1983 American dates his dream came true when Congress passed a bill, 78 to 22, to make Dr Martin Luther King's birthday a national public holiday, despite opposition from North Carolina's senator Jesse Helms (who had attempted to sully King's reputation) and Evan Meacham, the governor of Arizona. (Wonder later announced boycotts of the states until the governors introduced the public holiday.)

The national holiday would start in 1986, and it was a relieved and overwhelmed singer who said, 'Martin Luther King showed us, non-violently, a better way of life, a way of mutual respect, helping us to avoid much bitter confrontation and inevitable bloodshed. We still have a long road to travel until we reach the world that was his dream.' In his official statement Wonder declared, 'Somewhere Dr King is smiling, not because his birthday is a holiday, but because he, too, is convinced that we are moving in the right direction. I know that Dr King appreciates that this day is a day for all Americans to celebrate love, peace and unity. It's not the cure-all, but it is a healing aid.' Remarking that he was proud his fellow Americans agreed to honour King, he insisted celebrations begin straight away: 'Let's celebrate that we have the first holiday demanded by the people. Let's celebrate our democratic process that allows us these opportunities . . . and our collective effort that brought blacks, whites, reds, browns and yellows together – our new child.' Finally he thanked the millions of Americans who had supported his dream: 'We could never have accomplished this if you didn't have faith in yourself, your country and your fellow Americans. I just want to give you a standing ovation and my heartfelt thanks and applause.'

Motown finally released 'Happy Birthday' in celebration in November 1983. The 12″ single's flipside contained extracts from four speeches by King ('I Have A Dream', 'Drum Major Instinct Sermon', 'Dr King's Desired Eulogy', 'I've Been To The Mountain Top'). Despite 'Happy Birthday' being released in Britain during 1981 to become a number two hit, Stevie Wonder had refused permission for its American release until agreement was reached on King's public holiday. Motown in London had no choice but to reissue the single to counteract American imports flooding the market. Unfortunately, the 'Happy Birthday' used for the A-side was the original album track as opposed to the extended re-mix that was first released.

The Year 1984 started with more celebrations when a star-studded line-up including Ray Charles, Lena Horne, Joan Baez and Irene Cara performed at Washington's Kennedy Center on 8 January in a gala commemorating the life of Dr Martin Luther King. Alex 'Roots' Haley was responsible for the show's script, which traced King's career. The two-hour performance was filmed for American screening on 15 January. Stevie Wonder celebrated by performing at Washington's Capitol Center on King's birthday. It was billed as the 'people's concert', and the singer insisted that admission be pegged considerably lower than his usual ticket prices.

Meanwhile, Lionel Richie, whose career continued to soar, took a break from his recording commitments to host the eleventh American Music Awards ceremony in January, where he also received the Favourite Soul Single Award for 'All Night Long (All Night)'. The 1984 ceremony was dominated by ex-Motowner Michael Jackson, who won eight awards related to his *Thriller* project. He then went on to be nominated for a staggering twelve Grammy Awards for the same album and one for his narration of the MCA Records *E.T.* album in the Best Recording For Children category. Bob Dylan and Stevie Wonder were joint announcers for the Best Song category. When Dylan opened the envelope and handed the brailled card to Wonder to read the winner, he laughed, 'Bob, you've given it to me upside down!'

Lionel Richie then began performing in earnest when he signed a deal with the soft drinks company Pepsi Cola to promote his 1984/1985 concerts. His agreement with Pepsi Cola followed hot on the heels of a similiar deal the drinks company had made with The Jacksons. However, before Richie set foot on stage he was rebuked by the Promoters Association (which represents prominent black promoters in America) for not involving local black promoters in the tour. The Jacksons were similarly criticised – unlike Stevie Wonder who insisted on black personnel working for him during his European *Hotter Than July* tour, which caused embarrassment to Motown's predominantly white staff – although neither act was known to hire whites in preference to blacks. In the end, Richie agreed to six black promoters co-promoting his concerts, even though he believed he now appealed more to white audiences.

Stevie Wonder toured again, with June 1984 dates in Britain as part of an extensive European tour. The British dates, his first since 1980, spanned Birmingham's National Exhibition Centre (NEC); two nights at the Brighton Centre, East Sussex, followed by two concerts at London's Earls Court, dates in Dublin's RDS Hall, and two dates at London's Wembley Arena. Additional concerts were later added by the promoters Harvey Goldsmith

Entertainments and Kennedy Street Enterprises. Motown added to the tour schedule the news that the forthcoming album was completed and titled *'People Move Human Plays'*. It was unable to confirm its release, but was sufficiently convinced of its imminence to allocate the catalogue number STML 8040. To date the title has not been used but the musical contents were, by and large, released in 1985 under the title *In Square Circle*.

The June tour announcement coincided with the heart-breaking news that Marvin Gaye had been shot dead by his father at the family home in Los Angeles just before noon on Sunday, 1 April 1984, the day before his 45th birthday. Wonder received a phone call telling him of the tragedy: 'When you hear things like that you say, well, this is April Fool's Day, but on the other hand I knew [the caller] wouldn't be kidding about something like this.' He attended his friend's funeral four days later at the Los Angeles Forest Lawn Cemetery, with Gaye's family, Berry Gordy, Martha Reeves and Smokey Robinson, among others. During the ceremony Wonder told the congregation, 'Marvin was the person who encouraged me that the music I had within me I must feel free to let out', before singing 'Lighting Up The Candles', a song he had written twelve hours prior to Gaye's death: 'I felt something was about to go wrong. I didn't know what it was going to be . . . a possible losing of someone.' In fact, Stevie Wonder had spent the previous evening visiting Clarence Paul in hospital. He had composed the music to 'Lighting Up The Candles' but had no lyrics although he knew what he wanted to say. Paul's contribution and inspiraton enabled Wonder to complete the song that same evening.

The death of Marvin Gaye was a tragedy beyond words: that a father, a Baptist church minister, could so easily shoot and kill his own son seemed beyond belief. And it was this that his family and indeed Marvin Gaye's millions of fans had to try to come to terms with. Few succeeded. Stevie Wonder was later angry at negative stories circulating the industry about his friend's last days, and told *Rolling Stone* magazine: 'All those things people are saying about Marvin after he died are just incredible. When I die, I'm going to have my people gagged.' Numerous artists later paid tribute to the late singer on record, but neither Motown nor CBS

Records immediately cashed in on his death. Such was the respect that Marvin Gaye commanded from the industry and public alike.

Stevie Wonder decided to drop much of his early material from his European concerts; to test the new format he performed four shows in Detroit for a fee of $1 million. The performances, dedicated to Marvin Gaye, were filmed for a cable television special titled *Stevie Wonder Comes Home*.

In between his London performances, the Motown star met the media at a plush reception held at 'The Roof Garden' in Kensington; attended a Greater London Council rally claiming he 'supported any organisation that fights racism' and dubbed the GLC 'God's Little Children'; and took it upon himself to promote his new Wondirection act, two brothers Keith and Kevin John, as Ralph Tee reported:

> Those lucky enough to have popped into Gullivers in Mayfair would have heard a preview delivered by Stevie himself. He's stated before that Gullivers is his favourite club in London and in the words of DJ Graham Gold 'what a blinding night, the new track is a killer and the club went beserk!' Not a surprising reaction but then, in the words of the main man himself as he walked on stage to a deafening ovation at Earl's Court, 'Hey, it's only Stevie Wonder . . . give us a break!'

And after attending the Earl's Court concert, Tee wrote:

> One thing that's very apparent when watching [Stevie] live is his sense of humour, something you can't imagine and have to experience for yourself . . . Shortly after walking on stage . . . he announced, 'I've got some bad news for you – yesterday I quit the business.' So we're introduced to the new Stevie Wonder who proceeds to play some Country and Western and a touch of the Blues – both booed in good humour by the audience, even though both performances were brilliant . . . If it's not music that Stevie Wonder is in the main associated with, it's his support for the fight against racism . . . In concert his message was relayed through James Brown's 'Say It Loud, I'm Black And I'm Proud'. He requested his audience to shut their

eyes and got them to chant 'I'm black and I'm proud', 'I'm white and I'm proud', 'I'm me and I'm proud' which was well received and well responded to . . . For well over two hours non-stop he gave a well-balanced set covering his early era right up to the new one. In all he performed around twenty-four songs, a handful of which I felt were slightly spoilt by an almost over self-indulgent insistence on audience participation. There was even some rap introduced into the night courtesy of special guest Grandmaster Flash, and Stevie himself contributed a few verses amidst a rather dubious dance routine! There's no denying that Stevie Wonder is a superstar in every sense of the word. After twenty-three years in the business, he still manages to conjure up that Wonder magic with ease.

During his concerts, he explained to his audiences his involvement in the movie soundtrack for *The Woman In Red*. Dionne Warwick, soul stylist and vocal mouthpiece for Burt Bacharach and Hal David's most sensitive of compositions, was responsible for introducing him to the film's director Gene Wilder. Originally Wilder wanted him to contribute two tracks to the project; Wonder ended up completing seven! At first, he was hesitant in accepting the offer because he felt the project would result in Motown and Berry Gordy 'trippin' out'. However, when Gordy was assured the soundtrack would carry the Motown logo, he agreed to Wonder's involvement. Another version was reported that concerned Jay Lasker, then Motown Records' president: when the singer played the soundtrack to him, he rejected it because he expected a tailor-made studio project. Wonder explained that *In Square Circle* had been delayed to enable him to complete the soundtrack, but Jay Lasker stood his ground. Only when Wonder later agreed to include the track 'I Just Called To Say I Love You' did Lasker agree to the release of *The Woman In Red*.

A singalong, instantly memorable ballad, befitting the pop rather than soul chart, 'I Just Called To Say I Love You' was the first single to be lifted from Wonder's self-penned and produced *The Woman In Red* album, released in August 1984, and a month later in Britain. The single entered the British chart at number three, the highest position to be registered by a Motown single in the chart on both sides of the Atlantic. During the first week of the ballad's British release it sold over 130,000 copies, becoming Motown's fastest-selling single and registering as one of the ten best-selling British singles of all time. It was Wonder's first solo British number one and his first American chart-topper since 1977 (with 'I Wish' and 'Sir Duke'). This success spread across the world. For example, in Canada the single sold in excess of 300,000 copies, earning the singer a triple-platinum single, the first ever awarded. On the single's promotional video Wonder sat at his piano singing his words of love into a phone mouthpiece, which looked somewhat ridiculous. His diehard fans howled in dismay: their hero had turned prissy and mainstream, with flowery, predictable lyrics set to a juvenile melody. Was this the end of Wonder's determined music with social attitudes? Had Stevie Wonder sold out to the white man? Only time would tell.

The HMV record store in London's Oxford Street sold five hundred copies of Wonder's *The Woman In Red* album on the first day of release, signifying the pulling power of the number one single. Critics were unanimous in their reviews – the soundtrack was a classic Stevie Wonder release. Apart from 'I Just Called To Say I Love You', there were other jewels like his duets with Dionne Warwick, 'It's You' with all the trademarks of the chart-topper, and the laid-back 'Weakness'. Warwick, however, took solo lead on 'Moments Aren't Moments', which suited her sophisticated styling and presentation. Lashings of funky grooves came with 'Love Light In Flight' which one critic noted 'cooks in a musical pot of bubblin' synths and creamy vocals', while Ralph Tee pointed out in his review that, 'As with most of Stevie's albums, not every track is a killer, but it's certainly one of his most consistent.' The music was packaged in a gatefold sleeve advertising the movie, with the two inner sleeves carrying lyrics and a colour shot of Wonder talking on the phone, sitting at his Wonderland studio control panel where the soundtrack was recorded with backing vocalists including Susaye Green, Motown signings Gene Van Buran and Finis Henderson, and Timothy Hardaway. A second picture of the singer surrounded by keyboards covered the back sleeve. Both were taken by Ron Slenzak.

The *Woman In Red* was a romantic farce, starring Gene Wilder,

Charles Grodin and Judith Ivey, and was based on the screenplay *Un Elephant Ça Trompe Enormement*. Wilder played a forty-year-old city public relations officer who becomes infatuated with a beautiful woman in a red dress whom he sees each morning on his way to work. Though faithfully married, he phones her for a date. The girl on the phone isn't the woman in red and the plot is set. The praise showered on the soundtrack album rather over-shadowed interest in the film itself but, unlike Wonder's previous soundtrack for *The Secret Life Of Plants*, at least this time the film and soundtrack were simultaneously available. The album passed platinum status in America at the same time as Diana Ross' RCA/Capitol album *Swept Away* earned a gold disc. 'I Just Called To Say I Love You' went on to win an American Academy Award for Best Original Song, and was nominated for both a Grammy and an Oscar. The latter's eligibility was jeopardised because the song was penned in 1977 and only compositions written during the year prior to the Oscar ceremony were eligible. Stevie Wonder told the Awards Board that although the song was partly composed seven years ago, he had written it especially for the movie *The Woman In Red*. His explanation was accepted and the 1985 Oscar was his.

Stevie Wonder dedicated his Oscar to the imprisoned black leader Nelson Mandela, and told the United Nations audience of his feelings regarding the new South African working policies:

> If it is so important to have black labourers living near the industrial centres, why must they be separated from their wives and children while living in a shack? If the black people of South Africa really do want to live together all in one place, then why have so many given their lives and others protested to avoid these great new settlement camps? The resettlement camps are wrong. If they're so great, why don't the whites want to live there?

As a result of his controversial speech, the South African Broadcasting Corporation announced an airtime ban on all his records. The ban had the reverse effect in much the same way as a similar ban was imposed on The Beatles' records twenty years earlier following John Lennon's remark that they were more popular than Jesus Christ. Indeed, the day after the SABC's announcement, independent radio stations reported extensive airplay of Wonder's music, with record shops reporting increased sales. The singer's increasing activities in the political arena were seen to be further indication of his plans to make a significant contribution in this field.

Meanwhile, the singer himself was fending off the American legal system, when he was sued for $10 million by Lee Garrett and Lloyd Chiate, who claimed 'I Just Called To Say I Love You' was their composition which they wrote during 1978 while staying with Stevie Wonder at Hollywood's Regency Hotel. Reputedly Wonder heard the duo rehearsing and was given a demo tape of the track. In reply to the allegation he said, 'My music and integrity speaks for itself.' In May 1986 the lawsuit was dropped with no case to answer when it was decided the only similarity was the title.

The deceptively lazy, mid-tempo 'Love Light In Flight' was the second single extracted from *The Woman In Red* during November 1984; it stalled in the British top fifty and peaked in the American top twenty early in 1985. This was followed by the self-explanatory 'Don't Drive Drunk' track, issued in America on 12″ single only in December and on 7″ and 12″ single in Britain, where it made it only to the top seventy. Interestingly, the singer wrote this song before agreeing to work on the movie soundtrack, after hearing television commercials warning of the horrors of car accidents. 'Don't Drive Drunk' was later featured in a video commissioned by RCA in Spain, a joint effort between the American Department of Trade and the Chrysler Corporation. The Spanish government flew a film crew to America to shoot the thirty-second commercial for television use. And the single's marketing in Britain coincided with the government's Christmas campaign to ban drink driving. Although it did not officially form part of the campaign, its topicality added weight to its release.

To capitalise on Stevie Wonder's chart-topping love theme, Motown/BMG issued a compilation of previously released material under the title *Love Songs – 16 Classic Hits*. The marketing tactic worked when this album, released only in Britain, reached the top twenty. While this album flourished, Chaka Khan took 'I Feel For You' to the pole position across the world, but there was more to the mighty single than met the ear. More than 21 years after its release, excerpts from 'Fingertips Part 2' were used in the song, although experts could not decipher whether it was lifted from the 1963 live single release or a 1965 live concert recording. When questioned, Chaka Khan's spokesperson was unable to confirm whether Wonder's work had been rifled but admitted that Khan's producer Arif Mardin could 'well have been up to something' because he had slapped in an original Charlie Parker solo on her 'Night In Tunisia'!

Motown/BMG wasn't the only company to cash in on Wonder's chart-topping success. Island Records didn't miss the opportunity to publicise the release of their signing, Nigerian juju mainman, Sunny Ade and his *Aura* album which included Stevie Wonder playing on the title track. Ade and Wonder first met at the 1977 FESTAC event and it was there that the two agreed to work together. However, career demands meant regular postpone-ments by both artists and it was only now that the album was ready for release.

Following television coverage of the horrendous scenes of starving and dying people in Ethiopia, The Boomtown Rats' lead singer Bob Geldof was moved to approach the cream of British recording artists to contribute to a single about the tragedy and dedicate all royalties to Ethiopia's plight. The single 'Do They Know It's Christmas?', written by Geldof and Midge Ure, was recorded at London's Sarm Studios and released by Mercury/Phonogram under the collective name of Band Aid. The British public flocked to buy it, and 'Do They Know It's Christmas?' became a 1984 Christmas number one and an international million seller.

The British project prompted singer Harry Belafonte to organise a similar recording session in America. Michael Jackson and Lionel Richie wrote 'We Are The World' for the project and Quincy Jones conducted and produced the session held at the A&M Records studio in Los Angeles during 1985. Following the British lead, more than 45 major artists contributed their time to take part in the recording, including Diana Ross, Tina Turner, Smokey Robinson, Bruce Springsteen, The Jacksons, Dionne Warwick, Ray

Charles and Stevie Wonder, who had in turn asked Eddie Murphy to join them. The comedian turned down the invitation. 'Rebuffing a beloved blind man and a children's charity in one stroke didn't help a public image that was already beginning to show feet of clay,' Frank Sanello reported. 'Murphy's reason was understandable. He feared that because of the critical lambasting his musical efforts had received, in the "We Are The World" video he'd be stuck in the back row with the likes of Sonny Bono and LaToya Jackson and told to sing quietly.' In fact, Eddie Murphy was at one time a Motown recording artist when 'the beloved blind man' wrote and produced, 'Everything's Coming Up Roses', a track for his *How Could It Be* album.

After the tense recording session for 'We Are The World'. Stevie Wonder lightened up the occasion by laughing, 'It gave me a chance to see Ray Charles again. We just sort of bumped into each other!' And when the session started to run over time, he quipped that if the song wasn't completed on the last take he or Ray Charles would drive everyone home! In actual fact Stevie Wonder had driven a car under supervision and also piloted a plane of all things, as he recalls: 'I've flown a plane from Chicago to New York and scared the hell out of everyone. There was a pilot and he let me handle this one thing and I said, "What's this?" and we went Whooooosh . . .'

'We Are The World' by USA For Africa, released by CBS Records in April 1985, repeated the British single's success. Wonder says, 'Millions of dollars were raised because there was a cry of many people, and I'm not saying this because I was involved.'

Inside Motown and flushed with the success of the *Somebody's Watching Me* album and single in 1984, Rockwell (Berry Gordy's son Kennedy) plunged into the world of rock/pop with his second album *Captured*. Unlike his debut project, which included Michael Jackson, there were no outside influences to sway the artist's musical intentions, except Stevie Wonder who added vocal support to the track 'He's A Cobra', the first extracted single. 'We were in the studio doing a rough mix of the song when Stevie was walking down the corridor, and he came in with the backing singers,' Rockwell explains. 'Originally I said "no" to his involvement because I thought people would say I couldn't make a record without a top star on it. I really didn't think I needed Stevie but in the end I was delighted when he joined in. Who wouldn't be?' Stevie or not, the single bombed; undeterred, Rockwell tried again a year later with the album *The Genie* but his recording career was over.

Harlem's Apollo Theater in New York was the home for black performers from 1935 until 1976, when it closed, another victim of Harlem's urban decline. In its heyday the Apollo was the stronghold for black music and many of Motown's acts performed there, or as youngsters had snuck into the theatre to watch their idols in action. Following a $10 million rehabilitation project, Inner City Broadcasting, NBC and Motown Productions brought the venue back to life with a gala concert that coincided with the theatre's fiftieth anniversary. The concert, with $100 tickets and a list of invited guests that ranged through New York and Harlem politicians, society names and music industry moguls, was screened on NBC during May 1985, with the proceeds earmarked for the Ethiopian Relief Fund.

The stage spectacular included American acts and British guests, such as Martha Reeves, The Four Tops, Patti LaBelle, Billy Preston, Luther Vandross, George Michael, Stevie Wonder and Boy George. Following his solo spot, Wonder performed with Boy George, who wrote in his autobiography, *Take It Like A Man*: 'I'd been asked to duet "Signed, Sealed, Delivered" with Stevie and another undecided song with Luther.' The British star took an early flight to New York in the hope of rehearsing with the two stars, but discovered Stevie Wonder was recording in Los Angeles and wouldn't arrive at the Apollo until the day of the gala. An extremely nervous singer was then summoned to Wonder's dressing room:

> Stevie was hammering away at a keyboard and grunted a quick hello in mock Cockney. I stood rigid, wondering if I'd have to practise in front of his entire entourage. He sang 'Signed, Sealed, Delivered'. Even raw he sounded brilliant. I hummed along not daring to sing out. Five minutes of rehearsal convinced me we should try another song. Stevie persisted, 'You can do it, you can do it.'

Following a managerial discussion, Boy George persuaded Wonder to sing 'Part-Time Lover'. Even that brought problems for the British singer: 'On stage my white suburban tones were drowned out by Stevie. I shuffled around awkwardly, thankful it wasn't talent night.'

Boy George also reported that he again suffered in Stevie Wonder's presence during the after-show dinner. With photographers swooping close, Wonder grabbed him by the throat: 'probably rewarding me for my performance . . . I was angry that he'd made me ridiculous for a second time, and wondered how he'd managed to aim so well. Bastard, I bet he can see.'

Diana Ross flew to the concert by helicopter in time for the finale – 'I Want To Know What Love Is' with the participating artists and the New Jersey Mass Choir. A tearful member of the audience told an American magazine: 'In the middle of so much despair in Harlem, the Apollo revival comes as a hope for us all.' Wonder, who performed 'Fingertips' at the theatre when he was a mere eleven-year-old, told *People* magazine: 'The Apollo was like my home after school and I would study backstage between shows.' *Motown Returns To The Apollo* won an Emmy Award for Best Variety Programme.

It was rumour time again, a ploy Motown had mastered to perfection by now, when details of a new album titled *In Square Circle* were leaked to the music press. Stevie Wonder himself added credence during a performance at the annual NARM convention, when he annnounced the album's tracks would include 'Broken Glass', 'The Land Of La La', 'Part-Time Lover', 'Go Home' and 'Trying To Find My Whereabouts'. He then performed them, playing solo with a selection of keyboards, following which he was presented with the Artist Of The Decade trophy by NARM and a Golden Note Award from ASCAP. During the interim period through July and August, Wonder's name cropped up on third-party recordings. For example he played harmonica on the Eurythmics' single 'There Must Be An Angel (Playing With My Heart)' and contributed his composition 'I Do Love You' to The Beach Boys' eponymous album. He had also contributed harmonica and the services of his band Wonderlove to 'Feel It', a single by the British group Feelabeelia, signed to

Quincy Jones' Qwest label. Plus he had worked again with Jean Carn. 'In the four years we've had the track I haven't been able to tie him down for long enough, and he's actually started on two more songs for me which he hasn't got round to finishing yet,' she told *Blues & Soul* magazine.

> He never gets sleepy and I've been in a studio with him where he has been for three days and nights. In fact, he brought engineers to the studio in shifts and they would literally fall out of their chairs . . . He would only allow me to leave the studio to go to the hotel to change and eat. Then I'd have to go back because he'd say, 'You're my inspiration and if this doesn't go right it will be your fault.

In Square Circle was finally ready for release in September 1985. To prove the project's existence, the bouncy, finger-popping 'Part-Time Lover', with a bass line snatched from Hall & Oates' 'Maneater', was extracted as the first single in August. And again it was the mainstream buyers who elevated the single to number three in the British chart and to the American pole position: his 26th top ten single on *Billboard* magazine's chart. As an added sales incentive Wonder remixed and extended the song to eight minutes' playing time. The 12″ version, with Luther Vandross on the introduction, was also issued on cassette.

A straightforward collection of familiar songs, *In Square Circle* was Wonder's first serious album for five years, since *Hotter Than July*. Featuring Syreeta, Deniece Williams and Luther Vandross as support vocalists, it shot into the top five in Britain and America, where it went on to sell in excess of two million copies. It also won a Grammy for Best R&B Vocal Performance – Male in 1986 and several American Music Awards for the singer including Favourite Male Artist in the Soul and R&B categories. Stevie Wonder tactfully said the project's delay was due to his other commitments: 'I'd been working a lot on making Martin Luther King's birthday a national holiday and was also working on *The Woman In Red* soundtrack, and it just took me a long time to get the songs I wanted together.' He had also moved to Beverly Hills, while his children and their mother remained in New York. Among other things, he had jammed at a local restaurant with Sting's jazz outfit; watched the NBA playoffs (he laughed, 'When I leave a basketball game, I hear people say things like "What's he doing here?" or "You and the referee saw the same game", but the laugh's on them because I got the best seats in the house just to hear the game!'); watched movies, usually, those starring Clint Eastwood and Gene Wilder, where a colleague described the film's action to him; and done a host of other everyday activities.

'Go Home' was the second culled single in 1985; it reached the British top seventy and American top ten three months later. Its follow-up was the bitter-sweet 'Overjoyed' a five-year-old instrumental to which Wonder added lyrics for inclusion on the album: 'I usually come up with the music first and then come up with an idea about the song. I sing out loud and change it right away if it sounds like there's too many words.' Many of his ideas, he stated, originated from news broadcasts, everyday life, and the world's injustices: 'Unfortunately, some of the things that are negative in the news keep happening. Man never seems to learn.' The single was a top thirty American hit and top twenty British entrant in 1986. His views on apartheid were once more strongly aired on the album's two-year-old track 'It's Wrong (Apartheid)', which he recorded with a gospelly, call-and-response sound to encourage people towards taking positive action: 'You know it's wrong, like slavery was wrong, like the Holocaust was wrong.' He had kept the demo of this song close at hand and finished it with synthesisers, several African instruments and a synclavier. 'I then did a sequence for the chorus and verses and on top of that I sampled the cora.' The song also reflected his feelings when he was arrested for disturbing the peace on 14 February 1985 during a non-violent protest outside the South African embassy in Washington DC. With others he was protesting against 'the barbaric policies of apartheid'.

The funk-slanted 'Stranger On The Shore of Love' and his reflective 'Never In Your Sun' gelled well with 'I Love You Too Much', a jazzy track with strong lyrics, and the Caribbean-influenced 'Go Home'. A complex 'Spiritual Walkers', dedicated to doorstep religious fanatics, held an outstanding bass rhythm and chorus, while 'Whereabouts' was a poignant balled in the 'Lately' mould. 'The album represents who I am in this decade,' Stevie Wonder told *USA Today*'s Craig Modderno, 'but it also represents what I'm seeing in a lot of situations with a lot of people . . . the theme is that life and love are beautiful, but people have to work at making things happen all the time.' The 'Land Of La La', an amusing satire about Los Angeles, sold abysmally and merely struggled into the American top ninety. In Britain the title was afforded Wonder's first release in the personalised series carrying the record number Wond1. A further album cut, 'Spiritual Walkers', was scheduled in America but not issued. On the British front, 'Stranger On The Shore Of Love' (Wond2) followed 'Land Of La La', giving Wonder a top sixty placing in 1987 and signifying the album's final single.

Written and produced by Wonder at Wonderland, the music was presented in a full-colour package, this time with a profusion of pictures, particularly in the four-paged lyric leaflet which also carried the singer's comments and notes. Against a purple and blue backdrop, and with a vinyl disc stuck in the black gritted ground, Wonder, with a moustache, sat open-handed, with his braided hair tied back. Many believed this picture showed him sitting on the surface of an uninhabited planet with the disc as his spaceship. A sepia picture of Wonder spanned the inside of the gatefold sleeve, while the back shot showed him sitting cross-legged, wearing black and surrounded by dead leaves. *In Square Circle* was dedicated to the late Marvin Gaye, with Wonder printing four lines of 'Lighting Up The Candles' in the leaflet; however, the song was omitted from the project.

At the time of the album's release, Motown announced that Stevie Wonder was the only American artist to have reached the pole position with a debut album (Elton John led the British contingent), and to have enjoyed seventeen American number one singles more than any other Motown act: The Temptations were second with ten (nine of those produced by Norman Whitfield). He also had more records on catalogue than any other Motown artist, and every one of his albums released since 1973 had reached the top ten in the American pop chart.

Stevie Wonder's name was also linked to a British project: he led a host of international names including Dionne Warwick and

Ashford & Simpson to record tracks for an album celebrating the British musical *Time*, the brainchild of Dave Clark (drummer with the sixties group Dave Clark Five, and owner of the cult Friday night music shows *Ready, Steady, Go!* and the Dusty Springfield-hosted *The Sound of Motown*). The first single from the album was Cliff Richard singing Wonder's song 'She's So Beautiful', which peaked in the British top twenty.

Diana Ross was midway through her British tour, Lionel Richie had released 'Say You Say Me' from the *White Nights* movie, and Stevie Wonder was active once more, taking part in possibly the largest live phone call in history. During an Al Jarreau concert in Portland, Oregon, his 2,000-strong audience phoned Wonder. The two-way conversation of songs and poetry lasted thirty minutes and was carried on the sound system at the Portland Meadows outdoor amphitheatre.

Dionne Warwick touched Stevie Wonder's life once more by presenting him with the Allen K Jonas Lifetime Achievement Award during a black-tie dinner at the Century Plaza Hotel, Los Angeles. Mayor Tom Bradley and Warwick agreed Wonder should be the recipient of this prestigious award for his musical, social and philanthropic contributions to the world.

If this year closed on a high note, then 1986 started in spectacular fashion for Stevie Wonder when his personal dream became a reality, and his professional nightmare began.

Chapter 14

CHARACTERS

'Stevie is very picky'

Grady Harrell

'I would like to think of myself as a unity mayor'

Stevie Wonder

'Stevie's birthday concert was a very special event'

Wembley spokesman

For the first time ever, Americans celebrated the observance of the late Dr Martin Luther King's birthday as a national holiday on 15 January 1986. With Stevie Wonder's determination and unfaltering, tireless lobbying of Congress, a majority vote passed the bill to recognise this day. Concerts were organised in most of America's major cities to mark this remarkable achievement. However, not all states agreed with Stevie Wonder. For example, Arizona still refused to acknowledge the public holiday, which had angered him sufficiently that he upheld his boycott and encouraged other acts to do the same. Also during January Stevie Wonder hosted a televised celebrity gala that included Diana Ross, Elizabeth Taylor, Quincy Jones, Eddie Murphy and others. Although this was a great stride forward for Black America, there was still a long way to go to fulfil King's dream.

After appearing with Lionel Richie on Neil Diamond's television spectacular, when he sang 'Castle Of Love' at the piano and indulged in a few comedy sketches that were as uninspiring as the show itself, Stevie Wonder was linked to Smokey Robinson's

181

Smoke Signals album released in January 1986 which saw Robinson at his commercial best. Wonder co-wrote the track 'Hold On To Your Love' while a further track, 'Be Kind To The Growing Mind', featured The Temptations as backing vocalists. Robinson, Richie and Wonder then went on to narrate the three volumes of *The Motown Story* project, scheduled for release that year.

On his own recording front, Stevie Wonder was also riding high, though this time for another record company, when he joined Dionne Warwick, Gladys Knight and Elton John to record 'That's What Friends Are For', an American number one single and a top twenty British hit. Written by Burt Bacharach and Carole Bayer Sager, the song was originally one of five written for the 1982 movie *Night Shift*, and was first recorded by Rod Stewart. The new version went on to win the 1987 Grammy in the Best Pop Performance By A Duo Or Group category, whereupon the three attending American singers performed the song with Burt Bacharach at the piano.

Taking respite from his studio work, Stevie Wonder sang for his supper . . . When Diana Ross divorced her first husband Robert Silberstein in 1976, he publicly aired his views about the marriage, including his frustration over his wife's devotion to Berry Gordy: 'She's totally dominated by a man who has never read a book in his life . . . I just can't stand it anymore to hear them calling Stevie Wonder a genius. Whatever happened to Freud?' Ross moved on to marry Arne Naess, Norwegian shipping magnate and Everest climber, in February 1986, and the ceremony took place in a tenth-century Swiss reformed church in Romainmotier, a small village outside Geneva. Some 240 guests attended the service. This was followed by a lavish reception at the Beau Rivage Palace Hotel in Lausanne, where, after a lunch of roast veal and chocolate wedding cake, Stevie Wonder sang 'I Just Called To Say I Love You'. (This marriage also ended in divorce.)

Throughout their careers the two Motown artists have worked and socialised together. Another instance was Diana Ross's 58th birthday celebrations in 2002, dubbed as the 'Boxing Party On The Beach'. In keeping with the theme of the occasion, boxing gloves were distributed as invitations. For this special occasion, Wonder sang 'Happy Birthday' – naturally!

To promote *In Square Circle* Stevie Wonder toured America. The travelling show hit New York's Madison Square Garden during September, when his two sold-out performances won him the Gold Ticket for ticket sales in excess of one hundred thousand. Journalist Mark Webster watched the New York show:

> Even sitting in the quarter full stadium an hour before the concert started, my thoughts were idling with many things, but as the stadium filled up people slop[ed] in from all sides and I realised that all roads led to Stevie Wonder. The stage itself was a cluster of keyboards with synth machines and Stevie's grand piano catching the light like a chandelier as it turned slowly to face all sides of the building. Further out into the auditorium, video screens brought all the far-flung corners of the stadium into the stage while a supreme quadrophonic sound system highlighted the elaborate sequencing techniques instigated by Stevie's drummer. But for all the array of modern technology, it was only Stevie that anyone wanted to see . . . and only his magical tunes that they wanted to hear . . . He sang twenty years of music as if it was the first time!

From music to business, and on Christmas Eve 1986 Wonder met Berry Gordy to discuss Motown's future. A dispirited Gordy explained he had no option but to sell the company. As the singer had previously persuaded him to abandon plans to sell Jobete, he thought he could do the same now. But the situation was grim; there was no other course to take. Gordy, however, assured Wonder that Motown's heritage would be rigidly protected, so a reluctant singer agreed that MCA Records could purchase Motown before the deadline date of 31 December. During the remaining few days, Berry Gordy changed his mind and, according to Syreeta, decided to invest his personal money into the company to keep it operating. It was a welcome breathing space.

As 'Stranger On The Shore Of Love' stalled in the British top sixty and with the American tour over, Stevie Wonder returned to his studio to work earnestly on his forthcoming album titled *Characters*, whose sales he hoped would help keep Motown afloat. The company was struggling through an extremely lean period. So much so that it slipped to eighth position on the 1987 listing of top labels in *Billboard* magazine, earning only two gold albums during the year. The company's British situation was no better. Established acts such as Stevie Wonder, Lionel Richie and The Temptations failed to repeat past achievements, and once again, success enjoyed by artists like Smokey Robinson was confined to America. Motown relied on these acts to produce hits in order to offset the enormous costs involved in breaking new names. Thankfully, the company still attracted a great deal of attention from the public and competitors because of its musical history, but everyone realised that if Motown fell, the nosedive would be more catastrophic than that experienced by any other company. Stevie Wonder also planned to promote his new project with lengthy American and European tours.

Instead of filtering news to the media, Motown's publicity machine was strangely secretive about the progress of *Characters*. In fact, it was the artist himself who confirmed the project was finished when, in March 1987, he was involved in a demonstration with Quincy Jones and Nile Rodgers. It was a unique audiovisual demonstration linking two studios, 3,000 miles apart, involving Wonder's new anti-crack song, 'Stop, Don't Pass Go'. During the demonstration, a two-way audio/visual satellite connected Rodgers at the MSA Studio in New York to Wonder and Quincy Jones at Wonderland in Los Angeles. This technological break-through was intended to underscore the capability for multi-city digital audio recording that would remove geographical barriers and enable artistic collaborations. With his love of innovative technology, an excited Wonder told the media:

> In the beginning of communications, it instinctively happened that the message, the rhythm and the spirit was carried through the drums of Africa, and now in the twentieth century, it must be said that man's desire to spread the same message, rhythm and spirit must be accommodated. At best, in this being the first bi-coastal simultaneous recording in history, it is appropriate in our civilisation that we communicate energies of positiveness to the young and a brighter future for all.

As a precaution, a reluctant Motown had prepared another compilation in case *Characters* failed to materialise in July. Titled *The Essential Stevie Wonder*, the low-price release with 39 tracks spanning 1962 to 1971 was issued in dull, desperate packaging in Britain. 'Although it's great to have an almost definitive Stevie Wonder collection up to and including *"Where I'm Coming From"*, fans will have the tracks already,' one critic wrote. 'Motown considers some tracks to be in demand, but are they really? Doubtless Stevie's original version of Aretha Franklin's 1974 hit "Until You Come Back To Me" will be of great interest.' But that interest wasn't sufficient to chart the album.

True to his word, Wonder had made plans for a British and European tour: his first major dates since 1984. The original itinerary for May 1987 was re-scheduled for August and September due to contractual obligations to complete *Characters*. In other words, Motown insisted the album be delivered before he left America. The new dates included several nights at London's Wembley Arena, and later at the NEC in Birmingham. With these dates behind him, Stevie Wonder intended to undergo neurological surgery to remove a neuroma on his index finger.

Prior to leaving America Stevie Wonder performed at a benefit staged in Los Angeles for retinitis pigmentosa, the degenerative eye disease that had so far affected 400,000 Americans. As Ted Hull, his private tutor, had also suffered from the disease, Stevie Wonder agreed to perform a ninety-minute set, which included 'Front Line', dedicated to Vietnam veterans, and 'I Just Called To Say I Love You'. Bypassing his funk favourites, he concentrated on ballads ranging from 'My Cherie Amour' to 'Overjoyed' and, to the dismay of his audience, performed without a live support group, preferring to use a programmed computer. He then duetted with Julio Iglesias on 'My Love' (a track on the crooner's current album) which went on to be released as a single in August 1988. The benefit's proceeds topped $1.5 million and went towards the Los Angeles research and care facility called Wonderland.

To coincide with the sold-out 1987 British dates, 'Skeletons' was culled as the first single from *Characters*. The track marked the singer's return to an urban groove and stemmed from a bass riff he was working on one afternoon: 'It just kinda fell out, kinda similar to when I did "Superstition".'

Before Stevie Wonder stepped out on the Wembley Arena stage, four large, suspended screens showed white-gloved hands clapping against a black background, encouraging the audience to do the same. Through the performance he hit several low points, but his older material saved the show. New York ghetto footage was shown during 'Living For The City' and the computer-programmed 'Skeletons' was the last song, which, bearing in mind its unpopularity, wasn't a wise choice for a finale. It was widely felt that the music relied too heavily on technical input with fans fearing that much of the artist's live visual excitement was lost through his insistence on using computers in the studio and later on stage. Despite onstage promotion, 'Skeletons' (which featured no musicians, only Robert Arbittier's computer and synthesiser programme), described by DJ Graham Gold as 'masterful, riff-laden and heavily percussive', made it no further than the British top sixty, but became an American top twenty hit and an R&B chart-topper.

During one of the Wembley performances, Stevie Wonder took an unpredictable step, requesting help from a member of his audience in transporting a newly recorded track from London to Los Angeles. Barry Betts from Reading acted as Wonder's courier the next day by flying first class to Los Angeles where he delivered the tape personally to Michael Jackson. The track in question was 'Get It', planned as a duet between Wonder and Jackson for inclusion on *Characters* but it was not finished in time for Jackson to add his vocals prior to the start of his own world tour. These were recorded on the tape in Japan, whereupon Quincy Jones produced it at the CBS Sony Studio in Tokyo.

So, what of *Characters* itself? Released simultaneously in America and Britain during November 1987, it was a project blighted from its conception. The album contained ten tracks, with two extra titles – 'Come Let Me Make Your Love Come Down' and 'My Eyes Don't Cry' on the cassette and CD formats, a marketing ploy that annoyed vinyl buyers despite Wonder promising they would later be released as future B-sides. By adding this incentive, Motown, in keeping with other record companies, was trying to encourage the public to move into the new and more lucrative CD market as vinyl was becoming too expensive to use. Record companies eventually got their own way, pricing CDs at extortionate levels. In time, the public tired of constant over-pricing and sales slowly declined. By 2001 albums and 12″ singles were big business once again, slicing away a huge chunk of the CD market. The price of vinyl was no longer in question.

Characters was dubbed Stevie Wonder's 'concept album'; the artist explained his intentions: 'It's about many characters, politics and relationships, and I'm excited about the whole project. The album comes in two parts. Twelve songs now and more in a few months' time . . . Some of the songs are about ten years old, but most of them are recent. When you listen to it you'll find out things about me and things about yourselves.'

Written, arranged and produced by Stevie Wonder, the project was mostly recorded at Wonderland, with additional work completed in Los Angeles. 'You Will Know', a typical Wonder ballad and future single, was one of his personal favourites. Another was 'Dark 'N' Lovely', with lyrics by Gary Byrd, who said: 'It's about a people who live on Earth's motherland in the southern part of Africa . . . We deal with the regime of apartheid and that it's still a major struggle that we have yet to see the end to. We deal with the reasons why these people are oppressed [because] no one should be oppressed.' Redolent of sixties Motown, 'In Your Corner', complete with the shrill cat calls and saxophone break, was a pleasant distraction from the density of other tracks, and gelled easily with the moody, broody ballad 'With Each Beat Of My Heart' later considered to be the project's high spot. British singer Junior added vocal support, and blues guitarist B B King enjoyed a solo spot on 'One Of A Kind', a lively song with a light-hearted atmosphere. Michael Jackson was a strange choice of duettist for Wonder, and 'Get It' proved that. Classed by many as a sequel to Jackson's own 1983 hit 'Beat It', it was ruined, according to critics, by his irritating squeals and sighs, which he believed to be his trademark. In time, Michael Jackson's career was destined to plummet as quickly as it had ascended, but for reasons other than his music.

The static and samey 'Galaxy Paradise' was considered to be the album's low spot, whereas 'Cryin' Through The Night' carried the hallmarks of a Wonder standard, with catchy backing vocals and instant chorus. The final track, 'Free', recorded at the Westside Studios in London in between his city dates, offered a change of style as the clavichord, spinet and acoustic guitar produced an atmospheric feel, with a haunting sound that built into a cavalcade of voices. The two add-on songs were confusingly different. 'Come Let Me Make Your Love Come Down' was jumbled and bitty, tentatively held together by a solid riff, as Wonder growled his way through the maze that led nowhere, and 'My Eyes Don't Cry', although lacking that positive melodic path, was saved by Wonder's crafting of memorable hooklines.

The front picture on the gatefold sleeve showed the singer dressed in red and black, holding an embossed mask on a stick, against a backdrop of sculptures by Willa Shalit on a shelf that continued across the back cover where the embossed mask was the only raised sculpture. For the inner sleeve picture, Wonder, dressed in blue and sitting with a mask in his hand, was surrounded by other sculptured heads. This was rather uncomfortable to look at because most of the sculptures were eyeless. Song lyrics were printed around the album's inner bag, signed off by Stevland Morris's thumbprint. Trawling through the credits observers noticed two new names: Melody and Mumtaz.

An excited Jheryl Busby, Motown's new president, gushed. 'I believe in my heart that this album is his most inspired of the past ten years. We're going to stay with this, because we believe in it and because we want to see the album continue to live up to its acclaim.' True to the president's word, *Characters* was another distinguished seller, reaching the American top twenty, later passing platinum sales, and the British top forty, indicating perhaps that fans there were becoming less supportive of his musical crusades.

Unlike previous work, particularly *Songs In The Key Of Life* and *Innervisions*, *Characters* was felt by many to be a disappointing project, one of his regurgitated political and religious statements, and music that was saturated in technological programming. British journalist Jonathan King elaborated: 'I think the reason for his popular collapse is simple. He is enormously talented. But his real gift – pure, exuberant soul, so magnificent on "Fingertips" – has been replaced by cold, calculated technology.' Stevie Wonder replied that the album was unique, *because* of the technology and the way it was used:

> The Synclavier is a very current, [and] a very much used instrument in a lot of today's music. So too is the Fairlight, and other such synthesisers and computers which have become the marriage of technology of computer, keyboards and synthesisers. The way we use it, I feel, is very unique and that uniqueness will be heard on [the album].

While *Characters* was being recorded, Motown's chief executive Lee Young had spent time at Wonderland, when Wonder explained to him the symbolic meanings of the tracks as they were created. Young recognised a connection between the aural and visual music and suggested a television concept to the American music channel MTV. At the same time, Wonder's own video production unit was developing ideas designed to capture *Characters* on film. Carmen Efferson, president of Third Eye Films, explained: '[Stevie] wanted the impossible, something no one had seen on television before, and he wanted it in three months . . . MTV was thrilled with the chance to work with him because he's a performer of legendary proportions, and his music is so rich in imagery that it translates effortlessly to the screen.' Joining Wonder on this musical trip were Stevie Ray Vaughan, Jody Watley, Salt-N-Pepa and Motown signings Georgio and Brownmark. 'It started as Stevie's album listening party, but turned into a televised event,' said Lee Young. 'In fact, it was the biggest gathering of characters we'd ever seen.' The ambitious hour-long television special (which also debuted a new track 'In The Business' destined for *Characters II*) was screened at peak viewing time on 27 April 1988: the first of its kind aired on MTV.

With 1988 opening to disappointing mainstream sales of 'You Will Know', described by Graham Gold as 'typical Wonder wisdom put together over a gentle plodding rhythm, touching on the plights of drug addiction and single parent families', Stevie

Wonder knew he needed a musical rethink, and British critics believed his work should take on a lighter vein because fans wouldn't accept a future dominated by his continuing self-indulgence and consuming passion for computerised music.

Meanwhile, all credit to Motown in its perseverance in promoting tracks from *Characters*. No one was really prepared though for the poor public reaction to 'Get It', Wonder's much-publicised duet with Michael Jackson. In spite of the huge selling power of two international artists, the single struggled to reach the American top eighty during May 1988. British sales were better, with a top forty entry. Within the month, Stevie Wonder's duet with Julio Iglesias, titled 'My Love' was issued by CBS Records to flounder in the American top eighty, marking his final hit of the decade. In Britain it soared into the top ten, proving once more that mainstream music buyers had come to the rescue, but leaving Wonder's true fans disgusted with what they considered to be 'an unthinkable musical combination'.

Stevie Wonder tried to redeem himself when, in June he contributed to 'Nelson Mandela's 70th Birthday Tribute' staged at London's Wembley Stadium. Unfortunately, his act was blighted when his computer programme was stolen, which necessitated him revamping his act and which, in turn, meant the time allocated for his performance was ticking away behind scenes. When he requested extra time to perform a decent set, two of his co-acts Whitney Houston and Dire Straits reputedly refused to sacrifice one song each from their sets. Consequently his performance was short and somewhat shoddy. Disbelieving members of the audience openly cried when he was prematurely taken off the stage and reviewers were quick to highlight the circumstances behind Wonder's performance.

On his return to America, the month got worse for Stevie Wonder. For two years Berry Gordy had kept Motown financially afloat. Several major artists had defected to other companies, leaving Stevie Wonder, Lionel Richie and Smokey Robinson as the Motown prime sellers, even though their sales were erratic. And since returning to Motown, even The Four Tops and The Temptations failed to recapture past successes. The *New York Times* reported that Motown's annual turnover had nosedived from $100 million to $20 million and that at least half of that revenue had been generated from repackaging old material. During these two years Gordy had juggled offers from other companies including Virgin Records and, of course, the patient MCA Records, who had remained keen to conclude their original interest. By this time MCA Records had teamed up with Boston Ventures, an investment conglomerate, who offered eighty per cent of the asking price of $61 million and had also agreed to Gordy's contractual demands.

On 29 June 1988 the Motown name, its record catalogues and artist contracts were sold. Jobete, Stone Diamond, and the film and television operations were not part of the deal. 'He put his own personal money into Motown to try and save it because he felt a responsibility to us, to all the artists who were there,' Syreeta explained at the time. 'Nobody wants to put their baby out. It's like a father giving his daughter away in marriage, he knows he still has the connection but there's something there that's a little uncomfortable.' She also realised her days with the company were numbered and with typical frankness she said:

> When Mr Gordy sold Motown the new regime didn't want the likes of 'With You I'm Born Again', they went for a younger market. I'm not old by any means, but I'm not your teenybopper . . . we knew it just wasn't a thing that would work. I don't want to be moulded into something I'm not. I mean, I fought for my identity and freedom for a number of years so I certainly didn't want to be anywhere where they're going to put me in clothes that are slit from my toes up to my neck and where I'm not wearing underclothes because it's fashionable. That's not me.

As for Stevie Wonder, he made no public comment about the sale, preferring to adopt the 'business as usual' stance by previewing his pending American tour with sell-out dates at New York's Radio City Music Hall. He was then advised that, with The Rolling Stones, Otis Redding, Dion, Phil Spector, Bessie Smith and The Temptations, he would be inducted into the Rock and Roll Hall Of Fame in January 1989. At the fourth annual ceremony, Wonder attended with his children Keita and Aisha, and their mother

Yolanda Simmons, while The Temptations, with the line-up of David Ruffin, Otis Williams, Melvin Franklin, Eddie Kendricks and Dennis Edwards, stunned the audience with a resounding version of 'My Girl', one of their immortal singles.

'Free' was the only single released in 1989 and was a top fifty British hit. *Echoes* magazine's reviewer wrote: 'I don't understand why I'm reviewing a 1987 single. Have I missed something?' What he missed in actual fact was Stevie Wonder's inability to deliver his new album to Motown before embarking on a sold-out European tour. Or perhaps, as some suggested, the artist was showing his disappointment at the change in Motown's ownership by deliberately not delivering his next project on time.

Whatever the reason, Stevie Wonder was far from idle: his name cropped up as producer of two tracks on the new album *Come Play With Me* by RCA Records artist, Grady Harrell. And like artists before him, especially Jean Carn, Grady was astonished at his working schedule: 'Stevie is very picky, he's great and crazy at the same time, and working with him was a lot of fun. The amazing thing is that Stevie will work all night – we were falling asleep at the control board and at 7 a.m. he'll want you to do lead vocals. He'll go in and do a reference vocal at that time of the morning and sound like an angel.' A former employee also comments on Wonder's working practices: 'He plays his instruments all night. He eats when he wants and he sleeps when he wants. It's always dark to him, so he don't know breakfast from lunch and dinner.'

He also flew to Japan to sing at the popular Tokyo Song Festival and for the occasion composed the song 'Parents Of The World', the proceeds from which were donated to UNICEF. 'UNICEF is working to inoculate two million children in the Third World against disease and I feel that artists have the opportunity to do something in our own way to help situations like that,' Wonder told reporters. 'In the Western world we have a responsibility to communicate positively to those less fortunate.' He spoke further on the subject during a press conference held in Amsterdam at the start of his sold-out European tour, when he publicised his forthcoming involvement in a star-studded concert to be staged at the Hippodrome De Vincennes, Paris, during June in aid of the United Nations Children's Fund, with the proceeds earmarked for the Third World. Joining him were Elvis Costello, Tracy Chapman, George Michael, Bob Dylan and others; the midday to midnight concert was the city's largest rock gala, which also marked part of the French Revolution bicentenary celebrations. The gala was to be transmitted to fifty countries.

During the same conference Wonder also announced his intention to run for mayor in Detroit. Having been given the keys of the city on 24 December 1984, he felt he stood a good chance of being elected. He wouldn't run as a musician but as a caring, political figure: 'I feel that God has an even bigger plan for me, and I would like to move to the plan. I would like to think of myself as a unity mayor.' He could, he added, give something back to Detroit by stamping out the city's drug culture and solving the breakdown of family structures, something others had failed to do.

British dates throughout May 1989 kicked in with seven dates at London's Wembley Arena, and two each in Edinburgh and Birmingham. The tour coincided with Stevie Wonder's 39th birthday on 14 May. Most of the dates were sold out, but in Glasgow's SECC members of the audience left the theatre after one hour complaining of the terrible sound system. It was 25 years since Wonder, who now sported a ponytail, an untidy moustache and obligatory sunglasses, had performed in the Scottish city. The earlier performance was one he remembered well because someone had stolen his jacket. 'And it's long overdue,' he teased his audience. 'The last time I was here was with the Motown Revue and this man came into the dressing room and said, "I think you need your cleaning done." So I gave him my jacket and said, "You'll bring it back won't you?" Maybe he'll bring it back today!'

To cash in on the tour, Motown released 'The Collection', a shrink-wrapped eleven-CD box set (including three double sets) on Stevie Wonder's birthday. A special limited edition of five hundred, with each box containing an individual allocated number, covered his career to the present time. Box set number one was presented to the artist during his stay in Britain. The contents were: *Music Of My Mind, Talking Book, Innervisions, Fulfillingness' First Finale, Songs In The Key Of Life, Stevie Wonder's Journey Through The Secret Life Of Plants, Hotter Than*

July, *The Woman In Red*, *In Square Circle*, *Characters* and *The Essential Stevie Wonder*.

For his London shows, the Wembley Arena stage had been modified to represent Africa, the Black Continent. Stevie Wonder's guitarists and keyboard players stood in the Western Sahara region; his backing vocalists (Kimberley Brewer, Bridget Ryan and Keith John, who escorted the singer around the stage) stood from Zambia to South Africa, and the percussionists were placed in Libya. Wonder, with another smaller map lying across his grand piano, was stationed in the Southern Chad area in the middle of the stage, which slowly revolved during the performance. Spotlights encircled Wonder throughout, and searchlights danced at random. The sound system was reasonable and numerous cameras fed the giant video screens, now an obligatory fixture at his concerts because of the huge scale of the venues in which he performed.

For three hours Stevie Wonder wove his musical web through thirty years of legendary music. It was a familiar, welcoming and addictive evening. Wonder's endearing love and respect for his audience was capped by his sense of humour, particularly when he joked around using a British accent. In unashamed high spirits, the Motown star and his musicians encouraged the audience to join in the party atmosphere, which included him jumping on his piano stool and cavorting around the stage. It was an evening of non-stop celebration.

It was hailed the 'gig of the year' when his surprise guests, Chaka Khan, Billy Ocean, Paul Young, Cyndi Lauper and Aswad crept on to the stage as Stevie rounded off the marathon show. Khan grabbed his hand and burst into the traditional 'Happy Birthday'; the 10,000-strong audience gasped in amazement as three burly security men staggered on stage with a massive birthday cake in the shape of a baby grand piano. Weighing five stone, measuring five foot, made in Harrow, Middlesex, the keyboard had individually carved ivory and black keys, with a songsheet that carried the notes to 'Happy Birthday', while the lid was raised to reveal the words 'Happy Birthday Stevie'. The cake was later donated to a children's home.

A delighted birthday boy told his audience: 'Thank you all for giving me this incredible treat, I'm lost for words . . . I just like celebrating my birthday, and if I am touring at the time, I like to share it with the public.'

Among his presents was a £10,000 gift from the management of Wembley Arena. As the show over-ran by one and a-half hours, he had expected to be billed for the additional costs for staff, lighting, security and so on. But a Wembley spokesman announced: 'Stevie's birthday concert was a very special event and we don't want to spoil it by asking him to pay for the over-run. It was one big party and we are happy to let him have the time free!' Wonder's manager, Rod McGrew replied, 'On behalf of Stevie we are extremely grateful that Wembley should see fit to waive these charges in the spirit of celebrating a very special day in the life of Stevie Wonder by giving the gift of time.'

When the singer had finally left the stage and a reluctant audience had wound their way through the Arena to start their journey homewards, a party was held backstage in Wembley's Silver Mint Room, renamed the 'Birthday Bar' and decorated in party fashion, with food, drinks and a disco unit. The festivities ended at three in the morning. When his guests had left, Wonder played a cassette featuring birthday messages from Motown artists and staff and read his birthday cards, which all carried Braille inscriptions.

The birthday celebrations were screened by BBC-TV on two consecutive Saturday nights, 29 July and 5 August 1989, spanning a combined two hours. The BBC had been offered the opportunity of filming the performance after Wonder's management had watched the 'Behind The Beat' productions of concerts by Luther Vandross and Alexander O'Neal. Terry Jervis, the series producer, agreed to film the concert with just five days' notice. As Wonder's management wanted to keep the filming a secret from him to surprise him later, Jervis had the difficult task of working around the singer, whose hearing is so acute that any alien noise is immediately noticed. The task was completed without a hitch, other than Wonder saying after the birthday show, 'I feel so good about tonight, we should have recorded it!'

As the following day, Sunday, was Mother's Day in America, Stevie Wonder presented all the women involved in his tour with a gift: each of the thirty women was ushered into his Wembley dressing room, where he presented a bouquet to each, saying 'every woman is symbolic of motherhood'. As to his own life at this time, his relationship with Yolanda Simmons, mother of his two children Keita and Aisha, had ended, and his new partner, Melody McCully, had given birth to his son Mumtaz, first acknowledged in the sleeve notes of the *Characters* album. 'There's nothing I won't share with my children or their mothers,' Stevie said at the time. 'But I am not engaged and have no plans to marry.'

He also spoke to the press about a new eye transplant operation. Animal transplant experiments were rife at the time, despite desperate worldwide campaigns to stop the inhumane practices Stevie Wonder had offered himself as a human guinea pig for a new eye transplant operation that had been successfully carried out on animals and that he described as a radical technique that doctors believed was very close to becoming a reality. He told the *Sun*'s reporter Andy Coulson that he'd never given up the hope of being able to see:

'I was born prematurely and given too much oxygen in the incubator, which led to rogue tissue growing behind my eyeballs. Seeing has always seemed an impossible dream but thanks to advances in technology what was once impossible now seems possible. My doctors say that experiments including transplanting the eyes of different animals show promising results. Ultimately they believe this kind of experiment will lead to blind people having eye transplants that will make them see again.'

Despite mixed feelings about acting as a guinea pig in the first human experiments, Wonder believed it to be the biggest challenge of his life: 'I've been blind a long time and learned to cope with it. But the thought of being able to see always haunts me.'

Rolf Black, dean of the London Institute of Ophthalmology, was less optimistic: 'Transplant tests on reptiles have worked. However the human eye is very different but we hope full transplants will eventually be successful.'

While in Britain, Stevie Wonder appeared on Terry Wogan's BBC-TV chat show. Not a wise move. 'A dreadfully boring interview,' one reviewer wrote. When the enthusiasic studio audience welcomed the Motown star, he couldn't stop himself quipping, 'Maybe they think I'm Eddie Murphy!' Then, to relieve Terry Wogan's tedious questions, the singer's mother, Lula Mae, joined the show via a satellite link. Wonder also played hookey with his immediate entourage to explore London, soaking up the atmosphere and mingling with the public. One such adventure took them to Holloway, north London, where in the restuarant area of the Sea Chef, the singer and his party ate fish and chip suppers at £2.45 a time. The restaurant was actually reopened for two hours to allow them to eat in comfort, while fans packed the takeaway section of the shop to catch a glimpse of the star. The shop's proud owner Mustafa Caser remarked, 'Stevie said he was crazy about English fish and chips because of the batter.'

From Britain, Stevie Wonder took his show, supported by a team of one hundred people and twelve equipment trucks, through Europe and into Poland, Hungary and Czechoslovakia, making him the first Motown artist ever to perform in Eastern Bloc countries and the first to release an album (*Characters*) there. His initial performance at Czechoslovakia's Sparta Praha football stadium left 10,000 tickets unsold because the £11 ticket price was too expensive for his fans, but the Bratislava concert was a 40,000 sell-out show. 'I really was surprised,' the thrilled singer said. 'People actually knew my songs. I mean, they knew the words. I don't know if they understood them but I was very excited just knowing that they were familiar with my music.'

With record sales estimated at fifty million, a lucrative recording deal and money earned from touring, plus other business ventures and investments, it came as a surprise when Stevie Wonder began composing television commercials. He was, of course, accused of 'selling out' by certain quarters of the music business, but as he openly admitted to David Nathan: 'It's a lot more lucrative than a lot of other things I could do! I've sold out for money. And besides I had to do something while Michael Jackson was doing all the music and cleaning up with his record sales!' On a more serious level, he said: 'I have a policy with my attorney. He does the best he can with the business and the handling of money, and I do the best to deliver the goods.' On a daily basis, Stevie Wonder appeared to care little about money. By and large what he earned was ploughed into his music, staff salaries, his companies, and securing his family's future. Even with expert guidance he had been known to bail out his own business ventures with personal money. And, of course, his generosity to others also strained his resources.

At this point in his career, Stevie Wonder was also a heavyweight international name, with all the trappings of that status. He was a leader of his race, whether he liked it or not, and harboured plans to enter the political arena. Stepping into the next decade, he had achieved more with his music than most did in a lifetime. It was a daunting position for any individual to be in, yet for Stevie Wonder it was stimulating and challenging.

Chapter   15

GOTTA HAVE YOU

'Where was Stevie Wonder when David Ruffin needed him?'
quoted by Tony Turner

'I begged and begged [Stevie] to write something for me'
Diana Ross

'I feel there will never be an award great enough to give him'
Stevie Wonder speaking about Ray Charles

The next decade saw Stevie Wonder's recording schedules shot to pieces and his public appearances and guestings restricted. Sure, he started 1990 in fine fettle, with many high-profile activities but these petered off as the new decade got under way. His work with other artists continued but his later public appearances were confined to performing with others or at special functions. At the start of 1990 he was said to be formulating ideas for future projects, knowing that his musical style needed overhauling in the light of criticism aimed at his last album, *Characters*. Meanwhile, his back catalogue continued to sell at a steady pace, although his early work remained the most saleable.

Motown was celebrating again: this time the occasion was its thirtieth anniversary although compared to other years 1990 was relatively low-key. The company was minus Berry Gordy and its future dreams had yet to be realised. So this was a time of reflection and planning, of staff changes and office relocations. What a way to treat Motown, bewildered fans sighed. Had the death knoll been chimed? Certainly, it now seemed so, but in time the company would rise again thanks to a handful of well-chosen acts and, of course, its lucrative back catalogue.

During this period Stevie Wonder concentrated on benefit work by playing at the Great Western Forum to raise money for inner city education, and in New York where the proceeds were earmarked to help the homeless. When Paul McCartney was honoured with a Lifetime Achievement at the 1990 Grammy Awards, Wonder sang The Beatles' (and now his own) classic 'We Can Work It Out'. With Bonnie Raitt and Jackson Browne he sang a version of 'Amazing Grace' at the graveside service for Stevie Ray Vaughan when the blues guitarist was laid to rest in Dallas during August. An overflow crowd of one thousand mourned Vaughan, who had died in a helicopter crash in Wisconsin following a concert with Robert Cray and Eric Clapton.

Meanwhile, Whitney Houston, who had clashed with Stevie Wonder at Nelson Mandela's seventieth birthday celebrations in London, released her third album, *I'm Your Baby Tonight*. In an extraordinary career, she had become a multi-million-selling singer and performer thanks to the guidance of Artista Records founder Clive Davis. Like Berry Gordy before him, Davis groomed his singers into stars. He worked the same spell with Houston with help, of course, from her family, including her mother Cissy and aunt Dionne Warwick. Her previous work had attracted mixed reviews because critics felt she had dismissed her gospel upbringing to aim her music at the lucrative white audience. So, in an attempt to reclaim a footing in the black market with *I'm Your Baby Tonight*, she asked Stevie Wonder (whom she claimed was her lifelong idol) to produce one track, 'We Didn't Know'; the album's title song was produced by L A Reid and Babyface. Houston's ploy worked this time, but, according to soul fans, her subsequent work deteriorated rapidly. She had swapped the microphone for a film set, carving a niche as a credible actress, particularly with Kevin Costner in *The Bodyguard* (a film once offered to Diana Ross), but the strain of her professional and personal life took its toll, and she later turned to drugs for solace.

During the autumn Whitney Houston presented Stevie Wonder with the Carousel of Hope Award on behalf of the Children's Diabetes Foundation at a benefit held at the Beverly Hilton Hotel,

Los Angeles. He also received the Honorary Global Founder's Award for 'Don't Drive Drunk' from the Recording Artists Against Drunk Driving organisation. He then flew to Tokyo, Japan for two sold-out concerts.

In Britain writer/producer Ian Levine had opened Motorcity Records in tribute to Motown Records in Detroit. Levine's aim was to sign as many ex-company acts as he could. Syreeta was one. Now known as Mrs Torrence Mathis, she had written 'Searching For My Freedom' of which she said, 'The song has a heavy statement but Stevie used to write about heavy things, and he made the music work so that no one felt heavy about what he was saying.' Regrettably, success still eluded her.

After spending the first two months of 1991 in the studio working on his new album, now given the title *Conversation Pieces*, Stevie Wonder was commissioned by producer Spike Lee to compose the music to his forthcoming film *Jungle Fever*. Abandoning his own album, Wonder concentrated on the soundtrack at Wonderland, where he had a rough version of the film for guidance. 'If songs can touch the heart and pictures can tell a story,' he said, 'then maybe someday it will be said that the merging of both visions inspired people to reflect upon where we are, and dare to move this world forward making life a better place for everyone.' Working day and night, he completed the *Jungle Fever* project in time for its movie première in New York during June 1991, and two months later in London. Starring Wesley Snipes, Samuel L Jackson and Annabella Sciorra, the Universal Pictures film was typical of Spike Lee and his hard-hitting, no-nonsense approach to topical subjects such as mixed relationships. It was also his first 'crossover' film in Britain. Many critics believed the soundtrack was superior to the film itself, with Wonder's album appealing to fans of seventies music. The singer promoted the British release of the soundtrack by hosting a press conference in London's Pall Mall. With his hair in a ponytail and sporting a close-shaven beard, he performed a selection of songs at the piano for the selected members of the media.

The seventeen-year-old 'Fun Day' started the musical adventure both as an album track and single in September 1991. Perhaps surprisingly, the upbeat, singalong track, with a happy funk feeling did not make it beyond the British top seventy. In America it was the soundtrack's second culled single, and it bombed there too. (The first was 'Gotta Have You' which crawled into the top one hundred. Britain bypassed the release. As an album track 'Fun Day' led into 'Queen In The Black', a stimulating funk-edged track with acoustic guitar interludes. This, and the sensitive 'These Three Words' and 'If She Breaks Your Heart' – a light-weight song – were considered the album's high spots. On the other hand, 'I Go Sailing', wistful and reflective, and 'Each Other's Throat', a predictable stormer with a Wonder rap, were dismissed as album fillers and/or 'add-ons' which, of course, seemed understandable given the time available to Wonder to deliver the project. 'Chemical Love', already the subject of a video filmed at Hale House in Harlem, where babies born with HIV or addicted to drugs were treated, was a strongly worded song, with lyrics by Stephanie Andrews. And, at long last, 'Lighting Up The Candles', the song Stevie Wonder composed for the late Marvin Gaye, closed the album in a gentle and optimistic way.

Spike Lee had meticulously described his movie to Wonder, prompting the latter to write in the CD's notes: 'I was able to see this picture well enough to write the songs, even though [Spike] gave me the rough version in black and white . . . my ability to have been able to see this film so vividly without eyes could not have been done without him.'

Packaged in a multicoloured front sleeve of red, blue and green, with a black drawing of the singer rising from a high-rise skyline, the CD version carried a six-page booklet, crammed with lyrics and credits, while the black back cover held the track listing.

Music From The Movie 'Jungle Fever' peaked in the British top sixty in June 1991 and the American top thirty a month later. It was later replaced at the top of the R&B chart by Motown's new signing, Boyz II Men, with their *Cooleyhigh Harmony* album.

On the day the American première of *Jungle Fever* on 1 June, ex-Temptation and long-time drug user David Ruffin was found dead in a crack house. His body was driven in a limousine to the University of Pennsylvania Hospital, before being returned to Detroit. As there was no money available for a casket, an

Atlanta-based company (which had made Dr Martin Luther King's coffin) donated one. Michael Jackson paid for the funeral itself held at Detroit's New Bethal Baptish Church on Franklin Boulevard, newly named in honour of the Reverend Franklin and his daughters. Stevie Wonder joined Ruffin's family, friends and fans, and Motown colleagues who included The Four Tops, The Temptations, Martha Reeves and Mary Wilson, for a service that reached fever pitch, as author Tony Turner reported in his book *Lead Us Not Into Temptation*:

> 'By the time Stevie Wonder stood at the podium, the mass hysteria was reaching a peak. He sang a song that he announced was from his latest album – an outpouring of love for David. He sang it so fabulously, with only acoustical accompaniment that you could have heard a pin drop, and as soon as he was finished with this incredible wailing the congregation automatically rose to its feet and clapped. You would never have believed that this was a church, and that someone was being buried. I heard someone to my left mutter – 'Where was Stevie Wonder when David Ruffin needed him? David could have definitely used Stevie to write and produce a record on him.'

As Wonder sang, the lid to the coffin was closed. Motown had lost another artist and Stevie Wonder mourned another friend. With Dionne Warwick and Gladys Knight, he later performed at a Los Angeles benefit organised for the Ruffin family.

Stevie Wonder's early opinions on drug-taking remained unchanged. He faced it head-on at Motown and had accepted there was an active drug culture through all walks of life, particularly among people trying to cope with or obliterate periods of their lives because 'It's a better space for them to be in', he said. 'But there are people who haven't been through a private hell and they're into drugs.' He admits to once using marijuana to discover its effects: 'I was with a group of people that were very honest and not jiving about. They said, "Let's check this out." And I didn't like the experience of it. I was very paranoid, the music started getting louder and my mind said, "This is a drag." I didn't like it.'

While his own work struggled, Stevie Wonder injected a new lease of life into the career of Diana Ross. Following a shaky patch, she had returned to Motown as an equity partner, company governor and recording artist. When her RCA Records contract expired in 1989, she welcomed the new decade with an album titled *The Force Behind The Power*. Released in September 1991, her 58th album re-established her as the world's highest-selling songstress. Ross worked with three of the most sought after writer/producers – Peter Asher, James Carmichael and her friend Stevie Wonder. 'I wanted different sounds on the album [and] I thought these contrasting sounds would give it a unique texture,' she explained at the time. 'Over the years my relationship with Stevie has grown and blossomed. I respect his songwriting so much, I begged and begged him to write something for me. He finally did. It was a terrific song, "The Force Behind The Power". There's a tremendous message in that song and I believe that it will last for ever in my career and in my heart.' This track was so important to her that she named the whole project after it, abandoning the original title 'Change Of Heart'. Stevie Wonder also produced another track, 'Blame It On The Sun', written with Syreeta, which Ross had also wanted to record for some time. *The Force Behind The Power* and its spin-off singles, including 'When You Tell Me That You Love Me', returned Diana Ross to her rightful number one position and laid the foundation for her thirtieth anniversary celebrations in the music business during 1993.

The year 1991 saw Stevie Wonder receive several high-ranking awards. For instance, he collected the Diamond Award for Excellence at the first Celebration of African American Music Month held in Philadelphia. Then he received the Nelson Mandela Courage Award. Of his guestings this year, the most significant were singing 'These Three Words' on a CBS-TV special *Party For Richard Pryor*, and on Fox-TV's *Ray Charles: 50 Years In Music* where he sang 'Hallelujah I Love Her So' before duetting with Charles on 'Living For The City'. 'He has opened the door to so many hearts and has made the bridge possible in the gap that was between many different kinds of music,' Wonder said of his musical hero. 'I cannot believe that he received an award for my song "Living For The City". That song was alright but he deserves something even better than that. I feel there will never be an award great enough to give him and I just hope that he receives whatever we can give him while he is still a part of this earth.'

On stage he contributed to a Los Angeles benefit for Motown's first lady, Mary Wells, who was dying from throat cancer. Following the diagnosis in August 1990, Wells was unable to pay her medical bills, so the R&B Foundation and her former Motown colleagues and others, including Natalie Cole, raised money for her treatment. Mary Wells lost her battle against cancer and died on 26 July 1992. She was buried at Forest Lawn in Glendale, California.

Stevie Wonder's abandoned project, now re-named *Conversation Peace*, was publicly previewed when he sang tracks at the second 'Soul By The Sea' event, a televised concert for BET in Jamaica. He actually taped his appearance prior to the concert because he was heading off to Japan for a three-week tour. Other participating acts were The Temptations and newly signed Motown artists Gerald Alston, The Boys and Johnny Gill.

The biggest tour of 1992 started in Switzerland during May. Under the banner of 'European Natural Wonder', Stevie Wonder flew to Britain for concerts in Sheffield and Birmingham, and two dates at London's Wembley Arena, where Diana Ross followed him as part of her European tour. Gladys Knight was also performing in Britain at this time, with The Four Tops and Edwin Starr following two months later. Michael Jackson's high-profile British trek kicked off in July with dates at the open-air Wembley Stadium, with other British dates following. His Stadium audiences were approximately four times larger than those at Stevie Wonder's concerts in the Arena.

With no new album on release, Stevie Wonder, Wonderlove and his musicians were backed on stage by the Royal Philharmonic Orchestra's string section. *Blues & Soul* journalist Jeff Lorez who attended the concert reported:

> The theme for the evening, as has always been associated with Stevie, was that of world union through music, with Stevie's keyboard and piano rig set up within the prop of a small boat adrift at sea (the effect brought about by light blue silk sheets

and a wind machine). So, led by captain Stevie, the crew aboard the Natural Wonder set sail for the seas of spiritual, musical and social awareness. However, noticeable by its absence was the newer material, particularly from his most recent *Jungle Fever* set. [He] spent much of the early portion in non-communicado with the audience, letting the music speak volumes as he weaved together classic upon classic . . . Stevie previewed a track, the driving, funky, typically Wonderesque 'Woman Pleasing Man', from his forthcoming album and quipped 'People ask me, 'When's the new album out Stevie?' and I tell 'em, 'When it's ready'. That, of course, can never be soon enough.

Returning to America, the singer enjoyed his social life. He was one of eight hundred guests at Whitney Houston's marriage to the Rap singer Bobby Brown at her New Jersey mansion; he also performed at the reception attended by Aretha Franklin, Gladys Knight and Patti LaBelle, among others. Despite many upsets and separations, the marriage still stands at the time of writing.

Again, though, there were to be more deaths among Stevie's circle of friends and acquaintances during the early years of the decade. Fifty-three-year-old Eddie Kendricks died from lung cancer on 5 October 1992. The ex-Temptation, known for his falsetto voice, which was so beautifully highlighted on the group's early recordings, had undergone surgery in 1991 to remove his right lung, after which a full recovery was expected. Of the classic sixties Temptations line-up, three were now dead (David Ruffin, Eddie Kendricks, and Paul Williams who had reputedly committed suicide in his car during 1973), leaving Otis Williams and Melvin Franklin as the only surviving founder members. In 1995, Melvin Franklin died from heart failure, whereupon Williams recruited various replacement singers, culminating in the 2001 membership of himself, Barrington Henderson, Harry McGilberry, Terry Weeks and Ron Tyson – the last being a one-time group member in 1982.

The second Motown-related death in 1992 was that of 63-year-old Earl Van Dyke in Detroit, following a long battle against cancer. Apart from touring with most of the company's artists, Van Dyke was the leader of the house band throughout the sixties and early seventies and can be heard on hundreds of recordings. He also fronted several bands, and was a recording artist in his own right. His most notable singles were '6x6' revived in the seventies by public demand and 'All For You', which was used as the theme for the British pirate station Radio Caroline. During the eighties he had recorded for Ian Levine's Motorcity Records, and had continued performing until his illness forced him into retirement.

A galaxy of contemporary recording artists came together under the direction of Quincy Jones for *Handel's Messiah: A Soulful Celebration*. The project, recorded earlier in 1992 at Hollywood's A&M Studios, was released on Reprise Records in December, and boasted an all-star choir including Stevie Wonder, Chaka Khan, Johnny Mathis, Gladys Knight, Take 6, Jeffrey Osborne and The Sounds Of Blackness, among others. As well as the 'Hallelujah Chorus', the album featured contemporary interpretations from *The Messiah* such as Stevie Wonder and Take 6's version of 'O Thou That Takest Good Tidings To Zion'. A proportion of the album's profits were earmarked for the Children's Defence Fund.

Following this release, Stevie Wonder accepted yet another award. This time the Lifetime Achievement Award from The National Academy Of Songwriters, presented to him during a ceremony held in Los Angeles.

Still with no release date for *Conversation Peace*, Stevie Wonder kept a low profile for most of 1993, a year that started with the state of Arizona celebrating the 15 January as its first public holiday in honour of the late Dr Martin Luther King. Wonder lifted his boycott of the state and performed before approximately 17,500 people at the American West Arena in Phoenix. In June he travelled to Washington to perform at the Duke Ellington School Of Arts as part of their twentieth anniversary celebrations, and journeyed to Minneapolis to perform 'Maybe Your Baby' with Prince, during the latter's lengthy American tour.

From America, Stevie Wonder travelled to Ghana in December, where his much-hyped performance at the National Theatre in Accra was plagued with so many problems that a lesser artist might have marched off home. His music equipment was lost somewhere outside Ghana and his audience included unauthorised television crews, home-video users and fans carrying personal recording equipment. As security guards removed all unlicensed property, a grand piano was delivered to the theatre. A great fuss surrounded the tuning and checking of this in front of the restless audience. Eventually Wonder walked on stage to explain the circumstances for the delay and to apologise not only for his missing equipment but also for his orchestra which had also failed to arrive! Wearing an off-white African robe, he sang and played the impeccably tuned piano through a variety of classics, which were interrupted by the singer exchanging banter with his audience. Reviewers who started their notes with 'the gig that nearly didn't happen', showered praise on Stevie Wonder for his 'relaxed yet electrifying performance'.

During his absence, Berry Gordy paid tribute to Robert White, another of his in-house musicians, who died at the age of 57 in Los Angeles after complications following a coronary bypass operation. 'It's hard to say what our sound would have been like without Robert, and his contribution to the mix was vital,' he said. Another founding member of Motown's success had died.

Fans questioned why, given that Stevie Wonder had previewed songs from his new album, it was not ready for release. After all, he had been steadily working on it until the *Jungle Fever* project took precedence. Motown, now under new management following its sale to MCA Records and Boston Ventures, was also reluctant to offer any explanations except to say that an album was expected in 1995. It's interesting to note at this juncture that Stevie Wonder was one of a handful of artists to have stayed signed to the same record company since the start of his career. It was widely reported that he'd never been seriously tempted to leave Motown even though other companies had offered huge financial advances and incentives. He believed Motown to be his home and the source of his early inspiration, and his faith in the company had sustained him so far. But how would he survive without Berry Gordy? Time would tell.

Chapter   1   6

MY LOVE IS WITH YOU

'Music is a world within itself, a language we all understand'
Stevie Wonder

'He's my home boy from Detroit'
Aretha Franklin

'There's not too many living legends around that's in great shape
and healthy like Stevie'
Rockwilder

Satisfied that *Conversation Peace* was exactly what he wanted, a
relieved Stevie Wonder delivered the master tapes to Motown.
While the company dealt with its production and release, he
prepared to embark upon a long-overdue tour of America. These
dates were promoted as the 'Natural Wonder-Charge Against
Hunger Tour'. Wonder's opening night in Boston was a struggle.
He was suffering with throat problems, which meant he was
constantly spraying his mouth. However, with a New York string
section, his own musicians and support vocals from the group For
Real, Wonder showcased tracks from his pending album
interspliced with the most popular cuts from his most recent
projects during a performance that spanned two and a half hours.

While he was on the road EMI-America released *Movin' On Up*,
a collection of songs popular during the civil rights struggles of the
sixties. Wonder contributed to the compilation along with artists
such as Curtis Mayfield, Nina Simone and James Brown. Also on
release was the official single taster to *Conversation Peace* titled

'For Your Love'. The sloping ballad, which demonstrated middle-of-the-road tendencies, made it into the British top thirty in February 1995, and the American top sixty a month later.

Written and produced by Wonder, and largely recorded at Wonderland, *Conversation Peace* journeyed into a predictable mellowness on the opening tracks 'Rain Your Love Down' and 'Edge Of Eternity'. Many felt Wonder now lacked a contemporary edge, yet it was there in disguise. 'Taboo To Love', a compulsive, meandering ballad, was a million miles away from the expected Afro-rooted 'Take The Time Out' with Ladysmith Black Mambazo injecting the vital chant to complete the track. Mainstream or pop music was represented in the melodic 'I'm New' and 'Treat Myself'. Not, perhaps, a wise inclusion. If there was a throwaway title then 'My Love Is With You' was it. But as quickly as the album hit this low point, Wonder pulled it back with the jazz- and funk-influenced 'Sensuous Whisper' with Anita Baker as a guest vocalist, and with jazz touches from trumpeter Terence Blanchard and sax player Branford Marsalis. 'For Your Love' and 'Sorry' returned Wonder to the middle-of-the-road market, where he appears to be increasingly comfortable. Slicing into reggae with a calypso feel, Wonder introduced the appealing 'Tomorrow Robins Will Sing', leaving 'Conversation Peace', with joyous vocals from The Sounds Of Blackness, to close the unpredictable and often surprising musical journey.

Pale-coloured tiles, each showing an identical picture of the singer, covered the front of the CD packaging. In the middle of these tiles was a larger, darker picture outline, with a tiny coloured photograph in its bottom left-hand corner. This same picture was dotted on the eight-page insert, which carried the lyrics and recording details, while the back page, containing Wonder's credits, ended with text about the music, using the tracks as guidelines.

With the American tour over, Stevie Wonder flew to London during March 1995 to promote the British release of *Conversation Peace* and perform with others at Soho's Ronnie Scott's Club. This performance was broadcast on BBC Radio 1.

The world première, however, was held in Paris, where British journalists mingled with others from all over Europe at Le Meridien

Hotel. The singer hosted a press conference before being driven, with the media following, to the city's new Cité de la Musique where, dressed in purple, he previewed his new project. Wonder told Pete Lewis that this long-overdue album wasn't late, as many had thought, due to writer's block:

> Basically what I've done is just allow me the time to experience life as much as this business [allows] . . . While economically it is a great thing to have a record out every year-and-a-half and there are definite drawbacks if you don't . . . the many composers of hundreds of years ago didn't have records out every year-and-a-half. So I don't feel funny about the time that it takes me at all.

He also used the press conference to confirm that, rather surprisingly, he had abandoned plans to pursue a political career despite being keen to become the mayor of Detroit. He preferred to use his music, he said, as his platform.

Conversation Peace peaked at number sixteen in the American chart, passing gold status, and shot into the British top ten in March 1995. Also at this time, the extracted 'Tomorrow Robins Will Sing' bombed, failing to reach the top fifty in Britain. Sales-wise the album fell short of its prediction, and with no hit singles to bounce further sales, many felt the album, which was eight years in the making, to be a flop. Diehard fans, on the other hand, welcomed the return of their hero.

In June 1995, to coincide with the publication of Berry Gordy's autobiography *To Be Loved*, Motown released the compilation *A Tribute To Berry Gordy*. Wonder's '(You're My) Dream Come True' with The Temptations was one of several tracks by company artists. Also during June, Stevie Wonder returned to Britain to appear at London's Royal Albert Hall in support of the Royal Institute Of The Blind. His two-and-a-half-hour performance, backed by the Royal Philharmonic Orchestra, was a 'celebration of love and life' during which he sang his way through selections from his four decades of music, including a pair of tracks from *Conversation Peace*. Reviewers raved that he was a genius of the decade. 'British people really respect black music,' he once said.

'At one time I was thinking of quitting because the only place I got any satisfaction from an audience was over here. They appreciate you for real, no bullshitting. They don't have to smoke pot or get high to appreciate you. Whereas in the States, concerts have to be like some hallucogenic experience.' That respect was also reflected in his British record sales, which of late had led to higher chart placings than those in America. However, Stevie Wonder wasn't the only Motown artist in this situation: Diana Ross, Lionel Richie and Marvin Gaye likewise experienced waning American support during their careers. Perhaps, as one journalist noted, British fans were more loyal and that allegiance stayed for life.

In an attempt to recoup money from lost sales, and perhaps boost further interest in *Conversation Peace*, Motown released a double live CD titled *Natural Wonder* to catch the Christmas market. Recorded during the recent tour and showcasing concerts in Tel Aviv, Israel, and Osaka, Japan, with the Tokyo Philharmonic Orchestra, the release featured 24 songs spanning his career, together with 'Stay Gold' from the movie *The Outsiders* and previously unreleased tracks 'Dancing To The Rhythm', 'Stevie Ray Blues (a tribute to the late Stevie Ray Vaughan) and 'Ms & Mr Little Ones'. The CD's second side stood out as a 'greatest hits' package ('My Cherie Amour', 'Sir Duke', 'Superstition', 'I Just Called To Say I Love You' and so on) into which Wonder ploughed much spontaneity to ensure his familiar songs were heard with a vital freshness. 'Imagine how it was this night [of the recording]' wrote Ruth Adkins Robinson and Brian O'Neal in the CD notes:

> The learned young conductor steps up to the podium and raps sharply. All eyes are turned to Dr Henry Panion III as he raises his baton to begin the concert. Before him, the Tokyo Philharmonic Orchestra, all extraordinary, classically trained musicians, their upturned faces expectant. Behind Dr Panion, Stevie, his rhythm section and his backing singers, stood ready to embark on a concert designed in Stevie's complex mind. In *Natural Wonder*, aloof meets accessible and scholarly runs smack into the soul as the notes jump from the conductor's baton, head into the classical instruments and out into the souls of the audience.

'They were about to get a history lesson,' arranger Paul Riser said.

The CD's artwork, designed by Jackie Salway, included pictures of Wonder's work tools – harmonica and keyboard – in a montage of his surname, sunglasses, leaves and petals. A picture of him performing was slotted into the right-hand corner. Half of a yellow daisy dominated the back cover

From Israel and Japan, Wonder returned to America, where he performed a short hit medley following his induction into the Soul Train Hall of Fame, staged at the Shrine Auditorium, and at the *Billboard* Music Awards he performed 'Pastime Paradise' from *Songs In The Key Of Life* with Coolio, who had sampled it on 'Gangsta's Paradise'. The single went on to be voted the Best Rap Solo Performance at the February 1996 Grammy Awards ceremony, when Wonder also scooped the Lifetime Achievement Award and the Best R&B Song and Best R&B Vocal Performance for 'For Your Love'.

The only Stevie Wonder album released in 1996 was another to take advantage of the Christmas market titled *Song Review – A Greatest Collection* which Motown insisted was his first ever 'greatest hits' collection. Comprising nineteen classic tracks – 'Isn't She Lovely' (for which the synthesiser appeared to have been retouched), 'Supersitition', 'Part-Time Lover', 'I Just Called To Say I Love You' and so on – and covering ten albums, the release was intended as a replacement for the promised *Musiquarium II*. Wonder's best moments, however, were captured on 'Simply Say I Love U', a track on the new Motown artist Johnny Gill's album *Let's Get The Mood Right*, and on the duet with Babyface titled 'How Come, How Long' included on the latter's current album. The track was later issued in 1997 to become a British top ten single. Following this, the two artists performed at an MTV Unplugged concert at New York's Manhattan Center Studios, with the proceeds earmarked for the Phoenix House drug rehabilitation centre. 'I enjoy working with people but my expectations are too high.' Stevie Wonder once commented. 'I really don't want them to be like me and as a writer I'm protective about my melodies and lyrics. So, I expect to get things done the way I want it.' Actually, few artists have crossed the singer while recording, preferring to take his lead, knowing that the finished product will be faultless but not necessarily a million-selling item. It's also true to say that working with Stevie Wonder is an ambition of many artists but one that few achieve. Not because of his disinterest but through lack of time, as typified by Diana Ross's comment that she'd begged him for the 'longest while' to write 'The Force Behind The Power'.

Prior to his hit duet with Babyface in July 1997, Stevie Wonder was in the audience at the Rhythm & Blues Foundation's annual gala in February at the Hilton Hotel, New York. With tickets at $500 each, the black-tie event publicised once more the Foundation's determination to honour past artists from the R&B world, many of whom had to date not received the recognition they rightly deserved. In those cases money raised by the Foundation was presented to the honourees to help with, say, medical bills, and to provide financial aid in later years when they no longer worked. With Aretha Franklin as mistress of ceremonies, honourees and performing acts this year included The Four Tops, Smokey Robinson and the Miracles, Curtis Mayfield and The Spinners. Two months on, Wonder sang 'Living For The City' with George Michael at the VH1 Honours Awards ceremony at Universal City, California. After the two had performed at the Apollo reopening, this duet seemed to seal their mutual respect, which George Michael would take one step further in 1999.

A relatively quiet year, 1997 saw the elusive Stevie Wonder enjoying quality personal time, interrupted by his guest appearances and studio work. One personal outing attracted unexpected publicity when he and his family celebrated his daughter Aisha's birthday by dining at an unnamed New York restaurant. It was a midweek treat with few other diners and was perfect for the occasion. However, before they left the restaurant, someone pointed out the nearby piano, while someone else hooked up a microphone, in the hope that Wonder would oblige. Staff and diners waited until midnight when he gave in and sang 'Isn't She Lovely', originally penned in 1976 in celebration of his daughter's birth. With Aisha by his side, he then sang 'How Will I Know If She Loves Me' before dedicating both songs to his family.

By mid-1998 it became apparent that no new album was in the offing. Both Motown and the artist were surprisingly evasive on this issue. No major tours were planned either. In fact, the future looked bleak for the Stevie Wonder fan. During the next two years, Wonder's name usually cropped up when he attended award ceremonies, select performances, or made impromptu onstage guestings. A performance at the White House in Washington marked one of his more prestigious appearances, at a reception hosted by President Bill Clinton for Tony Blair, the British prime minister. Another was an appearance in Italy at the annual 'Pavarotti & Friends' War Child charity gala, followed by his participation in the celebrations for Nelson Mandela's eightieth birthday held in South Africa. Wonder performed two concerts dubbed 'Gift To The Nation' at Durban and Johannesburgh. He then kicked off the 1998 NBA's All-Star Weekend with a concert at Madison Square Garden, and a year later performed in Miami, Florida, in support of the Superbowl XXXIII at the Prop-Player Stadium.

Of the honours received during this time, the most notable included a Grammy award for Best R&B Vocal Performance – Male for 'St Louis Blues', and an Honorary Doctorate of Fine Arts presented by Rutgers University in New Jersey. And in December 1999 he was one of five artists selected for the distinguished annual Kennedy Center Honours. At 49 years of age, Stevie Wonder was the youngest person ever to be in the selection. 'Stevie Wonder is a musical genius who has been an integral part of American popular culture for four decades,' announced James A Johnson, chairman of the Center. He added that during his career Wonder had notched up almost as many chart singles and albums as Elvis Presley and The Beatles and, aside from his musically creative list of Motown hits and socially conscious albums, was responsible for paving the way for the concept album by black artists via pioneering recordings such as *Innervisions*. The award was presented during a dinner at the State Department, followed by a party for all the recipients hosted by President Clinton at the White House.

In his own musical absence, Stevie Wonder was heard on the group 98 Degrees' 'True To Your Heart', a top sixty British single in October 1998, and was sampled by actor/singer Will Smith. The track was 'I Wish' and was a top forty American hit. George Michael included Wonder's 'As' on his compilation *Ladies And*

Gentlemen. Described by one reviewer as 'oddly dispassionate', the song also featured Mary J Blige, was produced by Babyface to a George Michael arrangement and was funked up by Full Crew, to be culled as a single in March 1999; it reached the British top four. This signified his final hit single for Sony Records.

It wasn't clear why no new Stevie Wonder product was forthcoming. Even the rumours of a new album, his first for five years, that persisted during 1999 appeared to lack substance. Subsequently, Motown had to sustain his past popularity and selling power, so resorted to doing what they did best – they released a compilation. This time it was a deluxe four-CD box set titled *At The Close Of A Century* slotted in for March 2000 release. The black box carried a picture of the performing singer, dressed in a blue and gold braided shirt, with the release's title in blue lettering on the front, while a stick-on lyric sheet covered a picture of a young Wonder on the back. Compiled by Motown's Harry Weinger and dedicated to Ewart Abner, who had died in 1997, the retrospective collection was released to celebrate the singer's fiftieth birthday. The seventy digitially remastered titles included 'Fingertips Parts 1 & 2', 'Uptight (Everything's Alright)' and 'Until You Come Back To Me (That's What I'm Gonna Do)', 'My Cherie Amour', 'Never Had A Dream Come True', 'Superstition', 'Golden Lady', 'Creepin'', 'Sir Duke', 'Send One Your Love', 'That Girl' and 'How Come, How Long' with Babyface. The 96-page booklet was crammed with photographs and details of the special release. As magnificent as it obviously was, diehard fans bemoaned the absence of new material and were loath to purchase a further collection of old tracks, digitally remastered or not. Why no new material was included remained a mystery, particularly as Stevie Wonder has often made it known that he has stockpiled songs by the hundred. He had previously said that he intended to make public a selection of those songs that had been overlooked for past albums, or those that failed to meet the criteria of a particular concept. He had also stated that some of his demo recordings were actually superior to those commercially released:

I'd like people to be able to hear some of the stuff to get an idea of what I really meant to say. Even though songs have words I can't really tell what they mean when I'm on stage. They relate to whatever feeling I had when they were composed. Singing before a microphone in the studio, you have no real technique which is why I think some demos turned out better than the final performance.

For someone of Wonder's calibre with his quest for absolute perfection in music, this appeared to be a strange comment to make; perhaps, when forced to defend some aspects of his work, he felt that allowing his fans an insight into the music's creation would alleviate some of the criticism. 'Music is a world within itself, a language we all understand,' he once remarked. 'It doesn't belong to any one person or one people either. Music is a gift of life, is a toy to express our joys and sorrows. And even in moments of sorrow to give us peace and the ability to be strong enough with the joy that it sometimes brings.'

During this private time in his life, Stevie Wonder reflected on his fast-paced, highly successful career and wild and demanding lifestyle. His determination to fulfil his childhood dreams and ambitions, to pave a way for black entertainers in the cut-throat music business and to become a forerunner in musical expression, motivated him through the heady seventies and eighties. He obviously had no inkling of the heights he would reach, yet, he said, he felt able to cope with the extraordinary demands constantly thrown his way. 'I knew what the job was before I took it on,' he explained:

An artist knows what a job is before he takes it on, so you have to kinda hash all these things out in your mind. You know that you are going to have moments where there'll be personal things that aren't significant to anyone but yourself, but you still have to face the audience and do a performance. But as much as possible if you are happy with being yourself, and in being the artist that you are, then who you are is pretty much what comes from what you are as a person.

He recalled his 25th birthday when some sections of the media treated him differently. His music was given less coverage than his sexual attraction, particularly as one journalist noted he was now plagued with groupies. This wasn't new, Wonder replied, he had grown up with girls chasing Motown groups like The Temptations, and later himself, but to be called a sex symbol was indeed a fresh slant. 'The ladies love to look at his chest, his broad neck and his heavy black-rooted facial structure, with his strong high cheekbones,' Ira Tucker told Lee Underwood. Wonder, on the other hand, admitted that no matter how beautiful sex was, it was man's weakness: 'All of mankind should be a little above that. It should be like one of the lesser things that he thinks about, because man has let that rule the world.' Communicating mentally was, he believed, far more important than the sex act itself, 'because it heightens everything and makes what you do sexually so much better. Sex is a very intimate relationship that you share with the person you're with and that's what makes you feel good.'

To see how sex sold records, Stevie Wonder only had to be aware of the mainstream charts, which showed a huge diversity in music ranging from manufactured teenage groups oozing sex appeal, to pubescent girls, to rappers arrogantly dictacting to impressionable young minds. The record-buying public was attracted and influenced by both clean-cut and rebellious images. 'I feel that music has always been a reflection of society and only some people decide to go beyond that immediate reflection to write about things that are generally forgotten on a day-to-day level', Stevie Wonder told journalist Pete Lewis. The sexual connotations in lyrics were also a reflection of changing attitudes: '[because] I think that people are "doing it" more and talking about "doing in" . . . I mean, you got talk and gossip shows all over . . . people these days just wanna know. So I just think what is happening with music in general is a reflection of society as a whole.'

With such an open-minded attitude in music, it seemed surprising that the concept of establishing a black entertainment channel in Britain proved non-viable. In America the station BET guaranteed to support the varying styles of black music. In fact, most music videos for singles were produced with BET in mind. When the station celebrated its twentieth anniversary in June 2000 in Las Vegas, it was an all-star celebration. Hosted by comedian/actor Jamie Foxx, its contributors included Luther Vandross and Gerald Levert, but the evening's highlight was the honouring of Stevie Wonder and his music, in which artists sang his compositions as the build-up to him taking the stage to perform 'Do I Do' before a star-studded gathering joined him for 'Higher Ground'.

Two months later, the Washington-based Rhythm & Blues Foundation paid homage to another selection of R&B legends at their Pioneer Awards ceremony in New York. The late Marvin Gaye became the recipient of the legacy Tribute Award. Presented by Berry Gordy, the award was accepted by Gaye's children, Nona and Marvin III. Isaac Hayes, Dionne Warwick and Herbie Hancock, then presented Stevie Wonder with the Foundation's Lifetime Achievement Award. He delighted the audience by an impromptu performance. Betty Wright, The Chi-lites and The Impressions were among other acts honoured during the ceremony.

Stevie Wonder's next publicised appearances occurred during 2001, when in May he played before a celebrity audience including Cher, Billy Connolly and Dustin Hoffman, at the newly renovated Century Plaza Hotel in Los Angeles. He was also a surprise guest at a tribute evening held in honour of Aretha Franklin at New York's Radio City Music Hall. The two superstars duetted on 'I Just Called To Say I Love You' before an audience dotted with star names such as Janet Jackson, The Backstreet Boys and actress Sigourney Weaver. 'To have Stevie Wonder walk on to surprise us all like that was just too good,' glowed the Queen of Soul, 'He's my home boy from Detroit.' 'Aretha's got soul. She's been through it,' replied the home boy. 'Soul is something you can only get through experience, that causes you to be able to express yourself with feeling.'

'It's an exciting time and I wish we could do this every year for Detroit and we've got to do something to encourage people to embrace the city throughout the year,' an excited Stevie Wonder told thousands of people who had packed into the downtown Hart Plaza for a free concert in celebration of the city's 300th birthday during August 2001. In the eighty-degree heat, with spasmodic pouring rain, Wonder performed his Celebrity Homecoming Concert, which everyone agreed was a magical event.

In New York City on 11 September 2001, an American Airlines Boeing 767 with 92 people on board ploughed into the north tower of the World Trade Center. Eighteen minutes after the first crash a second plane plunged into the Center's south tower, where it exploded within seconds. It could have been a scene from an American disaster movie, but it wasn't. The terrorist assault was real; an act of war and a tragedy of extraordinary proportions. Firefighters, medical staff, members of the public and American and British office workers were killed in the twin towers that had dominated the Manhattan skyline for over thirty years, when they collapsed to the ground. Thirty minutes after the south tower tragedy, an American Airlines Boeing 757 carrying 64 people crashed into the west wing of the Pentagon in Washington. America burned with fire, fear and hatred. The terrifying nightmare and festering wounds remain unhealed as America seeks revenge from the most wanted man in the world – Osama bin Laden.

Many functions and events were hastily arranged to boost American morale and to raise much-needed financial help for the survivors and the dependants of those who died. As artists, actors and politicians performed and dictated, bodies were dug from the hell-hole known as Ground Zero, the spot where the twin towers had once stood.

One such event was a two-hour telethon screened on 22 September without advertisements across 31 American networks, in 156 countries and broadcast on 8,000 radio stations. Egos were put on hold as celebrity followed celebrity, applauding police officers, firefighters, airline crews, Pentagon staff, passengers and World Trade Center workers who had died in the atrocity. 'The people here tonight are not heroes or protectors of this nation. We are artists who are here to raise money and to honour the real heroes,' said Tom Hanks, who was joined by fellow actors such as Whoopi Goldberg, George Clooney, Robin Williams, Robert de Niro, Meg Ryan, Jack Nicholson and Goldie Hawn. Stevie Wonder was among the many recording artists involved, who also included Neil Young – who drew courage from John Lennon's 'Imagine' – Paul Simon, Sting, Mariah Carey, Wyclef Jean, Bono and U2, and Natalie Imbruglia. With Willie Nelson, Wonder led the massed stars for a rousing 'America The Beautiful' as the programme's finale.

During their careers, Stevie Wonder and Elton John have crossed paths several times, so it came as no surprise when the Motown star played harmonica and clavinet on 'Dark Diamond', a track on John's courageous and innovative CD *Songs From The West Coast*. Ex-Motowner Billy Preston played the organ on two further cuts, 'The Wasteland' and 'Love Her Like Me'. The CD was widely advertised in Britain and Elton John was even featured in a television advert for the Royal Mail.

However, in October, Stevie Wonder's personal life was dragged through the tabloids. An ex-girlfriend, Angela McAfee, filed a $30 million palimony lawsuit against him. She claimed he had pursued her for over a decade and had convinced her to drop her career as a wardrobe consultant in August 1996 to live with him. An American publication further reported, 'The couple verbally agreed five years ago that he would be the sole income earner and she would remain at home, the lawsuit said. They lived together until February when Wonder allegedly breached the agreement.' When the British tabloid, the *Sun*, ran the story on 6 October 2001 it claimed Stevie Wonder had passed on incurable genital herpes, a condition he had, reputedly, concealed from her and with which she was diagnosed in 2000.

The lawsuit also stated that McAfee had supported Wonder through personal and medical problems (none of which were publicly identified) and that he had agreed to provide lifetime support even if their relationship ended. In reply to the allegations, Laura Wasser, Wonder's lawyer, told the media that the claims were without merit and 'the only breach that has been made is one of Stevie's trust in someone he had heretofore called a friend.'

Six months later, the American courts ordered Wonder and McAfee to 'resolve their differences with the help of a mediator.'

The next year also started badly for the Motown star when he was dealt another personal shock. His mentor and close friend Hank Cosby died on 22 January 2002 at his Californian home. In July 2001 the producer/composer was admitted to Detroit's William Beaumont Hospital for triple bypass heart surgery. Then he underwent a further three operations to correct infections not detected following the original operation. He was survived by his wife Patricia, whom he had met at Motown, three sons and five grandchildren. Stevie Wonder played 'My Cherie Amour' at the funeral, attended by thirty mourners at the James H Cole Funeral Home, which stood next door to the Motown Historical Museum on West Grand Boulevard. 'He was very lucky he developed good working habits at an early age,' Cosby once said of Stevie Wonder. 'He is behind the piano every day for twelve to thirteen hours. How can anyone compete with that?'

Within six months another Motown musician died. After a long battle against cancer, Richard 'Pistol' Allen – who, with Uriel Jones, deputised for Benny Benjamin in the Motown studio – passed away on 30 June.

Also during June the British and Commonwealth nations were rallying in celebration of Queen Elizabeth II's Golden Jubilee. The year was packed with royal visits, functions and merchandise. Plans that were months in the making were realised for her British subjects when two free concerts were staged in the grounds of Buckingham Palace. One was a classical event, the other a pop concert featuring an impressive array of international artists, such as members of Queen, Phil Collins, Shirley Bassey, Tony Bennett, Paul McCartney and Elton John. Stevie Wonder and Aretha Franklin were also invited to join in the celebrations but they were absent on the night. In Detroit, revelries of another kind were in full swing. 'It is truly an honour to be at the Apollo,' Stevie Wonder told a capacity audience at the venue during the 'Comin' Home To Harlem' gala. Proceeds from the concert went to the Jazz at Lincoln Center, an organisation devoted to the music. Hosted by actress Whoopi Goldberg, Wonder played piano with Wynton Marsalis and his septet during 'Giant Steps' before singing a jazz version of 'Living For The City'. He also provided light-hearted moments: when grabbing the sheet music in front of him, he quipped, 'Didn't really need to read that right now!', and he referred to a backstage conversation with Marsalis which proved to be 'an eye-opening experience'. Other participating artists included Roland Hanna, Savion Glover and Vanessa Williams.

From elitist jazz to ground-breaking R&B: when Michael Jackson was inducted into the Songwriters Hall of Fame in June 2002, Stevie Wonder, already a member, received the Lifetime Achievement Award. Doubtless he smiled to himself at Jackson's induction, because the little boy used to sneak into Motown's studio when Wonder was recording and, he recalled, 'You could feel Michael's mind thinking.'

Also during the period Wonder began working in earnest on a new, as-yet-untitled album. The project was expected to feature in-demand producers such as Rockwilder, who had worked with Missy Elliott, and Raphael Saadiq, who said he'd been in contact with Stevie Wonder: 'We both work out of Los Angeles, so I just told him we need to get together. That's the icon right there, you've got to rub elbows with Stevie. You can't pass that up. There's not too many living legends around that's in great shape and healthy like Stevie.'

Once again Motown saw fit to remind the public that Stevie Wonder remains the most influential singer/composer of our time, by issuing a double CD titled *Stevie Wonder: The Definitive Collection*. Released in October 2002, the 38 tracks were dubbed by critics as the 'poor man's' version of the recently issued *At The Close Of A Century*. Indeed, the double CD actually carried a picture from that box set on its front sleeve. The American version was reduced to 21 tracks.

Stevie Wonder is the most faithful of all Motown's artists. He refused to leave the company he believed in, despite huge monetary temptations. On the other hand, some would argue that he has been foolish to remain with a company that is no longer the flagship of record companies. It's worth remembering, though, that Wonder is totally self-sufficient. He's in control of his music, his future and his destiny. Using Motown as the means to manufacture and release his records means he can work at his own pace without the worry of ensuring his work is delivered on time to record stores, radio stations, the media and so on. So maybe he was right to stay.

Also in Motown's favour, the company did sanction Wonder and Marvin Gaye changing the face of its music, and indeed black music generally. Their wealth of material is as vital decades later as it was when first conceived, and together the two artists have educated and influenced new generations of musicians and performers. Even today Stevie Wonder is still able to surpass the innovative music he has created, with his inquisitive mind always open to new ways of expressing himself.

His role as a world ambassador and his determination to help those in need regularly leads to clashes with politicians and world leaders. But throughout it all, Stevie Wonder remains solid:

> There are people who nobody cares about. They're black and white and they need a lot more love and understanding than they get. The trouble is many people take material things too seriously . . . and they're just thinking of themselves and nobody else. There'll be no future if we all don't learn to live with each other, and I'm going to try to bring people closer together.

And when asked if he had any more ambitions left to fulfil, he thought for a moment, then replied, 'Yes, I'd like to be able to braid my hair in less than ten hours.'

A TIME 2 LOVE

'I really had to squeeze my balls to get those high notes'
Elton John

'Without Stevie most of us never would have picked up a microphone'
Busta Rhymes

'Daddy, daddy, daddy, ok, that's enough!'
Kailand Morris

Welcoming in the new millennium with re-issued compilations and the promise of a new album 'soon', rumours were rife throughout the industry that Stevie Wonder was reluctant to present his new work to the world because he feared rejection. He had a point; his last album *Conversation Peace* in 1995 was just that – and it was mostly derogatory. Not only did it fail to hit its sales projection but produced poor selling singles. So, as Wonder wrestled with his confidence and viewed the changing musical world, he diversified by working with other acts.

In early 2000 he boosted his income by contributing songs to film soundtracks and compilations following the success of adding his version of 'If Ever' (originally intended for John Denver) to the *Down In The Delta* soundtrack. He joined acts like Ashford & Simpson, Luther Vandross and Chaka Khan in this 1998 film insight into a woman's pains in liberating herself and her family from a drug-infested, alcohol-ridden Chicago housing project. Starring Alfie Woodard, Al Freeman Jr and a fine supporting cast, it was writer Maya Angelou's first as director. Wonder also recorded 'Misrepresented People' and 'Some Years Ago' for *Bamboozled* in another star studded soundtrack that, this time included, Angie Stone, Prince and India. Arie with whom he would later work on his new project, suggesting that he was nervous about relying on his name alone to sell records. In fact, during the next few years her name cropped up quite regularly. (With a first name inspired by Mahatma Gandhi and a made-up second name, India.Aries mother Joyce was a former singer who had toured with Wonder. As a teenager India sang in church and mastered numerous instruments before creating her own music. She joined Motown Records during 1999 where her debut album was *Acoustic Soul*. Directed and penned by Spike Lee, the movie told the story of a frustrated African-American television worker who presented a black-face minstrel show in protest but, to his chagrin, it became a hit! Damon Wayans and Savion Glover led the cast through this dark, biting satirical look at the television industry.

'This is a really emotional moment. It's truly by the grace of God that all this has happened in my life' Wonder told his audience at the Hart Plaza on the banks of the Detroit River in 2001. 'I just want to thank you because you didn't even have to listen to any of my songs to understand my lyrics. Hopefully it brings joyful thoughts to your heart.' More than 500,000 people flocked to see his two-hour performance that was part of Detroit's 300th anniversary celebrations. This was his first show in the city for almost ten years on a bill that included updated versions of The Temptations and The Spinners. Kicking in with 'Master Blaster (Jammin')' and 'Higher Ground' before slowing the pace with 'Ribbon In The Sky', Wonder's act was varied and exciting. After an hour into the set he charged in at a funk pace for 'Superstition', 'Uptight' and everyone's favourite 'Signed, Sealed, Delivered (I'm Yours)'. Wonder closed with 'Happy Birthday' and 'Dancing In The Street', Motown's anthem immortalised by Martha and the Vandellas in 1964. Part way through the act, his ex-wife and Motown star Syreeta was introduced to sing her hit 'With You (I'm Born Again)'. Pledging his undying love for her by softly saying 'our love has never died. I loved you since the very first day we met', the words later became more poignant as within three years his beloved lady was dead. Following a two-year battle against cancer, Syreeta died on 6 July 2004 from congestive heart failure that was said to be a complication from her chemotherapy and radiology treatments. She was 58 years old and was survived by two daughters; Takiyah and Harmoni, members of Divine Hands, a dance troupe founded by their mother; two sons; grandchildren; her mother and sister. Dedicating a song to her on his next album, Wonder said it was one of the ways he dealt with her sudden passing – 'I just wanted a place of comfort'. Sadly, while Syreeta was fighting for life, his brother Larry was also diagnosed with a terminal illness. 'That was a low time in my life, knowing that my brother and Syreeta were not going to be here too much longer. We have to live until we die (and) I would prefer in my life to die living as opposed to live dying.'

To close 2001 his 'Merry Christmas Baby' (with Wyclef Jean) and 'I Love You More' (with Kimberly Brewer) were included on the fifth chapter of A&M's *A Very Special Christmas* album series which annually raises funds for the Special Olympics International organisation with a mix of live and studio performances. This worthy compilation boasted songs by Bon Jovi, Stevie Nicks, Dido, among others, who, with Wonder played 'live' on the TNT television gala named after the album staged in Washington DC. As remarkable as it seems, the star was nominated for a Grammy Award for a television commercial, where he duetted with India.Arie on a version of Mel Torme's classic 'Christmas Song'! On a more serious note, the Festive Season automatically conjured up memories of John Lennon being murdered by Mark Chapman on 8 December 1980. Admitting he'd experienced a 'bad feeling' after hearing the opening words to Lennon's immortal 'Imagine' ('Imagine there's no heaven') Wonder further explained – 'After he died I couldn't stop crying whenever I heard [that song], but I wasn't surprised he'd been shot. Chapman said he shot him because he said he didn't believe in Jesus, and when I heard 'Imagine' I thought somebody isn't going to like that.'

In mid-2002 and again with Ashford & Simpson, Barry Manilow, Sting and others, Wonder collected special awards from the prestigious Songwriters Hall of Fame during a New York ceremony. Michael Jackson also coveted an award but didn't appear. ('His truck wouldn't start,' quipped the emcee, Paul Williams, himself a noted composer and singer). Jackson's pal Liza Minnelli accepted the honour on his behalf, while singer Joan Osborne presented Wonder with the Sammy Cahn Lifetime Achievement Award, citing his devotion to political causes – 'His music and his life shows how we can best use artistry in fame'. A smiling Wonder responded with 'People said "Yeah, you write good melodies, but forget about writing lyrics. Who can read Braille anyway?' Within months he would present the Century Award to Sting at the Billboard Music Awards staged in Las Vegas.

Finally, in what appears to be his last collaboration of the early millennium, he joined Gloria Estefan on 'Into You', which, for a change, he didn't write. While in Britain, Wonder's last successful musical fusion was with Blue and Angie Stone on 'Signed, Sealed Delivered (I'm Yours)' a track extracted from the all-boy quartet's third chart-topping album *Guilty*. Recorded in Los Angeles the single peaked at number 11 in the UK chart, introducing the Motown star there to a new, younger generation. As an aside here, Elton John once said – 'Nobody can sing like Stevie does. I know. I actually recorded a version of 'Signed Sealed Delivered (I'm Yours)', and I really had to squeeze my balls to get those high notes!'.

Homage was also publicly paid in 2003 when Mary J Blige, Eric Clapton, Musiq and others recorded the exceptionally stunning tribute album *Conception: An Interpretation Of Stevie Wonder's Songs*. Meanwhile, behind the scenes, the man himself continued to beaver away recording and re-recording tracks. He also toured Japan where he tested new material in his sold-out performances.

Into 2004 and Wonder honoured Lou Rawls at an Evening Of Stars 25th Anniversary Celebration before guesting at Oprah Winfrey's 50th birthday bash. In April he performed at the International Conference Centre in Ghana, raising funds for underprivileged children, and at the Stockholm Jazz Festival. Meanwhile, Motown announced that the album *A Time 2 Love* was slotted in for release on 11 May. The date was quickly amended to 8 June. Following his performance on Oprah Winfrey's show to present three new songs, Wonder's record company confirmed his album was deleted from its July release schedule. A new date hadn't been set. As if that wasn't enough for soul fans to think about, Ray Charles died on 10 June. 'He gave the world a lot of love in his music' Wonder said of his childhood inspiration. 'I often wish for an end to hate and the cure for hate is love. Ray Charles expressed much love in his music'. Eight days later he performed at his funeral, and the next month bid farewell to Syreeta, before singing 'I've Had Some Good Days' at the funeral of ex-Motown artist Rick James. On a happier note, Rod Stewart persuaded Wonder to play harmonica on 'What A Wonderful World', a track on the second volume of his Stardust: *The Great American Songbook* compilation. Upon his return to America from a Scandinavian tour, Stevie Wonder musically supported Democratic candidate John Kerry in his US Presidential Campaign at the Joe Louis Arena, Detroit. Addressing the rally attendees, Wonder said he was backing Kerry because 'we can celebrate peace, not talk about destruction, where we can be a country again that the world will have great respect for. It is time for change.' It wasn't – George Bush, who Wonder had met, was re-elected. 'He knows my politics and I know his' he told The *Guardian's* Simon Hattenstone who believed Wonder was now ambivalent about politics, preferring to use the words 'social justice'. 'I just basically say what I feel about a position or thing. The bottom line is that "when we do the right thing by each other, then God will do the right thing by us". I truly feel that way.' Fifteen years ago, the singer was first bitten by the political bug when he announced his intention to run for mayor of Detroit, believing he had a good chance of being elected. For some reason, he abandoned this but Martha Reeves, his ex-baby sitter, didn't. She became the first Motown star to take on a political role in the city.

From politics to anger. In a rare public outburst Wonder blasted Detroit-born rapper Eminem for ridiculing Michael Jackson in a video promoting his 'Just Lose It' single, lifted from the *Encore* album released during November 2004. The song made light of the child molestation charges against Jackson (he was later found not guilty) while the promotional video showed Eminem impersonating Jackson as children jumped up and down on him in bed.

This wasn't something Wonder approved of, as he fumed – 'Kicking someone when he's down isn't a good thing. I have much respect for his work, although I don't think he's as good as 2Pac. I was disappointed that he would let himself go to such a level.' He further told Billboard magazine that Eminem's success could be attributed to the continued support from underprivileged groups and African-Americans. 'He has succeeded on the backs of people predominantly in that lower pay bracket; people of colour.' The American Black Entertainment Network banned the video claiming it was 'inappropriate to disparage a celebrity', while the *Los Angeles Times* called it 'a playful look at celebrity voyeurism'.

Motown gleefully announced *A Time 2 Love* would be issued in April 2005 while the Recording Academy and the Entertainment Industry Foundation staged Grammy Jam, a musical event celebrating the music of their 22-time Grammy winner at Los Angeles' Orpheum Theatre. The performers were impressive – George Duke, Herbie Hancock, George Benson, Randy Jackson – and these, with others, performed jam-style with Stevie Wonder. Proceeds from this unusual gala were earmarked for the National Arts and Musical Education Initiative, which provided funding for exemplary arts programmes.

On Boxing Day 2004 the world's most powerful earthquake in over forty years erupted underwater off the Indonesian island of Sumatra. It sent walls of water barrelling across thousands of miles causing death and devastation in coastal areas like Sri Lanka's tourist resort of Kalutara and Southern India. The death count was 216,000 people, while many others were left stranded without homes, food or help. The natural tragedy touched hearts and wallets the world over. One of Stevie Wonder's first appearances of the New Year was to help organise and join a star-studded concert for survivors of the Asian tsunami. Tagged 'The Concert Of Hope', the gala attracted high-profile names like George Clooney, Madonna and Elton John. Wonder sang 'A Time 2 Love' with India.Arie and his lifetime friend Diana Ross closed the concert with the anthemic 'Reach Out And Touch (Somebody's Hand)'. In Britain, 60,000 fans watched stars like Keane, Charlotte Church and Liberty X performing at Cardiff's Millennium Stadium where 1.2 million pounds was raised with the final total reaching 200 million pounds. It was the UK's biggest charity concert since Live Aid 20 years earlier. However, at this time no one envisaged that within six months Bob Geldof would once more rally his brothers and sisters in music. Before this happened, Wonder switched music for fashion to support his wife Karen Millard-Morris (they married in 2001) at the unveiling of her Kai Milla's women's collection which was body conscious without being crass. 'I wanted it to be slightly provocative but quiet. The Kai Milla look is elegant, luxurious and sophisticated without being contrived or uptight' she told the attending media. Also an accomplished painter, the understated designer founded the Milla Design Group in 2004 and her creations have been purchased by the rich and famous including Christina Aguilera, Eva Mendes and Salma Hayek.

The Stevie Wonder travelling promotional circus attempted to get underway with the promise that *A Time 2 Love* was ready to deliver to Motown. In readiness for affording it the maximum promotion possible, Wonder intended to travel across America stopping in select cities along the journey to perform in small venues, ending with a huge celebratory concert in New York City's Central Park. The album wasn't delivered; so Motown extracted a first single 'So What The Fuss' in May 2005. The keys-driven song features Prince on bass and En Vogue on support vocals including the introduction interaction. To promote the single's release two videos were filmed. The first was the traditional music video, while the second was accompanied by a video description technique. For the first time in music history, Wonder released a descriptive audio track – a visual narration of the video – recorded by hip-hop artist Busta Rhymes. 'Until now music videos have been very one dimensional for those who are blind or with low vision. Now all music video fans will be able to apply their vision to my video thanks to the descriptive technique and of course, a great narration by Busta. For me, the entire concept is indicative of what happens when you go beyond the status quo and open yourself up to what's possible.' Busta Rhymes: 'Only Stevie could come up with a way to let fans that have never seen a video take part in the whole vibe. It was a great project to work on from start to finish. Without Stevie most of us never would have picked up a microphone.' The single entered the British singles chart at number 19; in America the charting process is less refined due to the several formats of radio like crossover and urban radio. In actual sales, suffice to say, it sold badly.

The poor chart placings weren't in the Wonder game plan, particularly as so much emphasis had been directed towards the forthcoming album. This taster would do little to encourage other than his diehard fans to purchase it, and merely added fuel to the argument 'Does a new Stevie Wonder album really matter than much anymore?'

When *A Time 2 Love* was postponed again, its creator took the most unusual step and delivered a second track for single release. Titled 'From The Bottom Of My Heart' it was, in actual fact, the song Motown wanted to release first because its natural, sing-along chorus was reminiscent of 'I Just Called To Say I Love You'. Wonder had resisted, claiming – 'I didn't want to do what one would typically expect, and I don't regret it.' The song failed to repeat it's chart-topping predecessor so he performed 'So What The Fuss' at the 2005 NBA Finals when he joined Will Smith, Alanis Morrisette and Kelly Clarkson in a live broadcast on the US network ABC at 9pm. Speaking from his dressing room at the Palace of Auburn Hills, he told journalists that he believed the message of love not sex was overdue in today's 'pop' market-place. 'I'm a married man; I understand. The way the world is right now, we need more love, and musicians have the responsibility to espouse a more positive message.' He discovered love at an early age, he said, 'when it was not so soon that I shouldn't have known, but not too late to be unaware.' He might sing of love, he said, but refuses to play his own music when making love, believing it to be a tacky gesture on his part. 'I can't make love to my own stuff. I'm gonna do Luther (Vandross) or Beyonce, but I don't need no music to get my groove on!'

On 13 May 2005, Wonder's 55th birthday, he became a father for the seventh time. His wife Karen gave birth to a son. They named him Mandla Kadjaly Carl Stevland Morris, at the suggestion of the star's friend, the former South African president Nelson Mandela. Their first child, Kailand, was born four years ago. He met his second wife in a nightclub, and when she moved to Washington, they remained in contact as Wonder told *Blues &*

Soul's Matilda Egere-Cooper. 'We got together again and I blew her mind and that was it. She's got a little sexy thing going on. Capricorns and Taurians are very compatible. But I didn't base it on the sign thing (when I met her). I based it on other things. She had a nice personality.'

So had Tiger Woods who held the singer's hand to stand on stage before 7,000 people in Las Vegas. On 23 May he headlined the golfer's annual charity event, which raises $1 million each year for his children's charities. With the words 'The most important thing we can do as men and women is make the investment in children' Wonder opened his show that included old and new material and a guest appearance from last year's headliner, Prince.

Also around this time, Motown's new boss, Sylvia Rhone, continued to hound her artist to release his work because the original delivery dates had passed without event and record stores and fans wanted to know what the problem was and, indeed, was the album actually worth the wait? To her credit, Rhone had already coaxed the two singles from him and on the strength of that had spent $200,000 on billboards (including the prestigious Sunset Boulevard site in Hollywood) advertising the album's imminent release. However, Wonder was adamant – nothing would be released until he was ready, and if his non-delivery drained resources from other artists, so be it – 'Obviously Motown would have liked to have had it yesterday ... the creative process is delicate and the reason they haven't got it is I'm not ready to give it to them. However long it takes me, I'm giving the very best that I can and I won't settle for less. My feeling is that this is my statement. Other artists I have nothing to do with. So much has happened in the last year (that) it caused me to think differently about how I would organise the record. Time is making the album better. I can only apologise in that I did say it would be ready on this or that date.' On the upside, since the first deadline was missed, jazz flautist Hubert Laws and Paul McCartney were added to the list of contributors.

Two decades after Live Aid spearheaded the campaign to abolish poverty that continues to blight our planet, Bob Geldof again took up the challenge by raising public consciousness to international debt relief. And once more artists from all musical avenues supported him. Saturday, 3 July 2005 was the day the world linked arms. Live8 was the biggest event in the history of entertainment, with free concerts staged in eight countries with an international audience of 3 billion people. In London's Hyde Park 205,000 peopled watched Paul McCartney, Elton John, Robbie Williams, Pink Floyd and other high-ranking artists, while audiences around the world watched concerts in Japan, Germany, Canada, Russia, France, Italy, South Africa, and , of course, America, where in Philadelphia Will Smith told the world – 'Let's end poverty in Africa. George Bush are you listening?'

A leading voice in the fight against world hunger, Stevie Wonder (who wasn't a contributor to Live Aid) was an obvious choice to headline the American leg that also included among others, Destiny's Child, Alicia Keys, Jay Z and Bon Jovi. With a funky, highly charged set and backed by an eleven-piece group, he performed 'Master Blaster (Jammin')' and 'Higher Ground' before strutting his stuff in a choreographed routine with two of his daughters. 'Signed, Sealed, Delivered (I'm Yours)' followed, then 'A Time To Love' and 'Shelter In The Rain' before closing with 'Superstition'. 'People are still arguing and fighting about dropping the world debt, and it's a joke to me' he told Simon Hattenstone. 'It's a joke because look at how much has been taken from Africa. God has given every continent on this planet some natural resource we can use to survive, for trading or whatever. But the world powers go and turn over the areas and take whatever they do (and) work out those ridiculous contracts.' A week later, many of those same world leaders attended the G8 summit in Scotland to thrash out making poverty history and to increase international aid. While they did this, they dined on the finest cuisine Scotland had to offer.

Within days the city that so willingly opened its arms to Live8, was bombed by terrorists. Three bombs exploded on underground trains outside Liverpool Street and Edgware Road stations, and on another travelling between King's Cross and Russell Square. The final explosion ripped a double decker bus to pieces near King's Cross. 'We're living in a mad world where people do crazy things. The God I believe in doesn't believe in bombing, and the Allah that I respect for Muslims doesn't believe in terrorising innocent people' he said following the 7 July atrocity which killed 52 and injured 700 people.

Hardly a month had passed from Live8 when Wonder became one of many figureheads helping another American tragedy – this time not man-made, but rather Mother Nature losing her temper. Hurricane Katrina hit Florida, and spawned several tornadoes on its deadly journey to the Gulf of Mexico, with winds up to 175 mph, before whipping through Louisiana to hit New Orleans and the coasts of Mississippi and Alabama. It was the most destructive and costliest natural disaster in the history of America, and the deadliest since the Okeechobee Hurricane in 1928. The official death toll (December 2005) was 1,383 with 4,000 people missing. The world witnessed the devastation as it happened and reeled at the incompetence of the Bush government in dealing with the tragedy. Another aspect that emerged from intense media coverage was the numbers of black people left to flounder in Katrina's wake, while it appeared whites were systematically helped to safety. Wonder admitted to The *Guardian* reporter that there was still a divide – 'and in certain instances it is economics and class, and in other instances it's racial. When every single person can feel when they see a black kid being beaten up by a white kid that this could be one of their own kids, when people start to care like that, we'll be moving forward.'

Releasing the album track 'Shelter In The Rain' was his way of feeling because all net proceeds from its sale would go to his Foundation for Hurricane Katrina Relief Efforts to be distributed to Habitat for Humanity, United Negro College Fund, National Urban League and the Bush-Clinton Katrina Fund. 'God gave me that song as a gift. When I heard about the hurricane I was really hurt and was hoping to do what I could. Things we could never have imagined were happening. It's sickening to know that no matter how much we've grown, we've grown very little.' Ironically, 'Shelter In The Rain', featuring gospel singer Kirk Franklin, was intended as a duet with Syreeta 'but she decided that as she was having more bad days than good days she wanted me to sing it...Even though we were not married, we were still family.' The Rolling Stones, who were touring America at the time, donated $1 million to the American Red Cross Disaster Relief Fund. A number of other like-minded celebrities made similar donations.

A Time 2 Love – or as one fan put it 'a clock to heart' – met with mixed reviews upon its release in October 2005. Always criticised for the long time-span between his new albums, this time Stevie Wonder broke his own record with a ten-year wait! 'Ten years is a long time but I think when you're in it and you're doing life, you don't really see how long that is. But a lot of personal family stuff happened and a lot of changes happened – good, bad, and wonderful. That's why I don't regret the time. Perhaps if I'd done ten years doing nothing but music between 1995 and 2005, what I had to say by 2005 might be boring.' Wonder admitted to scrapping songs that he felt were inferior, re-working old songs and writing new material but as he got older, he said, creativity became harder although he knew he still had plenty to say – 'it's when you stop living that you don't have anything to say.'

So, was it worth it? *Rolling Stone* magazine gushed 'It's Wonder at his prime', while The *Sunday Times* noted it as 'Gloopy balladry and formulaic funk, both serving lyrics of banal sentimentality or vapid sloganeering have threatened his pioneering reputation.' A little harsh perhaps, although signs of past repetition can be heard, likewise Wonder's determination to preach to music. Nonetheless, in the light of musical trends, *A Time 2 Love* proudly stood with the finest, and for soul fans, the album was a gift from God, no matter the denomination. As the star himself insisted, the time was now perfect for the release – 'because there is a need now, more than ever, to bring love back to the forefront. We are all suffering because there's war, hatred, terrorism in the world … I'm happy with the reaction I've received. To me music is music and you do whatever feels good and right. For those who have constructive criticism I can relate to that. But for those who have just nonsense to say, I'm not even thinking about it.'

With his receding hair corn-rowed from the back of his head to below his shoulders, the heavily-framed smiling singer sits astride a chair on the front cover of *A Time 2 Love* – the raised symbols drawn by himself. Dressed in black, he holds a harmonica in his right hand, against a two-toned brown background showing his name. A sombre sleeve; a dark, brooding invitation to the music within representing some of the best and worst Motown's icon had to offer. Song lyrics and music credits are listed in detail in the booklet, while a serious portrait shot of Wonder closes it. A further track listing and thumb print pictures of the singer are featured on the back of the actual CD. The design was his creation. (In the days of vinyl this generous 15 track CD would have been called a double album). 'It's been an ongoing project and is something I started ten years ago, and something that has come from life experiences. The joy, pain, moments of sorrow and moments of happiness' he said of the release, before choosing favourite titles like the opening track 'If Your Love Cannot Be Moved' featuring Kim Burrell. 'I love her voice. We knew each other from a few years ago. I told her there was a song (I) wanted to try on her. We talked about my writing stuff for her and this song was made for her voice.' And quite openly Wonder acknowledged the influences of Dr Dre, Luther Vandross and Lauren Hill here; the haunting orchestra and voices weaving through the melody. 'Please Don't Hurt My Baby' which he started when he was eighteen years old ('and I kept messing with it') is a hard-hitting tale of infidelity and its tawdry repercussions. The song 'How Will I Know' with his daughter Aisha which was penned on a Tuesday morning in New York ten years ago following 'a wonderful night of making incredible love because I wanted to know what my partner felt about me. I used to sing the song around the house, and so Aisha memorised the lyrics. It turned out she sang better than me. She has such a sincere voice and it was a wonderful experience." His daughter also joined him on 'Positivity' with which he remembered his dear friend and singer Minnie Riperton, who died from breast cancer in 1979 and who encouraged Wonder to be positive about life – 'we have to have hope; as without hope we become hopeless.' The final track he commented upon was 'Passionate Raindrops', an infectiously boppy song, which Motown believed was too repetitious and should be dropped. 'I made the decision to keep it' Wonder said. His son Kailand can be heard clearly on the soulful 'Sweetest Somebody I Know'. The four year old burst into the studio yelling 'daddy, daddy, daddy, ok that's enough'; much laughter followed. The album is well balanced, enjoyable, intense and light-hearted. Throughout there are themes of time and how we choose to spend it, and love and how we use it. When the album closes it starts again; the last track mirrors the first; like a clock, like life.

Following its release, father and daughter visited Tokyo ('Japan is like my second home. If there is such a thing as reincarnation, I probably was Japanese in a previous life'), before hitting London where Wonder held a press conference at London's Savoy Hotel. He followed this with a one-off concert with a ten piece band for BBC Radio 2 at EMI Records' famous Abbey Road Studios where fifteen years earlier he had presented his 'Hotter Than July' album to the world. He also undertook several television appearances with a promise to tour the world.

A Time 2 Love soared into the American album chart at number five, selling 121,000 on the way. Its two biggest competitors were Rod Stewart with the *Great American Songbook/Thanks For The Memory* at 193,000 copies sold, and Ashlee Simpson at the pole position with her second album *I Am Me* which shifted 220,000 copies. His last album *Conversation Peace* peaked at number sixteen in 1995. Within a week *A Time 2 Love* had dropped eight places. British sales appeared no better because the album hit number 24 in its first week, before dropping to number 43. Universal/Motown must have harboured grave misgivings about the viability of further promoting *A Time 2 Love*, unless a hit single could be plucked from its grooves. Even though sales remained sluggish, Wonder and his work were nominated for five Grammy Awards. He was also nominated for a sixth for 'So Amazing', his duet with Beyonce Knowles, which was included on the compilation *An All-Star Tribute To Luther Vandross*. The singer died in July 2005 and artists like Elton John, Patti LaBelle and Celine Dion paid homage to one of the world's finest soul stylists who, over his astonishing career, had sold 30 million records worldwide .

Although he hadn't released a new album for ten years, Stevie Wonder insisted he's not slowing down, nor does he plan to retire. His future includes recording jazz, gospel and children's albums, writing a musical, and remaining a leading figure in the fight for his many causes. He also wants to add more Grammy awards to his collection because the late composer Henry Mancini, who had received thirty in his lifetime, used to tease him saying – 'You still have a long way to go!'

BRITISH SINGLES DISCOGRAPHY

Compiled by Graham Betts

Year of release	Title	Label	Chart position
1963	**Little Stevie Wonder** 'Fingertips Part 2' 'Fingertips Part 1'	Oriole 1853	–
	'Workout Stevie, Workout' 'Monkey Talk'	Stateside 238	–
1964	'Castles In The Sand' 'Thank You (For Loving Me All The Way)'	Stateside 285	–
	Stevie Wonder 'Hey Harmonica Man' 'This Little Girl'	Stateside 323	–

Tamla Motown Series

1965	'Kiss Me Baby' 'Tears In Vain'	TMG 505	–

	'High Heal Sneakers' 'Music Talk'	TMG 532	–
1966	'Uptight (Everything's Alright)' 'Purple Raindrops'	TMG 545	14
	'Nothing's Too Good For My Baby' 'With A Child's Heart'	TMG 558	–
	'Blowin' In The Wind' 'Ain't That Asking For Trouble'	TMG 570	36
	'A Place In The Sun' 'Sylvia'	TMG 588	20
1967	'Travelin' Man' 'Hey Love'	TMG 602	–
	'I Was Made To Love Her' 'Hold Me'	TMG 613	5
	'I'm Wondering' 'Every Time I See You I Go Wild'	TMG 626	22
1968	'Shoo-Be-Doo-Be-Doo- Da-Day' 'Why Don't You Lead Me To Love?'	TMG 653	46
	'You Met Your Match' 'My Girl'	TMG 666	–

	'For Once In My Life' 'Angie Girl'	TMG 679	3
1969	'I Don't Know Why' 'My Cherie Amour'	TMG 690	14
	'My Cherie Amour' 'I Don't Know Why'	TMG 690	4
	'Yester-Me, Yester-You Yesterday' 'I'd Be A Fool Right Now'	TMG 717	2
1970	'Never Had A Dream Come True' 'Somebody Knows, Somebody Cares'	TMG 731	6
	'Signed, Sealed, Delivered (I'm Yours)' 'I'm More Than Happy (I'm Satisfied)'	TMG 744	15
	'Heaven Help Us All' 'I Gotta Have A Song'	TMG 757	29
1971	'We Can Work It Out' 'Don't Wonder Why'	TMG 772	27
	'Never Dreamed You'd Leave In Summer' 'If You Really Love Me'	TMG 779	–
1972	'If You Really Love Me' 'Think Of Me As Your Soldier'	TMG 798	20
	'Superwoman 'Seems So Long'	TMG 827	–

1973	'Superstition' 'You've Got It Bad Girl'	TMG 841	11
	'You Are The Sunshine Of My Life' 'Look Around'	TMG 852	7
	'Higher Ground' 'Too High'	TMG 869	29
	'Living For The City' 'Visions'	TMG 881	15
1974	'He's Misstra Know-It-All' 'You Can't Judge A Book By Its Cover'	TMG 892	10
	'Don't You Worry 'Bout A Thing' 'Do Yourself A Favour'	TMG 908	–
	'You Haven't Done Nothin'' 'Happier Than The Morning'	TMG 921	30
	'Boogie On Reggae Woman' 'Evil'	TMG 928	12
1976	'I Wish' 'You And I'	TMG 1054	5
1977	'Sir Duke' 'Tuesday Heartbreak'	TMG 1068	2
	'Another Star' 'Creepin''	TMG 1083	29
	'As' 'ConTusion'	TMG 1091	–

1979	**(with Diana Ross, Marvin Gaye, Smokey Robinson)**		
	'Pops, We Love You'	TMG 1136	66
	'Pops, We Love You' (inst)		
	'Send One Your Love'	TMG 1149	52
	'Send One Your Love' (inst)		
1980	'Black Orchid'	TMG 1173	63
	'Blame It On The Sun'		
	'Outside My Window'	TMG 1179	52
	'Same Old Story'		
	'Master Blaster (Jammin')'	TMG 1204	2
	'Master Blaster (dub)'		
	'I Ain't Gonna Stand For It'	TMG 1215	10
	'Knocks Me Off My Feet'		
1981	'Lately'	TMG 1226	3
	'If It's Magic'		
	'Happy Birthday'	TMG 1235	2
	'Happy Birthday' (Singalong)		
1982	'That Girl'	TMG 1254	39
	'All I Do'		
	(with Paul McCartney)		
	'Ebony And Ivory'	Parlophone R6054	1
	'Rain Clouds'		
	'Do I Do'	TMG 1269	10
	'Rocket Love'		
	'Ribbon In The Sky'	TMG 1280	45
	'The Secret Life Of Plants'		

	(with Charlene)		
	'Used To Be'	TMG 1287	–
	(solo Charlene)		
	'I Want To Come Back As A Song'		
1983	'Front Line'	TMG 1289	–
	'Front Line' (inst)		
1984	'I Just Called To Say I Love You'	TMG 1349	1
	'I Just Called To Say I Love You' (inst)		
	'Love Light in Flight'	TMG 1364	44
	'It's More Than You' (inst)		
	'Don't Drive Drunk'	TMG 1372	62
	'Don't Drive Drunk' (inst)		

European Series

	'Part-Time Lover'	ZB 40351	3
	'Part-Time Lover' (inst)		

(with Dionne Warwick & Friends featuring Elton John and Gladys Knight)

	'That's What Friends Are For'	Arista ARIST 638	16

(Solo Dionne Warwick)

	'Two Ships Passing In The Night'		
	'Go Home'	ZB 40501	67
	'Go Home' (inst)		
1986	'Overjoyed'	ZB 40567	17
	'Overjoyed' (inst)		

	'Land Of La La' 'Land Of La La' (inst)	WOND1	–

1987	'Stranger On The Shore Of
	  Love'
	'Did I Hear You Say You
	  Love Me'
		WOND2	55

	'Skeletons' 'Skeletons' (inst)	ZB 41439	59
1988	'You Will Know' 'You Will Know' (inst)	ZB 41723	–
	(with Michael Jackson) 'Get It' 'Get It' (inst)	ZB 41883	37
	(with Julio Iglesias) 'My Love' **(solo Julio Iglesias)** 'Words And Music'	CBS JUL102	5
1989	'Free' 'Free' (inst)	ZB 42855	49
1991	'Fun Day' 'Fun Day' (inst)	ZB 44957	63
1995	'For Your Love' 'For Your Love' (inst)	TMG CD1437	23
	'Tomorrow Robins Will Sing' 'Tomorrow Robins Will Sing' (remix)	M8603732	71
2003	'Signed, Sealed, Delivered (I'm Yours), (Blue featuring Angie Stone & Stevie Wonder)		11

BRITISH ALBUMS
DISCOGRAPHY

Compiled by Graham Betts

Year of release	Title	Label	Chart position
1963	**Little Stevie Wonder**		
	Tribute to Uncle Ray	Oriole 40049	–
	Recorded Live – The 12 Year Old Genius	Oriole 40050	–
1964	*The Jazz Soul Of Little Stevie*	Stateside 10078	–
1965	**Stevie Wonder**		
	Hey Harmonica Man	Stateside 10108	–
	Tamla Motown Series		
1966	*Uptight*	STML 11036	–
1967	*Down To Earth*	STML 11045	–
	I Was Made To Love Her	STML 11059	–
1968	*Greatest Hits*	STML 11075	25

	Someday At Christmas	STML 11085	–
1969	*For Once In My Life*	STML 11098	–
1970	*My Cherie Amour*	STML 11128	17
	Live	STML 11150	–
	Live! At The Talk Of The Town	STML 11164	–
	Signed, Sealed And Delivered	STML 11169	–
1971	*Where I'm Coming From*	STML 11183	–
	Greatest Hits Volume 2	STML 11196	30
1972	*Music Of My Mind*	STMA 8002	–
1973	*Talking Book*	STMA 8007	16
	Innervisions	STMA 8011	8
1974	*Fulfillingness' First Finale*	STMA 8019	5
1976	*Songs In The Key Of Life*	TMSP 6002	2
1979	*Stevie Wonder's Journey Through The Secret Life Of Plants*	TMSP 6009	8
1980	*Hotter Than July*	STMA 8035	2
1982	*Stevie Wonder's Original Musiquarium Volume 1*	TMSP 6012	8
1984	*The Woman In Red*	ZL 72285	2

1985	*In Square Circle*	ZL 72005	5
1987	*The Essential Stevie Wonder*	WL 72585	–
	Characters	ZL 72001	33
1991	*Music From The Movie 'Jungle Fever'*	ZL 71750	56
1995	*Conversation Peace*	M 5302382	8
2000	*At The Close Of A Century*	M153 992-2	–
2002	*Stevie Wonder – The Definitive Collection*	M066502-2	16
2005	*A Time 2 Love*		5

BIBLIOGRAPHY

Boy George with Spencer Bright. *Take It Like A Man: The Autobiography of Boy George* (Pan Books, 1995).

Davis, Sharon. *Motown: The History* (Guinness Books, 1988).

— *I Heard It Through The Grapevine: Marvin Gaye. The Biography* (Mainstream Publishing, 1991).

Franklin, Aretha and Ritz, David. *Aretha: From These Roots* (Villard Books, 1999).

George, Nelson. *Where Did Our Love Go?: The Rise and Fall of the Motown Sound* (St Martin's Press, 1986).

Gordy, Berry. *To Be Loved: The Music, the Magic, the Memories of Motown: an Autobiography* (Warner Books Inc., 1994).

Herman, Gary. *Rock 'N' Roll Babylon* (Perigee Books, 1982).

Hirshey, Gerri. *Nowhere To Run: The Story of Soul Music* (Pan Books, 1985).

Larkin, Colin. *All Time Top 1000 Albums* (Guinness Publishing, 1994).

Norman, Philip. *Elton – The Definitive Biography* (Arrow Books, 1992).

Reeves, Martha and Mark Bego. *Dancing in the Street: Confessions Of A Motown Diva* (Hyperion, 1994).

Ritz, David. *Divided Soul: The Life of Marvin Gaye* (Michael Joseph Ltd., 1985).

Robinson, Smokey. *Smokey: Inside My Life* (Headline Book Publishing PLC, 1989).

Sanello, Frank. *Eddie Murphy: The Life And Times Of A Comic On The Edge* (Birch Lane Press, 1997).

Spector, Ronnie and Vince Waldron. *Be My Baby: How I Survived*

Mascara, Miniskirts, and Madness, or My Life As a Fabulous Ronette (MacMillan London Ltd., 1991).

Swenson, John. *Stevie Wonder* (Plexus, 1986).

Taraborrelli, J Randy. *Call Her Miss Ross: The Unauthorized Biography of Diana Ross* (Sidgwick & Jackson, 1989).

Turner, Tony with Barbara Aria. *Lead Us Not Into Temptation* (Thunder's Mouth Press, 1992).

Whitall, Susan and Marsh, David. *Women Of Motown: An Oral History (For the Record)* (Avon Books Inc., 1998).

White, Adam and Fred Bronson. *The Billboard Book Of Number One R&B Hits* (Billboard Books, 1993).

Williams, Otis with Patricia Romanowski. *Temptations* (G. P. Putnam & Sons, 1988).

Wilson, Mary. *Dreamgirl: My Life As A Supreme* (Sidgwick & Jackson, 1987).

Blues & Soul magazine – interviews, reviews, comments by Bob Killbourn, David Nathan, John Abbey, Kwame Braithwaite, Mick Clark, Ralph Tee, Mark Webster, Graham Gold, Jeff Lorez, Pete Lewis, Roger St Pierre

Chatbusters magazine – Alan Taylor, John O'Dowd, Robert Dennis, Rockwilder

Disc – Phil Symes interviews

Melody Maker 1980 – Geoff Brown review

New Musical Express 1973

Newsweek (undated) – Maureen Orth interview

Rolling Stone magazine 1973, 1984

Soul magazine (undated) – Lee Underwood interview

The *Sun* 1989 – Andy Coulson interview

The *Sun* 2001 (uncredited)

USA Today 1986 – Craig Modderno interview

Variety magazine 1979

Early UK and US Stevie Wonder news clippings and interviews researched were often badly damaged through age – therefore, credits may have been omitted and for this the author apologises. However, she would like to thank the following, whose names were legible: Penny Valentine, Alex Kanakaris, Lon Goddard, David Breskin, Alan Lewis, Ben Fong-Torres and Nick Kent.

VISUAL CREDITS

The author is extremely grateful to the following for kindly providing and/or granting permission to reproduce the visuals contained in this book. While every effort has been made to establish and contact all copyright holders, it is possible that an oversight has occurred, and for this I apologise. I will, of course, be pleased to correct any omission in future editions of this publication.

Motown Record Corporation/Motown Records, Motown International, EMI Records, Peter Vernon, Justin Thomas, the Sharon Davis Collection, Dave Godin, Keith Harris, the late Graham Canter, Marshall Arts and Stevie Wonder's fans who have contributed so willingly.

INDEX